SEIZE *the* FIRE

Heroism, Duty, and Nelson's Battle of Trafalgar

ADAM NICOLSON

HARPER PERENNIAL

NEW YORK • LONDON • TORONTO • SYDNEY

HARPER PERENNIAL

First published in Great Britain in 2005 by HarperCollins Publishers.

First U.S. hardcover edition of this book was published in 2005 by HarperCollins Publishers.

P.S.™ is a trademark of HarperCollins Publishers.

HarperCollins books may be purchased for educational, business, or sales promotional use. For information, please write: Special Markets Department, HarperCollins Publishers, 10 East 53rd Street, New York, NY 10022.

First Harper Perennial edition published 2006.

Library of Congress Cataloging-in-Publication Data is available upon request.

ISBN-10: 0-06-075362-5 (pbk.)
ISBN-13: 978-0-06-075362-7 (pbk.)

06 07 08 09 10 RRD 10 9 8 7 6 5 4 3 2 1

Praise for *Seize the Fire*

"A beguiling discourse on the character of the English at that time, illustrated by their behavior amid the shocking realities of war at sea. Nicolson's eye for detail creates a compelling readability—recalling Sir Arthur Bryant at his best—with the freshness and perception that gives his own writing its quality. . . . Of the hundreds of books written about Nelson and Trafalgar over the past two centuries, perhaps a dozen will be worth rereading at the tercentenary. This is one of them." —Tom Pocock, *The Spectator* (London)

"Written in the same kind of graceful prose as *Sea Room*. . . . In producing a narrative full of suspense and vivid, raw descriptions of the butchery, Nicolson masterfully avoids the kind of dry intellectualism into which this type of book can so easily slip. There are so many examples of sublime writing that it would be invidious to select any particular passage. Mercifully, [*Seize the Fire*] is also devoid of trendy historicism, and succeeds in explaining to a generation with little appetite for war just why Nelson was deified."
—Paul Riddell, *The Scotsman* (London)

"The story of the battle—the terrifying broadsides, the shattered rigging, the dying Nelson, Hardy's valedictory kiss—has been told before, but rarely with the literary aplomb and almost cinematic realism that are to be found in Adam Nicolson's new book. . . . In evoking the look and sound of the ships; the lives and loves of their commanders; and the horrendous, pulverizing reality of naval war; Nicolson can equal anything to be found in the novels of Patrick O'Brian. His book brims with statistics that alternately fascinate, awe, and appall. . . . Few will be more reflective or thought-provoking than this."
—John Adamson, *The Sunday Telegraph* (London)

"Adam Nicolson's [*Seize the Fire*] does not aim to flesh out this skeleton with a blow-by-blow account of the battle. Instead, he takes a philosophical and literary approach, attempting the difficult task of describing the mental landscape of the people involved, and 'why and how the idea of the hero flowered,' and in this he succeeds exceptionally well."
—Roy Adkins, *The Independent on Sunday* (London)

"There is no shortage of books about Nelson, but Nicolson's is not just another run-through of a rousing but familiar story. Argued with vigor and written with grace, it is an illuminating piece of interpretative cultural history."
—Lucy Hughes-Hallett, *The Times on Sunday* (London)

"Of the books marking the bicentenary of . . . Trafalgar, Adam Nicolson's can claim to be one of the most original." —*The Week* magazine

"Nicolson brilliantly characterizes each navy—British, French, Spanish—as an expression of the countries to which they belonged. . . . Vivid."
—*Country Life* magazine

"Vibrant and welcome addition to the admittedly already large library of Nelsonia." —Jonathan Bouquet, *The Observer* (London)

ALSO BY ADAM NICOLSON

Seamanship

God's Secretaries: The Making of the King James Bible

Sea Room

Perch Hill: A New Life

Restoration: The Rebuilding of Windsor Castle

Wetland Life in the Somerset Levels

CONTENTS

ILLUSTRATIONS

A First Rate Taking in Stores, 1818 by Joseph Mallord William Turner, R.A. *Trustees, Cecil Higgins Art Gallery, Bedford, England.*

Nelson's Undress coat, *National Maritime Museum, London, Greenwich Hospital Collection.*

Admiral Sir Cloudisley Shovell (1650–1707) by Michael Dahl, 1702. *National Maritime Museum, London.*

Admiral John Byng (1704–57) by Thomas Hudson, 1749. *National Maritime Museum, London.*

Rear-Admiral Sir John Jervis, Lord St Vincent (1735–1823) by Sir William Beechey, 1787–90. *National Maritime Museum, London.*

Admiral Charles Middleton, Lord Barham (1726–1813) British School 19th Century. *National Maritime Museum, London.*

Rear-Admiral Sir Robert Calder (1745–1815) by Lemuel Francis Abbott, 1797. *National Maritime Museum, London, Greenwich Hospital Collection.*

Vice-Admiral Sir Thomas Fremantle. *National Maritime Museum, London.*

Rear-Admiral Sir Alexander John Ball (1757–1809) by Henry William Pickersgill, 1805–9. *National Maritime Museum, London, Greenwich Hospital Collection.*

Sir William Beatty (*c*1770–1842) by Arthur William Devis, *c*1806. *National Maritime Museum, London.*

Captain Henry Blackwood (1770–1832) by John Hoppner, 1806. *National Maritime Museum, London, Greenwich Hospital Collection.*

Sir Thomas Masterman Hardy (1769–1839) by Domenico Pellegrini, 1809. *National Maritime Museum, London.*

Rear Admiral Sir Thomas Troubridge (*c*1758–1807) by Sir William Beechey, 1804–5. *National Maritime Museum, London.*

Portrait of Captain Henry W. Bayntun by Sir William Beechey, 1805. *Louisiana State University Museum of Art, Anonymous Donor's Purchase Fund, 59.8.*

The Battle of Trafalgar 21st October 1805 by Joseph Mallord William Turner, 1824. *National Maritime Museum, London, Greenwich Hospital Collection.*

Portrait of Pierre Charles de Villeneuve (1763–1806) engraved by Gilles Louis Chrétien. *Bibliotheque Nationale, Paris, France.* www.bridgeman.co.uk.

Commander-in-Chief of the Real Navy, Federico Gravina (1756–1806). Anonymous 19th Century. *Museo Naval, Madrid.*

Commodore Cosme de Churruca. *Museo Naval, Madrid.*

French naval officer Jean-Jacques Etienne Lucas (1764–1819) *c*1800. *Getty Images.*

Rear-Admiral Sir Horatio Nelson (1758–1805) by Lemuel Francis Abbott, 1800. *National Maritime Museum, London, Greenwich Hospital Collection.*

Rear-Admiral Sir Horatio Nelson (1758–1805) by John Hoppner, *c*1800. *National Maritime Museum, London.*

Vice-Admiral Horatio Nelson (1758–1805) by Sir William Beechey, 1801. *National Maritime Museum, London, Greenwich Hospital Collection.*

Horatio Nelson, Viscount Nelson by Guy Head, 1798–1799. *National Portrait Gallery, London.*

Horatio Nelson, Viscount Nelson by Sir William Beechey, 1800. *National Portrait Gallery, London.*

Vice-Admiral Horatio Nelson (1758–1805) 1st Viscount Nelson by Matthew H Keymer, 1801. *National Maritime Museum, London.*

Nelson in conflict with a Spanish Launch, July 1797 by Richard Westall. *National Maritime Museum, London, Greenwich Hospital Collection.*

The Battle of Trafalgar, 21 October 1805: End of the Action by Nicholas Pocock, 1808. *National Maritime Museum, London.*

The Death of Nelson 1806 by Benjamin West. © *National Museums Liverpool, The Walker Museum.*

The Death of Nelson, 21 October 1805 by Arthur William Devis, 1807. *National Maritime Museum, London, Greenwich Hospital Collection.*

HMS *Victory* towed into Gibraltar by Clarkson Stanfield, c1850s. *National Maritime Museum, London.*

Lord Nelson's funeral, 1806. *Courtesy The National Archives.*

ACKNOWLEDGEMENTS

Any book of this kind relies entirely on the work of scholars over many decades and I happily acknowledge my debt to all those who have written about the 1805 Royal Navy in the past. In particular, the outstanding volumes of naval records produced annually since 1893 by the Navy Records Society make any exploration of this extraordinary and fascinating world the greatest of pleasures. I have quoted extensively from those records and I gratefully acknowledge the permission to do so. Anyone wishing to become a member of the Society, and receive the annual volumes as part of their subscription, should apply to the Hon. Secretary, Department of War Studies, King's College London, Strand, London WC2R 2LS.

I would also very much like to thank my editors, Susan Watt and Hugh Van Dusen, as well as Katie Espiner, Marie Estrada, Vera Brice, Amanda Russell and Helen Ellis, all of whom have, with practised skill, guided this book through its various paths. Caroline Dawnay and Zoe Pagnamenta remain sources of great encouragement, for which I am immensely grateful.

PREFACE

There is a long tradition of English violence. More Catholics were burned at the stake in 16th-century England than in any other country in Europe. A higher percentage of the population died in the English Civil War than in the French Revolution. The suppression and brutalisation of the Scottish Highlanders after Bonnie Prince Charlie's rebellion in 1745–6 was the scandal of enlightened Europe. All this was part of the nation from which Nelson came. He was able at Trafalgar, as he had been at the Nile and Copenhagen, to summon a scale of aggression from his fleets that seems to have drawn on the deepest levels of common consciousness among his men. This is a difficult area to address, but essential: how does one read into the behaviour of a fighting fleet the deep half-conscious preoccupations of the people who man its ships? How do the semi-understood but widely inherited ideas about purpose, violence and victory, which are present in any evolved society, shape the way men behave in battle? Battle is not simply a question of ideology, military expertise or technology. Deeper and more personal forces are in play and intimate battle, of the kind Nelson invited and created, inevitably engages men at their innermost levels.

By 1805, the sequence of violent and revolutionary events in Europe over the previous fifteen years had established in England – or, to be strict, re-summoned – a form of millenarian fever which had not been seen since the 17th century. The template for this fever came from the prophets of the Old Testament, from Deuteronomy, Daniel, Ezekiel and Isaiah in particular, and from the Book of Revelation which draws on them. Deep in the Jewish tradition, and radiantly powerful in those books, is the idea that a moment of fearful justice will come, when the wrath of the divine descends on earth. It will know no compromise. Its very violence is a measure of its goodness.

> If I whet my glittering sword, and mine hand take hold on judgment; I will render vengeance to mine enemies, and will reward them that hate me. I will make mine arrows drunk with blood, and my sword shall devour flesh; with the blood of the slain and of the captives, from the beginning of revenges upon the enemy. Rejoice, O ye nations, with his people: for he will avenge the blood of his servants, and will render vengeance to his adversaries.

That is the tradition drawn on by the blood-drenched visions of the end of time in Revelation. In this shared vision of the Judaeo-Christian-Islamic world, the moment of utter violence gives way to the moment of utter peace, the tranquillity of the Kingdom of God, the future dream time of the millennium, when all striving is over and all wickedness banished. There will be no peace until the violence is done. Peace is inaccessible without the violence, because violence is righteousness in action. Apocalypse is the route to millennium.

These movements have always emerged in English history at periods of flux and crisis: during the Peasants' Revolt, early in the 16th century during the first years of the Reformation, in the lead-up to the Civil War in the mid-17th century, in the 1790s and again in the 1820s and 30s at a time of widespread uncertainty over the reform and democratisation of British political institutions. Never were they more powerful than in the years before Trafalgar. The twinning of apocalypse and millennium, of violence leading to peace, is everywhere you look. For English radicals, the French Revolution was itself a sign that the time had come when blood would be shed and peace would descend on all men. The Pitt government, bearing down heavily on any hint of revolutionary thought, was, in this cosmic drama, the agency of evil. House-to-house searches were made; registers of lodgers compiled; citizens denounced for 'incivism' if they did not sign a declaration of loyalty to the constitution. Semi-compulsory collections, for all the sailors and the troops, were set up as a means of testing loyalty to the government: if you were loyal you gave in your flannel waistcoats, mitts, drawers, caps, shirts, stockings, shoes, trousers, boots, sheets and greatcoats. If you did not, your loyalty fell under suspicion.

By the mid-1790s, as the pressure of the law came down, and as radicalism was driven underground, there was an eruption of millenarian fantasy. Richard Brothers, a retired naval lieutenant on half pay, spoke to the people. His books and pamphlets went through edition after edition on both sides of the Atlantic. 'All nations have drunk of the wine of the wrath of Babylon's fornications,' he told his giddy listeners, 'and the kings of the earth have committed fornication with her, and the merchants of the earth are waxed rich through the abundance of her delicacies.' His words were, in a subterranean way, pregnant with extreme violence. One evening he saw 'a large River run through London coloured with human blood.'

These were the 'signs of mercy' – the violence was beautiful – and after them there was to be an era of universal brotherhood. 'All shall be as one people, and of one mind . . . The time is come, and now is the whore of Babylon falling, and will fall to rise no more. Go forth then, ye Sons of Eternal Light, and instruct the Sons of Ignorance and Darkness . . . There shall be no more war, no more want, no more wickedness; but all shall be peace, plenty and virtue.'

In 1795 the Privy Council had him arrested and put in a lunatic asylum. His disciples clamoured year after year for his release. But his following continued. A prophet called Ebenezer Aldred, with flowing grey hair, floated in the Thames distributing his booklets of doom. The lost tribes of Israel surfaced in Birmingham and Wapping. Robert Southey sarcastically described how 'One madman printed his dreams, another his day visions; one had seen an angel come out of the sun with a drawn sword in his hand, another had seven fiery dragons in the air, and hosts of angels in battle array.'

For the non-enfranchised masses of early 19th-century England, these visions felt like access to a new and potent reality; and it is from those social levels that Nelson's fleet was manned. In 1801, the most powerful of all these movements erupted in the West Country (the navy's principal recruiting ground). Joanna Southcott, a Devon farmer's daughter, became the conduit for incantatory and apocalyptic visions which gave rise to a national movement both among the poor and among the frustrated English radicals. The repressions of the Pitt regime had pushed political radicalism inwards, into the visionary world. 'O England! O England! O England!' Southcott called,

> The midnight-hour is coming for you all, and will burst upon you. I warn you of dangers that now stand before you, for the time is at hand for the fulfilment of all things. But of mine enemies I will tread them in mine anger, and trample them in my fury; for the day of vengeance is in my heart, and the year of my redeemed is come. The earth shall be filled with My Goodness, and hell shall be filled with My terrors . . . My fury shall go forth – and My Loving-kindness shall save to the utmost all them that now come unto ME.

There were at least 100,000 Southcottians in England in 1804–5, but they were far from unique. The country was filled with violently apocalyptic religious movements, many of them versions of Methodism: Ranters, Jumpers, Tent Methodists, Magic Methodists, the Bryanites, Independent Methodists. All of them understood that divinely sanctioned violence was a route to the resolution of all pain. The violence was explicit. One oath sworn in Lancashire by political radicals took its opaque and magical rhetoric from Ezekiel: 'The sword, the sword is drawn: for the slaughter it is furbished, to consume because of the glittering.'

Such language might be used to justify genuine political revolution in England. But wherever it has appeared, millenarianism has always been able to divert its energies, to flick from radical to conservative, from subversive to patriotic, from democratic to nationalistic and back again. The energy of millenarianism acts beyond the political. This varying focus of the apocalyptic vision was certainly the mood in 1790s England, when members of angry mobs could just as easily turn on prominent radicals as on figures of the Establishment. It did not take much of a shift in consciousness to apply the millenarian rage not to the removal of the Pitt regime but to a defence of England against the wickedness and bloody excesses of revolutionary and Napoleonic France.

Battle, sacrifice, the glittering sword, the rivers of blood, the midnight hour, the dangers that stand before you: all those were real enough at Trafalgar and the new millennium of peaceful dominance they led to was not something in the next world but in this – the unrivalled creation of a God-blessed, ragingly commercial British empire. This was not the millennium of political freedom and equality of which the radicals in the 1790s had dreamed; but it was the only apocalypse and the only millennium which the British regime could allow.

It is possible to see Nelson instinctively responding to this deep and half-hidden current in English thought and belief. The apocalyptic tradition required a conjuring, wise, intuitive, violent and triumphant leader. Nelson fulfilled some of those expectations. A high conception of his destiny in life, and of his relationship to the cosmic and the divine, was not alien to him. In his youth he had experienced precisely a visionary understanding of what that role was. In mid-1776, as a 17-year-old on board the *Dolphin*, desperately thin, only just emerging from a life-threatening attack of malaria, he had experienced an extraordinary visitation, a moment of understanding:

> I felt impressed with an idea that I should never rise in my profession. My mind was staggered with a view of the difficulties I had to surmount and the little interest [meaning connections within the navy] I possessed. I could discover no means of reaching the object of my ambition. After a long and gloomy reverie, in which I almost wished myself overboard, a sudden glow of patriotism was kindled within me, and presented my king and country as my patron. My mind exulted in the idea. 'Well then,' I exclaimed, 'I will be a hero, and confiding in Providence I will brave every danger.'

Then, as Clarke and McArthur, his first biographers, who heard this story from a friend of his, Richard Bulkeley, in Ludlow, went on: 'The spirit of Nelson revived; and from that hour in his mind's eye, as he often declared to Captain Hardy, a radiant orb was suspended which urged him onward to renown.'

Robert Southey glossed it still further, saying that Nelson

> knew to what the previous state of dejection was to be attributed; that an enfeebled body, and a mind depressed, had cast this shade over his soul; but he

> always seemed willing to believe that the sunshine which succeeded bore with it a prophetic glory, and that the light which led him on was 'light from heaven'.

The overlapping tissues of belief, expectation, reinterpretation, self-aggrandisement and wish-fulfilment are subtly layered here. Stripped to essentials, though, Nelson felt led onwards through his fighting life by a prophetic and visionary fire. He, like Southcott and the others, called to England. He too was the friend of all. He too saw himself standing on a stage, habitually referring to himself in the third person. He too was calm in the face of danger and catastrophe and accepted the working of destiny as a fact of existence. He too presided over events of devastating and bloody violence. He too called on God as his guide and witness, far more often, to judge by the correspondence preserved in the Admiralty files, than any of his fellow flag officers. Nelson's heroic conception of himself was, on one level, as the prophetic agent of apocalypse and millennium.

England by 1805 was certainly drenched in that imagery. The angel of rage and the tradition of justified wrath had become commonplaces of the English mind. Nelson fulfilled the expectations of an archetype. His sense of daring and the totality in his style of battle; his understanding of the need for destruction as a route to creation; the acceptance of self-sacrifice; his portrayal of the enemy as profoundly wicked; his ideal of England as a place of beauty and goodness: all of that fuelled his immense popularity at home. He seemed to fulfil the archetype which a national mood had prepared for him. In England, there was a need for a hero like him who was a saviour, a man not from the established ruling class but outside it, sharing its patrician grace, but a less distant and more demotic figure than that. The figure of 'Nelson', the fleet-burning conjuror of victory, in some ways described and in some ways floated free of the anxious, methodical, endlessly attentive, systematic and careful man that Horatio Nelson, like many other naval officers, actually was. Even in the weeks before Trafalgar, informed opinion protested at this singling out of Nelson by the populace. The *Naval Chronicle*, in its issue for July and August 1805, regretted 'that ill-judged, and over-weening popularity, which tends to make another Demi-god of Lord Nelson, at the expense of all other officers in the service, many of whom possess equal merit, and equal abilities, and equal gallantry.'

Any description of Trafalgar cannot confine itself to the facts of rigging and armament, weather and weight of broadside. Other, less material expectations are just as potent a presence in battle as the concrete realities of a ship in action. This book addresses that underlayer, the subtlest and slipperiest of historical levels: pre-conceptions, and the way they shape present behaviour. It is an attempt to describe the mental landscape of the people who fought and commanded at one of the great battles in history and it asks, in particular, why and how the idea of the hero flowered here.

Answers are inevitably complex, rooted in part in the twin classical inheritance of the ruthless, Greek, Achillean hero, who burns and destroys without thought to his own welfare; and the Roman, Virgilian hero, who is in many ways a schematic opposite of the Greek. He is civic where the Greek is ragingly individual. He serves the state, not his own self-driven destiny. He too must use violence but his violence is limited and proportionate. He conforms and conserves where Achilles dislocates and destroys. Like Cincinnatus, called to save Rome in her hour of crisis, the Roman hero returns, after he has performed his task, to the farm and the plough from which the needs of state had summoned him. (The Trafalgar fleet, from Nelson and Collingwood down, is full of men dreaming of trees, fields, gardens, peace and home.) When Jane Austen, the sister of two naval officers, has her heroine in *Persuasion* marry Captain Wentworth, she loves him because he belongs to 'a profession which is, if possible, more distinguished in its domestic virtues than in its national importance'. Wentworth looks after her as a Roman hero should. The Roman is part of a system, social and considerate. He sees himself as a servant. Like Aeneas, he carries his father, his nation on his shoulders. If Achilles is crisis and destruction, Aeneas is support and love.

That twin inheritance, the Virgilian and the Homeric, are both in play at Trafalgar and both are fused there with the contemporary passion for a burning apocalyptic fire. It is not usually done, either by naval or literary scholars, to put William Blake and Nelson in the same bracket – Blake openly despised Nelson, virtually as a war criminal – but to do so, and to understand their shared relationship to the visions and desires of contemporary England, is to understand both why Nelson was the object of so much love and hope in England – one of the first examples of a media-driven frenzy for a star – and why the men of the fleet he commanded fought and killed with such unbridled intensity and passion.

Scarcely anyone in England in 1805 could be more distant from Nelson than William Blake: the one, radical, poor, impractical and 'hid', as he described himself, buried in an artisan subculture of radicals and mystics outside any conceivable Establishment; the other deeply conservative, courted by the government, the most public figure in England. And yet, at this deeper level, at the level of the vision of the radiant orb, there is an astonishing and intimate connection between the imageries on which they both drew.

Neither trusted the old ways. 'The Enquiry in England,' Blake said, 'is not whether a man has talents and genius, but whether he is passive and polite and a virtuous ass and obedient to noblemen's opinions in arts and science.' Nelson could have said that. But it is in Blake's concentrated encapsulation of the apocalyptic vision that he seems to be speaking most directly for the heart of the Nelsonian idea. Far more than the ranting prophets, whose language seems either mad or second-hand, Blake says conceptually what Nelsonian battle put into action. Nowhere is this more intense than in Blake's *The Marriage of Heaven and Hell*, acid-etched by him into his copperplates in the decade before Trafalgar. They are a summary of Nelson's method of battle:

> Energy is eternal delight.
>
> Prudence is a rich, ugly old maid courted by Incapacity.
>
> The tygers of wrath are wiser than the horses of instruction.
>
> Without contraries is no progression.
>
> The road of excess leads to the palace of wisdom.
>
> He who desires but acts not, breeds pestilence.
>
> The wrath of the lion is the wisdom of God.
>
> The nakedness of woman is the work of God.
>
> Exuberance is Beauty.

In these revolutionary stabs at truth, which strip away the graceful hypocrisy of the Enlightenment, something of the Nelsonian soul is laid bare. As statements, they are deliberately primitive, beneath and beyond the elegances of civilisation, just as Nelson's method of battle subverted the conventions of 18th-century warfare. Nelson lived and died for the 'portions of eternity' represented by love, violence and the destructive sword. He saw friendship as man's most nurturing condition and devoted years of his life to cultivating intimacy with his fellow officers. Capable of intense sensuality, he loved the nakedness of a woman as an almost holy thing. The road of excess was not in itself the palace of wisdom, but certainly led there. He believed in action, not dwelling on action. His method was exuberance and the tigers of his wrath were undaunted by the horses of instruction.

Buried deep in the assumptions of England, was a spirit of daring and ferocity. Within the ferocity was a sense of cosmic beauty. That is the spirit of Blake's greatest lyric, written ten or eleven years before Trafalgar, virtually unknown at the time, but full of a sublimity, a beauty in terror, which Blake's publicly acknowledged contemporaries, most of them still engaged with the courtesies of the 18th century, could never have encompassed.

> Tyger Tyger burning bright,
> In the forests of the night;
> What immortal hand or eye,
> Could frame thy fearful symmetry?
>
> In what distant deeps or skies.
> Burnt the fire of thine eyes?
> On what wings dare he aspire?
> What the hand dare sieze the fire?

Those are precisely the questions to which Nelson and his Trafalgar fleet could give answers in the affirmative. This fleet was, if anything, a model of 'fearful symmetry'. Here burned the ardour of destruction. Here were men who might aspire, who both confronted and delivered apocalyptic violence, who looked on battle not as a necessary evil but as a moment of revelation and truth. For James Martin, a 26-year-old able seaman on the *Neptune*, 'Now the moment was fast advancing which was to Decide wether the Boasted Herosum of France and Spain or the Ginene Valour of free Born Britains was to Rule the Main . . . Death or Victory was the Gineral Resolution of our Ships Crew.'

In that light, the story of the British victory at Trafalgar is of a fleet of ships and men who, in a heroic mould, part Greek, part Roman, part Hebrew – the three-pronged roots of European violence – both dared to seize the fire and to use their apocalyptic inheritance as the fuel for lives of honour.

Part I

MORNING

October 21st 1805
5.50 am to 12.30 pm

1

ZEAL

October 21st 1805
5.50 am to 8.30 am

Distance between fleets: 10 miles–6.5 miles
Victory's heading and speed: 067°–078° at 3 knots

Zeal: passionate ardour for any cause
SAMUEL JOHNSON, *A Dictionary of the English Language*, 1755

At 5.50 on the morning of 21 October 1805, just as dawn was coming up, the look-outs high on the mainmasts of the British fleet spied the enemy, about twelve miles away downwind. They had been tracking them for a day and a night, the body of their force kept carefully over the horizon, not only to prevent the French and Spanish taking fright and running from battle, but to remain upwind, 'keeping the weather gage', holding the trump card with which they would control and direct the battle to come. All night long, British frigates, stationed between the two fleets, had been burning pairs of blue lights, every hour on the hour, as pre-arranged. It was the agreed signal that the enemy was standing to the south, just as was wanted, straight into the jaws of the British guns.

Twenty minutes after the first sighting in the light of dawn, Nelson signalled to the fleet: 'Form order of sailing in two columns.' This was the attack formation in which he had instructed his captains over the preceding weeks. His next signal, at 06.22, confirmed what they all knew was inevitable: 'Prepare for battle'. Twenty minutes after that, the French frigate *Hermione,* standing out to the west of her own battle fleet, peering into the dark of the retreating night, signalled to her flagship, the *Bucentaure*: 'The enemy in sight to windward.' For all 47,000 men afloat that morning, it felt like a day of destiny and decision. Most ships in both fleets were already cleared for action.

The French and Spanish were about twelve miles and the British about twenty-two miles off the coast of southwest Spain. The nearest point was Cape Trafalgar, an Arabic name, meaning the Point of the Cave, Taraf-al-Ghar. From the very top, the truck, of the highest masts in the British fleet, two hundred feet above the sea, you could just make out the blue smoky hills standing inland towards Seville. The wind was a light northwesterly, perhaps no more than Force 2 or 3, blowing at about 10 knots, but that was enough. A man-of-war would sail with a breeze so slight it could just be felt on the windward side of a licked finger. On the day of the battle, only the very largest ship, the vast Spanish four-decker, the *Santísima Trinidad,* did not respond to her helm. Most had just enough steerage way to manoeuvre. The sky was a pale, Neapolitan blue, with a few high clouds, and it was warm for the autumn. By midday, the Spanish meteorologists, recording the temperature in the Royal Observatory just outside Cadiz, would log 21° Celsius, about 70° Fahrenheit. In all ships in both fleets, men would strip to the waist. There was only one ominous element to the weather: a long, stirring swell was pushing in from the southwest, 'the dog before its master', the sign of a big Atlantic storm to come.

Twenty-six British ships-of-the-line were bearing down from to-windward. One more, the *Africa*, captained by

Henry Digby, the richest man in the English fleet, who had won for himself £60,000 of prize money by the time he was thirty, perhaps £3–4 million in modern terms, had missed Nelson's signal in the night, had got out of position and was now coming down from the north. The main body of the fleet was arranged a little raggedly, in two rough columns, 'scrambling into action' as one of the British captains described it afterwards, 'in coveys' as a Spaniard remembered it, as though the British fleet were a flock of partridges drifting in from the western horizon.

Nelson was already on the quarterdeck of *Victory*, a slight, grey-haired 47-year-old man, alert, wiry, anxious and intense, five feet four inches tall and irresistibly captivating in manner. Before battle, the remains of the arm he had lost in a catastrophic fight against the Spanish in the Canaries eight years before tended to quiver with the tension. 'My fin' he called it, and on his chairs he had a small patch particularly upholstered on the right arm, where he could rest this anxious stump. Like most naval officers, he was both tanned – the word used by unfriendly landlubbers to describe captains and admirals in Jane Austen's *Persuasion* is 'orange' – and prematurely aged, worn out by the worry and fretfulness of his life. At regular intervals, he would be struck, quite unexpectedly, by a terrifying and debilitating nervous spasm, his body releasing, in a surge of uncontrolled energy, the anxiety it had accumulated day by day. Only three weeks before Trafalgar, one such attack, suddenly coming on at four in the morning, had left him feeling enervated and confused. 'I was hardly ever better than yesterday,' he wrote to his lover Emma Hamilton,

> and I slept uncommonly well; but was awoke with this disorder. The good people of England will not believe that rest of body and mind is necessary for me! But perhaps this spasm may not come again

these six months. I had been writing seven hours yesterday; perhaps that had some hand in bringing it upon me.

The burden of work was unremitting. Drawings of the cabins of naval commanders of this period show pile on pile of papers, logbooks, files, notebooks, charts, musterbooks, and orderbooks. It was a navy that ran on paper.

No one who met Nelson thought he looked like a hero should. Lady Spencer, sophisticated wife of a distinguished First Lord of the Admiralty called Nelson 'a most uncouth creature.' His general appearance, she thought – and this was a woman who loved and admired him – 'was that of an idiot.' He was the most feared naval commander in the world. In the previous seven years he had entirely destroyed, in brutally close action, both a French and a Danish fleet, with scarcely a thought for his own or his crews' safety. 'I consider the destruction of the Enemy's Fleet of so much consequence,' he had written within the last few months, 'that I would willingly have half of mine burnt to effect their destruction. I am in a fever. God send I may find them.' Naval warfare had not known such application since the wild mêlées of almost two centuries before. Nelson's declared purpose, in letter after letter, was simple and total: 'annihilation'. The spirit of Achilles was in him.

He was dressed this morning, as ever, in the coat on which the four stars of his orders of knighthood were embroidered in sequins. There was a drama to his presence. This was not Horatio Nelson, the smallish son of a Norfolk parson, the desperately anxious, self-justifying, sometimes jealous, sometimes squabblingly argumentative man he could so often appear from his letters; nor the extraordinarily unbuttoned lover; nor the friend of his brother officers and subordinates to whom, in an endless and ubiquitous cascade of ease and intimacy, he could bind himself with a single letter or even a look. This, as his orders still preserved in the Admiralty files in London repeatedly describe him, was:

> The Right Honorable Lord Viscount Nelson K.B. Duke of Bronte in Sicily, Knight of the Great Cross of St Ferdinand & of Merit, Knight of the Order of the Crescent & of the Illustrious Orders of St Joachim, Vice-Admiral of the White and Commander in Chief of His Majesty's Ships and Vessels employed and to be employed on the Mediterranean Station.

Here was the Trafalgar amalgam, Achilles as the servant of the state, an intense and passionate man, in whom one of the forms which passion took was the precise and unending attention to the details of order and organisation on which successful war depended.

The slowness of it would surprise us today, a murderous punch delivered at just about walking pace. The British ships, with all sails set, were moving at no more than two or three miles an hour. Ships' boats rowed the frigate captains over to the flagship. In most ships, breakfast and then lunch were served to the men. According to Nelson's particular instructions, all the men were given wine not the mixture of rum and water known in the navy as grog. As each swell came through, picking up the starboard quarter, travelling the length of the hull and then dropping the bow in the trough that followed, the huge rectangular bodies of the ships-of-the-line, built more for strength than speed, wooden blockhouses with oak walls three feet thick, their length no more than three or four times their beam, surged forward for a moment, only to fall back into a low, lazy wallow. Swell in light airs slats and bangs at sails and yards. From the slow scraping to and fro of an unoiled block, the creak of the main-top irons, the 'frequent *crack, crack* of the tiller' as the helmsman adjusted to each swell, the snatch and tug of a gust at the canvas, the pulling of the hard-eyes at the shackles on deck, everyone on every ship would have known that a storm would be on them before a day or two was out.

For over six steady hours, the two fleets watched each other growing larger, filling ever more of the eyepieces of their telescopes. A few miles out from the Spanish coast, and keeping warily away from the line of reefs and shoals which rim that shore between Cadiz and Cape Trafalgar, the combined Spanish and French fleet of 33 ships-of-the-line had been, according to orders received from Napoleon himself, attempting to make their way down into the Strait of Gibraltar and then on into the Mediterranean, heading for southern Italy where they were to land the 4,000 French soldiers they had on board. This force was to secure Naples and guard the Emperor's southern flank as he invaded central Europe.

The Combined Fleet was not in good order. They had inched out of Cadiz over the previous 36 hours, intently watched by Nelson's guard-dogs, every move, every hoisting of a yard, every bending of a sail transmitted by flag signal to the admiral waiting over the horizon. But the wind conditions had been difficult, their manoeuvres had been poorly executed and by this morning several ships had slipped far to leeward of the line. Mutual contempt prevailed between French and Spanish officers. The French considered the Spanish incompetent, the Spanish thought the French treacherous. Much of this fleet had fought an action together against a British squadron in July, in which two Spanish ships had been captured by the British, the result, the Spanish thought, of French failure to defend them. The French of course saw it only as evidence of Spanish hopelessness at sea. An atmosphere of anxiety and gloom had settled on them all. As the Spaniards had left the final angry Council of War in Cadiz, two days earlier, they had bowed to Villeneuve, the French Commander-in-Chief 'with a resigned demeanour, like gladiators of old Rome, making their salute in the arena: "*Ave Caesar, morituri te salutant!*" Hail Caesar, those who are about to die salute you.'

The asymmetry between British confidence and Franco-Spanish despair, at the very beginning of the battle, is the governing condition of Trafalgar. The battle was lost and won before a moment of it was fought. This was a meeting the British had desired for at least two years, a chance to establish their command of the world ocean. But it was a meeting which their enemies, as they quite explicitly repeated in dispatch after dispatch to Madrid, Paris and on to Napoleon's mobile headquarters, then in Germany, did not desire at all. The French and Spanish commanders knew, as if it were their destiny, that a catastrophe awaited them.

In the light of this, what happened at Trafalgar is, on one level, not complicated: a highly ambitious, confident and aggressive English battle fleet found and attacked a larger combined French and Spanish fleet whose morale was broken, and whose command was divided and without conviction, and heavily defeated it, by killing and disabling very large numbers of its officers and crew. In some ways, that was all: a pack of dogs battened on to a flock of sheep.

It is an easy description and in some ways inaccurate. The sheep were armed, brave, obstinate and frightening and did dreadful damage to the British attackers. Nevertheless there is a kernel of truth in it and the description raises questions. Why were the English so ambitious, so confident and so aggressive? Why were these crews, about half of them there against their own will, prepared to accept the level of risk which their commanders offered them? Why, in their different ways, were the French and Spanish so broken, so pusillanimous, so defeatist? Why did the British manage to kill ten times more of their enemy than they did of the British? How by 1805 had the Royal Navy become the most effective maritime killing machine in the world? And how had the French and Spanish, each with their long, dignified and noble naval traditions, become their quivering and broken victims?

There are technological answers to these questions, to do with ships and guns, but they are not enough. Two British ships, the *Berwick* and the *Swiftsure*, both in fact fought on the French side during the battle. They had been captured from the British during the war. The British *Belleisle* had begun life as the French *Formidable*, captured off the Breton coast in 1795. Many of the British ships had anyway been built as copies of French men-of-war. The British *Achille* for example was a precise copy of the French 74-gun ship *Pompée*, which had been captured by the British in 1793. The Spanish fleet had in large part been built by renegade Catholic Irishmen, using British ship-building techniques, even in the Spanish yards in Cuba, and including the greatest ship of all, the four-decker *Santísima Trinidad*, entirely constructed of sweet-smelling Cuban cedar.

Technology does not distinguish the fleets – or at least not sufficiently. What makes them different are the people on board. Trafalgar is a meeting of men. It is in the men that the difference lies between aggression and the need to defend; between the desire to attack and destroy and the desperate fear for one's life; between the ability to persist in battle when surrounded by gore, grief and destruction and the need to submit to the natural instincts to surrender; and between a reliance on an old-fashioned tactical method of defence – the well-closed-up line – and a hungry, searching and disconcerting inventiveness which blew that defence into atoms. The day of Trafalgar was one in which three complex variations of the early 19th-century European frame of mind was put to the test.

Both French and Spanish regarded the British with fear and contempt. When the Spanish declared war on Great Britain in 1797, the Madrid government had explained its decision to go to war by describing how

> that ambitious and greedy nation has once more proclaimed to the world that she recognizes no law but that of aggrandizement of her own trade, achieved by her global despotism on the high seas; our patience is spent, our forbearance is exhausted: we must now turn our gaze to the dignity of our throne . . . We must now declare war on the King of England and the English nation.

The values that were in conflict here are obvious enough, and reminiscent of 20th-century European attitudes to America: British amoral commercial ruthlessness set against the dignified, aristocratic patience and honour of old Spain. It is the repeated note in the contemporary Spanish view of Britain, confirmed after an incident in October 1804, when Spain was reluctantly in alliance with France but not yet formally at war with Britain, and which established the British fleet in Spanish eyes as little more than state-sponsored pirates.

A powerful group of four British frigates under the command of Captain Graham Moore, as commodore of the squadron, was cruising off Cadiz, with orders to detain any Spanish ships they should fall in with. Early on the morning of 5 October, they spotted four large Spanish frigates coming in from the west and making for Cadiz harbour. After an initial parley, in which the Spanish refused to surrender, the British rapidly savaged their opponents. They had come from Montevideo, with four million South American gold dollars on board as well as hides and furs. Two of the Spanish frigates were captured, described as 'torn to pieces' when later brought into Spithead, and one of them, the *Mercedes,* blew up, killing everyone on board.

What scandalised Spanish opinion more than anything else, though, were the civilian casualties. The wife of a colonel of artillery was wounded in the battle and died of her wounds when a prisoner in England. On the *Mercedes* were a large number of 'Spanish gentlemen and 19 ladies,' as it was reported in the *Naval Chronicle*, 'with their families, from Lima, returning to Old Spain, who, with the Spanish Captain, his wife, and seven children, all unfortunately perished in the explosion which took place.' The presence of these people was known to the British commodore, but he had no hesitation, once the Spaniards had refused his invitation to accompany him to an English port, in making, as he described it in his dispatch, 'the signal for close battle, which was instantly commenced with all the alacrity and vigour of English sailors.' Moore was acting entirely in accord with British government policy. As Lord Harrowby, the British Foreign Secretary informed the Madrid Court, 'it was an act done in express orders from his Majesty, to detain all ships laden with treasure for Spain.' Spain was paying reluctant subsidies to France and so her bullion was seen by the British as war material. Heartlessness at sea, and never more than when in pursuit of gold, was British policy. Nelson himself was described by the deeply conservative and nationalistic Spanish poet Francisco Sánchez Barbaro as '*el tirano del mar*' and '*el héroe más bárbaro y tirano*'. In the daily *Diario de Madrid*, the British in general were seen as '*los arrogantes usurpadores de la libertad de los mares*'. It seems, in retrospect, a perfectly legitimate description.

The language and perception was shared by the French. 'The sea must become free like the land,' the revolutionary zealot André Jeanbon Saint-André had told the French fleet in Brest in January 1794.

> Deploy therefore all the force and power which the People, whom you have the honour to represent, can give to exterminate the most miserable of its enemies, the speculators of London, the oppressors of Bengal, the disturbers of public peace in Europe. Ships, cannon, sailors: such must be your rallying cry.

Far more than any war of the 18th century, this was a triangular, ideological conflict. A post-revolutionary, authoritarian regime in France, profoundly subversive of all the accepted nostrums of pre-modern European society, was allied in Spain with the most conservative and backward of all the European powers, the trailing partner in the alliance, against a Britain which already embodied a distinctly modern Atlanticist set of values – commercial, libertarian, amoral and aggressive – but which remained, nevertheless, dressed in some very old-fashioned 'King and Country', monarchist 18th-century Establishment clothes.

Spain was the poorest, weakest, most inefficient and most antique of the three. It remained in 1805 a profoundly conservative country. The radical changes that had already occurred further north in Europe scarcely impinged, except in the most superficial of ways, on the style, thinking and government of the country. Spain was without a middle class. Enormous armies of desperately poor landless peasants languished at the bottom of society. A hereditary aristocracy remained, at least in theory, the dominant class, motivated by little except a kind of piety towards the crown, its institutions and the Roman church. The Spanish navy was officered by those aristocrats and manned by those peasants – a plebeian/patrician polarity on which the working of modern, high technology men-of-war, with highly complex systems of both sailing and fighting the vessels, could not easily rely.

On top of that, the Spanish aristocracy had learned to exist in a kind of dependency culture. Spain itself, scarcely developed from its own medieval poverty, had relied for two and a half centuries on the wealth it had extracted from the New World. Six or eight generations of its leading families had come to understand that no effort was required in order to enjoy the fruits of life. They had become indolent. Work was anathema to them. The hereditary offices which they still held were performed for them by low-grade administrative clerks. Unlike in England, the aristocracy was still difficult to penetrate. Soldiers, bankers and lawyers had yet to enter its ranks. It had become, in a word, effete.

Spain had lagged behind. Professional people were still miserably paid and of low standing, treated as minor functionaries. The productive cycle which had been developing in Britain for a century or more between higher growth, better standards of living, rising expectations, a hunger for world markets and a burgeoning economy had scarcely begun in Spain. Disease still reigned: although plague had finally disappeared in the 1720s, 'flu, smallpox, typhoid, dysentery and malaria continued to sweep through the country. Deeply symptomatic of a country going nowhere, of opportunities scarcely presenting themselves to Spanish youth, almost a quarter of Spaniards simply never married. There was no future for them to look forward to. As a result of high death rates and a low birth rate, the population of Spain had increased by little more than half during the century. In the same period, the number of English had doubled. The two countries were not even in the same arena. In the light of this, Nelson's famous insult to the Spanish has often been misinterpreted as pure racism. 'The Dons may make fine ships,' he wrote in 1793, '– they cannot however make men.' But this is not, as it might sound, a reflection on Spanish virility. It is a description of a demographic fact. The supply of good, strong, well-fed men, with a high level of ambition and enterprise, was simply absent. 'They have four first-rates in commission at Cadiz,' Nelson went on, 'and very fine ships, but shockingly manned. I am certain if our six barges' crews, who are picked men, had got on board one of them, they would have taken her.' He was probably right.

Navies reflect the societies from which they come and at Cadiz in October 1805, Villeneuve, the French commander, was in despair about his Spanish allies. Their ships were in such poor condition, he reported to his friend Denis Decrès, Minister of Marine in Paris, that they should never have been sent to sea. Scurvy and dysentery were rife. One of the disadvantages from which Spain suffered, compared with its northern rivals, was the ability of tropical and Caribbean diseases to survive in the homeland. Yellow fever, which would habitually kill up to twenty per cent a year of the naval manpower of all nations when stationed in the Caribbean, could not survive the cold of southern England. In Spain it felt at home and Cadiz itself had been subject to a yellow fever epidemic that had been raging across the whole of southern Spain since the spring. More than a quarter of the thirty-six thousand people in Malaga, for example, had died of the sickness. With social systems collapsing across the whole of southern Spain, there was no food in Cadiz and few stores for refitting the ships. There was little money with which to pay crews, or any bounty for those who might be persuaded to volunteer. The people on board the Spanish ships, Villeneuve told Decrès, were ridiculous. Barely ten per cent were sailors. 'It is truly painful to see such strong and beautiful ships manned with shepherds and beggars, and to have such a tiny number of real seamen. The fleet is not in a state to perform the services appointed to it. The Spanish are quite incapable of meeting the enemy.' Intriguingly, the percentage of qualified seamen on British ships, when first leaving port, might not on occasions have been a great deal higher. The Spanish rarely put large fleets to sea but the British blue seas policy, pursued since the early 18th century, by which fleets were kept for years at a time blockading the ports of continental Europe, transformed those incompetent landmen into effective and coherent crews. On both sides, policy reinforced demography.

In common with other European navies, the Spanish had more ships than they could man. Unavailability of skilled labour, rather than the lack of funds, limited the effectiveness and power of their navy. Like the French, the government had for fifty years organised a register of all acknowledged seamen, on whom the state could call in time of war. But, inevitably, in Spain as in France, the state did not have the mechanisms to enforce the scheme. The demands made by the register could be all too easily cheated. Poorly paid officials depended on bribes as an essential part of their income, and repeatedly the men did not appear. The savage discipline habitual in all navies – fifty strokes while lashed to a cannon for the first attempt to desert; consignment to the galleys for the second – did little to encourage subscription.

Vice-Admiral Jose de Mazarredo wrote to the King in May 1801, describing his predicament when finding himself at sea with no more than sixty sailors with any experience out of a crew of five hundred, the rest being fishermen and off coasting vessels 'without training or any understanding whatsoever of a ship's rigging or routine on board, such as securing a topgallant sail to the yardarm or taking in a reef.' It was a stumbling, untrained mass of ill-assorted peasantry with which the aristocrats of the Spanish officer class put to sea in October 1805. Spanish gun crews were able to fire one round every five minutes from each of their 32lb cannon. Most British crews could manage a round every ninety seconds. The best could reduce that time by a third.

The Spanish commander, Vice-Admiral Federico Carlos Gravina, was a Sicilian, and spoke a strongly accented

Italian as his mother tongue – a trait he had in common with Napoleon – but his father, the Duke of San Miguel, was a Spanish grandee of the first class, as was his mother's father. Gravina inherited the right on both his mother's and his father's side, to wear his hat in the presence of the King. He was, in many ways, an antique himself, laden with a sense of honour, duty and a particularly Spanish form of fatalism. 'There are disasters that may be honoured as victory,' the 19th-century Spanish nationalist Manuel Marliani later wrote of Trafalgar. It was a catastrophically self-fulfilling frame of mind.

Threads and fragments of the European Enlightenment had found their way into Spain. The Spanish navy had conducted long exploratory scientific voyages through the Pacific, which bear comparison with those of James Cook on behalf of the British Admiralty; and there was, for example, a modern and efficiently run meteorological observatory outside Cadiz. But these were superficial changes. The traditional structures remained in place. Of the two hundred and twenty-seven ships built for the Spanish Royal Navy in the eighteenth century, a third of them had been named after saints, others after the Mother of Christ, several after key elements of church doctrine: the Spanish Royal Navy was proud of nothing more than the *Salvador del Mundo*, and the *Purísima Concepción*. Here at Trafalgar, the *Santísima Trinidad*, the largest ship in the world, was the flagship of Rear-Admiral don Bernardo Hidalgo Cisneros, the *Santa Ana* carried the flag of Vice-Admiral don Ignacio Maria de Alava. In the Spanish fleet, Catholicism and aristocracy clasped each other in an embrace of pure retrospection.

The Spanish hierarchy had been exposed to, and clearly knew about, more modern approaches to war – and life – but didn't take them up. After the execution of Louis XVI, Spain had been briefly allied with Britain against France.

Gravina had visited Portsmouth in 1793 and had been introduced there to the extraordinarily beneficial effects that citrus juice could have on the health of sailors. The British sailors were known as 'limeys' for the very reason that they drank citrus juice drinks. Nelson would sip lemonade as he died. But Gravina ignored the advice. It was not what the Spaniards did. Lime and lemon juice was never introduced to the Spanish fleet and scurvy continued its wild career among their sad, impoverished crews.

There was one final element in Spanish naval tradition that would on the day secure their defeat. The navy itself, despite playing the essential role in the creation and maintenance of the Spanish overseas empire, on whose income the Spanish state itself relied, was not regarded, as it was in England, as 'the first service'. The theatre in which true nobility in Spanish arms could be enacted was on land. Seamanship, the handling and running of a ship, was considered secondary to the fighting that could be done once the sailors had manoeuvred the warriors into position. The captain of a Spanish ship did not concern himself with sailing matters. That was the business of a junior officer, the pilot, to whom all aspects of seamanship were delegated. The captain was in charge of the soldiers on board, of whom there were inordinate numbers. As a result, the Spanish men-of-war at Trafalgar were not ships but floating fortresses, castles in transit, commanded by a clique of officers for whom victory might have been preferable but who considered nothing more honourable than an exceptionally bloody defeat. On 20 October, Gravina listed the men on board his flagship, the *Principe de Asturias*: Infantry troops 382; marine artillerymen 172; officers and men 609. Even nominally, without taking into account the goatherds and the sweepings of Cadiz, almost half the men on board the Spanish flagship at Trafalgar were not seamen.

Set against the Spanish pieties, the names of the French

ships proclaimed a different culture: the great inheritance of Greek and Roman heroes, the beauties of France herself, the burning ardour of revolutionary zeal, the glories of empires which France had conquered and, like the masterpieces Napoleon was gathering in the Louvre, could adopt as her own. There was not a Christian idea or reference among them.

In October 1805, though, there was some mismatch between the trumpeting of these glories and the actual condition of the fleet. The flagship, the *Bucentaure*, was named after the great gilded barge of the Doge of Venice, the ancient republic finally humiliated by Napoleon in 1797. But the *Bucentaure* had been struck by lightning and all her masts were in a fragile condition. Nor were there any timbers in Cadiz with which to replace them. She wasn't alone in her fragility. Most of the ships of the French fleet had been sent to sea, as Villeneuve wrote to the Ministry, with 'bad masts, bad sails and bad rigging', and, overall, his account of the force under his command was full of unintended irony:

> The *Formidable*, the *Mont Blanc*, the *Fougueux*, [meaning the *Ardent*], and the *Swiftsure* [a ship captured from the British, and left with its earlier name as a taunt to the enemy] all need docking. The *Scipion* [the name of the two greatest and most aggressive of Roman generals] and the *Aigle* [the symbol of imperial dominance] want rerigging. The *Pluton* [the King of Hell] and the *Héros* can scarcely sail. The *Indomptable*, the *Achille* and the *Berwick* [another British capture] all have weak and incompetent crews.

It was a depressing audit, the rhetoric floating free of the vessels it adorned. 'There is not a ship,' the admiral wrote, 'with less than sixty sick on board.'

These were not temporary aberrations. There were deep and systematic failures in French naval administration of which all this was the outward sign. There had been French successes in the past: they had been defeated by the British Royal Navy during the Seven Years War between 1757 and 1763, but after radical reorganisation and major investment had out-fought and out-manoeuvred the British during the American War of Independence. In the revolutionary and Napoleonic wars, which had begun in 1793, they, like the other Europeans, had been consistently defeated by the Royal Navy, and at an extraordinary cost in human lives. It has been calculated that in the six major battles between British fleets and their French, Spanish, Dutch and Danish enemies (First of June 1794, Cape St Vincent 1797, Camperdown 1797, The Nile 1798, Copenhagen 1801 and Trafalgar 1805) the British lost a total of 5,749 men killed and wounded, of whom 1,483 were killed in battle. In the same engagements, their enemies lost 38,970 killed, wounded and taken prisoner, of whom 9,068 were killed in battle itself, a figure over six times greater than the number of British dead.

At Trafalgar that disproportion rose to an unprecedentedly high ratio of very nearly ten times the number of French and Spanish dead to English, but that Everest of slaughter was only the culmination of a consistent pattern. Over more than twelve years, in a wide variety of conditions and theatres of naval war, the British had savagely outkilled their opponents.

Much of what follows will attempt to explain that imbalance, but there can be no doubt that the travails and evolutions of France herself were at least partly to blame. Before the Revolution, the French navy had been in far from perfect condition, without an effective central board of control – nothing to match the British Admiralty – and consistently struggling to source the large number of complex materials needed to equip a fleet. French shipbuilders had, throughout the 18th century, designed light, fast and efficient ships, the envy of their British enemies and widely copied by them. But the sourcing of the necessary materials had consistently imposed strains which were not met. The 74-gun ship had by the end of the century become the workhorse of all navies – heavy enough to confront anything, fast enough to pursue any other ship-of-the-line. But to create a 74-gun ship required 100,000 cubic feet of timber for the hull, 168,000 pounds of hemp for the rigging, 33,750 pounds of copper to sheathe that hull, keeping it clean and fast, and 4,800 pounds of nails to fix the entire elaborate assemblage together. About 3,400 trees, from about 75 acres of woodland, were needed for each ship. Ninety per cent of that was oak, half of it straight, for the keel, stempost and the heavy planking; half of it curved, for the knees and breasthooks on which the integral strength of a ship-of-the-line relied.

The supply system was the foundation of any navy and throughout the 1790s the British had applied the screw. Ship timber was being imported into Britain from the Adriatic, masts and hemp from North America, and large quantities of materials were carried from the Baltic. Decks were made of 'good Prussia deals' and the British Admiralty always specified that 'all the Iron-work shall be wrought of the best Swedish iron'. By the end of the century, the number of British merchantmen sailing south from the Baltic to British ports had reached the astonishing total of 4,500 every year, the majority of them laden with naval stores: corn, tallow, hides, hemp and iron. Commerce was not only the purpose and prize of the long war against France; it was its method.

The cost of the fleet to the British Treasury was enormous: in 1805 alone, £2.9 million was spent on the pay of the 107,000 seamen and marines in the Royal Navy;

another £2.96 million on their food; but fully £4.68 million was spent on repairing the wear and tear of vessels which were maintaining the blockades around the European shores. By comparison, only £400,000 was spent on ordnance, on the guns and their shot which would do the damage at Trafalgar. It was the very bodies of the ships themselves, and the materials of which the ships were made, which imposed the financial strain, demanding from the British government more than a third of its total annual expenditure.

The French struggled and failed to keep up. Even by the measure of looking after their own men, they failed. In 1801, Admiral Ganteaume in command of the premier fleet in France, the Brest squadron, wrote imploringly to the minister:

> I once more call your attention to the terrible state in which the sea men are left, unpaid for fifteen months, naked or covered with rags, badly fed, down in the mouth; in a word sunk under the weight of the deepest and most humiliating wretchedness.

Since the late 17th century, the French state had reserved large slices of their native oak forest for those hulls, but it was not enough and they ransacked Italian oakwoods and Corsican pinewoods for their needs. The catastrophes of the 1790s had exacerbated the problem. When the British Admiral Lord Hood burnt nine French ships of the line and removed three more from Toulon in December 1793 (he had already taken one 74, an earlier *Scipion*, which soon sank) he also burned untold quantities of slowly maturing French oak from those government forests, stacked in the Toulon yards, and even larger quantities of mast- and spar-timber from the Baltic. The total destruction in 1798 of the French Mediterranean fleet at the Battle of the Nile, and in a series of individual ship actions after it, were both key elements in a form of attritional warfare which left the French naval establishment bruised, bleeding and diminished. The figures make it clear enough. In 1793, Britain had 135 ships-of-the-line and 133 frigates, the French well behind with 80 ships-of-the-line and 66 frigates. By 1801, at the peace of Amiens, the number of British warships had risen to 202 ships-of-the-line and 277 frigates. France at the same moment had 39 ships of the line and 35 frigates. Attrition had exacted its price.

In many ways, Trafalgar had been won at Toulon and the Nile. More, though, than technological and material failure, the long unrolling political crisis in France during the last years of the 18th century meant that the navy did not have the necessary depth and consistency of support it needed. The failing monarchy, the Revolution, the Terror, the string of half-competent administrations in the late 1790s and the coming to power of Napoleon – the 'land animal' as he was called – all, in their different ways, failed the French navy.

In the 19th century, it was often said by French conservative historians that the triumphant French navy of the American War of Independence was destroyed by the Revolution and the chaos that followed. That is not true. The endemic weaknesses stretched back into the management and structures of the pre-revolutionary navy itself. The French officer corps was traditionally formed into two divisions: *l'épée* and *la plume*, the fighting and the administrative arms. Each regarded the other with contempt: the pen thinking the sword incompetent, the sword regarding the pen as common. The British Board of Admiralty had a hint of the same division between politically appointed civilians and experienced, fighting 'sea lords', but further down the ranks of the Royal Navy, fighting tasks, sailing tasks and administrative tasks were all performed, at different stages, by the same individuals.

The three core demands of a navy – to supply and fit itself; to survive the sea; and to kill the enemy – were understood in Britain to be part of a single integrated whole. In both Spain and France, that single organism was institutionally divided into conflicting and competing parts.

This was largely a reflection of social structure. In England, the officers of the navy came from a broad spread of English society, stretching from the lower reaches of the aristocracy through the landed gentry and professional classes to (occasionally) the genuinely poor. Of Nelson's great predecessors in the 18th century, for example, Sir Cloudesley Shovell, who ran his fleet up on rocks off Scilly, was the son of a Norwich merchant; Byng, who was shot for cowardice off Minorca, was the son of a Kentish gentleman; Vernon was the son of a London merchant; Anson from Staffordshire gentry; Hawke the son of a barrister; Rodney from a family of army officers, and with his mother's father a judge; Howe was the second son of an Irish peer; Lord Hood was the son of a vicar, like Nelson himself; Lord Barham's father was a customs officer; St Vincent's a lawyer; and Lord Cornwallis was the fourth son of a peer, who like his brothers had been educated at Eton.

Those are the great men of the 18th-century navy. There is a drift towards high social status among them, but it is a far from exclusive set. Their mixed social origins are evidence of a kind of responsive elasticity in the hiring and promoting strategies of the Royal Navy. Nothing could have been more different in the Marine Royale of Bourbon France. There, any access to the officer corps was, as in Spain, rigidly restricted to members of the aristocracy. Access to the Grand Corps was through the élite trainee cadres of the *Gardes de la Marine* and the *Gardes du Pavillon*.

In the British navy, the test to become a junior officer, a lieutenant, depended on having spent at least six years at sea as a midshipman and an ability to answer a series of disturbingly sea-based questions. As the standard form of words approving a promotion to lieutenant expressed it, the candidate had to prove that he could

> Splice, Knot, Reef a sail, work a Ship Sailing, Shift his Tides, keep a Reckoning of a Ships way by Plain Sailing and Mercator, Observe by the Sun or Star, find the variation of the Compass and is qualified to do his Duty as an Able Seaman and a Midshipman.

In May 1805, one young man, William Badcock, was sent forward by his captain Thomas Fremantle of the *Neptune* to sit his exam. He was in a state of extreme nerves and the three captains on the examining board allowed him to sit quietly for a few moments so that he would do himself justice. Then they began.

> I was desired to stand up, and consider myself on the quarterdeck of a man-of-war at Spithead – 'unmoor' – 'get underway' – 'stand out to sea' – 'make and shorten sail' – 'reef' – 'return into port' – 'unrig the foremast and bowsprit, and rig them again'. I got into a scrape after reefing for not overhauling the reef tackles when reefing the sails [because unless those tackles were overhauled, the sails would not set fair]. However they passed me, and desired me to come again the next day to receive my passing certificate. I made the captains the best bow I could and, without staying, to look behind me, bolted out of the room . . .

* * *

For the young French aristocrat officers of the *gardes*, there was no equivalent. They were given an education in the great ports of Brest, Rochefort and Toulon and the curriculum they followed was essentially mathematical. They studied hydrography and the customs of the shipbuilding trade in both England and Spain, but no history, nothing about fighting or sailing tactics. There were daily sessions set aside for both dancing and fencing. Any suggestion that a French officer would know how to steer a ship, reef a sail, splice a warp or make a Single Diamond Knot, a Sprit-Sail Sheet Knot, a Carrick Bend, a Midshipman's Hitch, a throat seizing, a mouse for a stay or puddings for yards, would have drawn as quizzical a look from him as it does from us. All those tasks, and tens more, described in detail and with diagrams in the midshipman's *vade mecum*, '*The Young Sea Officer's Sheet Anchor*', first published in Leeds in 1808, but drawing on centuries-long expectation, were required to be known by an officer in the British Royal Navy. There was a naval academy in England established at Dartmouth, but it was not the usual or favoured route to a successful naval career. The British training ground was at sea.

In this was the core difference between the middle-class British and upper-class French and Spanish officer corps. For an aristocrat, failure in battle does not erode his standing or his honour. He remains, as long as he has behaved with courage, the man he was born to be. For the younger son of the English gentry, or of a lawyer or merchant, as most British naval officers were, there is no such destined luxury. If he fails at sea, his standing is diminished; he has not won the prize money which will set him up at home; his name is not gilded with honour; he has failed in the same way that a failing entrepreneur has failed. To preserve his honour and his name, he needs to win. Victory is neither a luxury nor an ornament. It is a compulsion and a necessity.

The young French *gardes*, convinced of their genetic and social superiority, often behaved with a kind of violent arrogance which more senior naval officers could scarcely control. In 1774, a senior naval administrator, Vice-Admiral Laurent Jean-François Truguet condemned it.

> The spirit of independence, of contrariness, of egotism which has long distinguished the different classes of naval officers, and which is so opposed to the good of the King's service, certainly is borne in the companies of the *gardes de la marine* and *du pavillon*; they perpetuate it in carrying it with them to all ranks.

No one should suggest that the officer corps of the ancien regime in France was made up of exclusively self-indulgent young blue bloods. There were a few officers of non-aristocratic lineage – *les bleus*, as they were called, contrasted with *les rouges* of the *gardes* – even if they were looked down on and excluded from the most valuable commands. In the 1780s there had been half-hearted attempts to recruit and promote men with a regard more to their skills than their names. There were officers among the aristocrats of great resource, ingenuity, courage and dedication to their profession. And the pre-revolutionary aristocracy was more open to recruitment from the bourgeoisie and the professional classes than is sometimes realised. Fully two-thirds of French titles dated back no further than the 1620s.

Nevertheless, the higher ranks in the French navy were strikingly incompetent. Fleet commands were more often than not given to old and decrepit admirals. Only three of the 22 vice-admirals promoted between 1715 and 1789 had ever commanded fleets at sea and the rank of lieutenant-general, a pivotal fleet position, was equally carelessly filled with the clueless: only eighteen of the sixty-eight *lieutenants-généraux* appointed between 1720 and 1784 had held seagoing commands. The man in charge of the navy as a whole, the Admiral of France, was the Duc de

Penthièvre, a relative of the king, who had never been on board a ship and treated the navy merely as a useful source of income.

It would be a mistake, though, to think of the French naval officers as doing little more than living out a self-deluded, aristocratic fantasia. It is true that they were deeply attached to and proud of their aristocratic traditions. It is equally true that there was fierce regional conflict between the Breton aristocrats and the Provençal aristocrats with which the Brest and Toulon fleets were officered. And it is true that to many of them their membership of the Hospitallers of St John of Jerusalem, or the Knights of Malta, the order of military Christian Knights founded in the 12th century as one of the vehicles of an ardent Christianity fighting Islam in the Mediterranean, was of equal importance to them as their duties with the French navy.

But these educated and professional men were inevitably alert to the forces of the Enlightenment unfolding around them. Their élitism had adopted modern dress and many of the Grand Corps thought of themselves as modern scientific men. In the 1780s, the French naval officer began to take up serious modern studies in navigation, the fixing of longitude, the rationalist understanding of the essence of sea-battle and other aspects of the sea, cartography and ship-building, as well learning and exercising in gunnery and fleet tactics. But, whatever its dress, the attitudes remained élitist, a step away from the antique Spanish grandeur, but at least as far removed from the British practice, which, from the very beginning, engaged the young midshipmen with the workings of the ship and its men.

The overall commander of the combined French and Spanish fleets at Trafalgar came from precisely such a tradition, as did his two deputy admirals. All three were aristocrats. Pierre-Charles-Jean-Baptiste-Silvestre Villeneuve was, until 1793, *de* Villeneuve, when he quietly dropped the incriminating preposition. He became what all self-preservative aristocrats in revolutionary France became, a '*ci-devant*', a Heretofore. But there was little he could do to disguise his patrician origins. He was a grandee from Provence, in all probability a pious Catholic, perceptibly well bred, reserved in manner, exquisite in dress and refined in demeanour. One ancestor had fought alongside Roland in the pass at Roncesvalles; others had been on the crusades. He was the 91st Villeneuve to be a Knight of Malta. He was an educated man, who would quote lines from the great French tragedians, with an alert and supple sense of irony at the predicament in which the revolutionary era had placed him, and with a devastating sense of honour and duty which would, in the end, be his downfall. Napoleon, comparing these qualities with his requirement for all-consuming ardour, called Villeneuve a *poltron de tête*, an intellectual coward, a man perhaps too refined for the brutalities which the moment required of him.

The navy of which Villeneuve was now a part was scarcely recognisable from the one he had joined as a boy. After 1789, it became an obvious target of revolutionary rage. It was a symbol of royal power in the French provinces, easily attacked by the populace when in harbour, and it was an organisation boiling over with the discontent and argumentativeness on which revolutionary movements feed. The Bourbon navy had never been able to pay the notoriously corrupt and self-confident dockyard workers and government authority soon broke down in the yards at Toulon and Brest. Throughout the 1790s, the British Admiralty had exactly the same problems with the skilled, articulate workforce in the British dockyards, the same economic and social energies bubbling up on both sides of the English Channel. In Britain, such stirrings were controlled by a careful imposition of state authority.

Trouble-makers were excluded; many of them were imprisoned on charges framed according to new anti-collectivist legislation rapidly passed by a Pitt government in political panic. It was called, at the time, the 'White Terror': Habeas Corpus was suspended in 1794 and again in 1798; a Treason and Sedition Act was passed in 1795, an Unlawful Oaths Act in 1797, a Corresponding Societies Act in 1799. Public meetings were banned and spies recruited. In the Royal Navy itself, uncompromising punishments were dealt out to the 47 ringleaders of the naval mutinies in 1797. Those men were mostly hanged, according to explicit Admiralty orders, by men from their own ships: men forced, by the authority of the state, to hang their own friends. By such methods, dissent was effectively suppressed in Britain until after Waterloo.

In France, though, the revolutionary state itself could not, at least initially, impose such repressive order on the popular will. Instead it faced an ideological conundrum: how could it discipline the popular will on which its own legitimacy was said to be founded? In the revolutionary navy, all citizens were to be eligible for all ranks. The habits of deference were to be banished by the ideals of equality. Discipline based on authority was to be replaced by discipline based on voluntary compliance. As Napoleon later reflected from St Helena, 'It was part of the political religion of the France of that day to make war in the name of principles.' For the old officer class, it was a catastrophe and their response was to abscond. By November 1791, 403 of Brest's 600 officers were absent, most without leave. The following February, one captain of a ship-of-the-line in Brest wrote anonymously to the Minister of Marine in Paris:

> A terrible fate awaits those who will command ships in the future, because they will be disobeyed and

> scorned with impunity. What has happened aboard various ships proves that juries can excuse faults of any kind: the most complete revolt becomes a crime that is scarcely punishable. These offences are recent, and no order of things permits the hope of a happier future.

In 1792, only 2 out of 9 vice-admirals, 2 out of 18 rear-admirals, 42 out of 170 captains and 390 out of 750 lieutenants remained at their posts. Those who did found themselves with nowhere to turn. 'The tone of the seamen is wholly ruined,' Admiral Morard de Galles wrote on 2 March 1793. He had been at sea in his flagship when her headsails were carried away in a storm, and it became imperative to wear ship, taking her stern through the wind on to the other tack. 'If I had a crew such as we formerly had,' Morard wrote to the Minister,

> I would have used means which would have succeeded; but despite exhortations and threats, I could not get thirty seamen on deck. The army gunners and greater part of the marine troops behaved better. They did what they were told; but the seamen, even the petty officers, did not show themselves.

Naval affairs reached their deepest crisis when in September 1793 a Jacobin mob murdered a naval officer in Toulon and washed their hands in his blood.

The sequence of revolution and mutiny, the punishment and emigration of officers, followed by the rolling waves of political chaos, gave fruit to the Reign of Terror, instituted by decree on September 5 1793. 'It is no longer, as under the Old Regime, the man that you obey,' the National Convention's Committee of Public Safety told the people, 'it is the law; it is *la Patrie*.'

The Convention appointed a ferocious revolutionary zealot, André Jeanbon Saint-André, as its representative responsible for rebuilding the Republic's navy after the chaos of the early revolutionary years. 'Because all here was gangrenous,' he told the fleet in Brest in October 1793, 'all needed the scalpel of patriotism, the billhook of Republicanism.' Guillotines were set up on pontoons among the fleet so that the crews could see the punishments dealt out to the mutinous. A form of naval terror was instituted, during which the language of French naval administration reached new depths of Orwellian doublespeak: 'Do not think that we usurp your rights,' Jeanbon told the men who were to be executed

> when we defend them; to assist you is not to oppress you; to break your chains like this is not to attack your liberty! They say we exercise arbitrary power; they accuse us of being despots: Despots! Us! Hah! Doubtless, if it is despotism which is necessary for the triumph of liberty, this despotism is political regeneration.

Politically-vetted instructors attached to each ship taught republican virtues to the fleet. French sailors in the 1790s had to learn a new Rousseauesque and totalitarian catechism:

> Work, the principal good of the free man; virtue, the torch of revolution and the foundation of republican government; nature, the source of the virtuous man's sweetest pleasures; la Patrie, to which our duty directs everything: force, talent, virtue, luck.

The French fleet was governed by an ideology of terror and virtue. Political commissars sailed with the admirals. All movements of the fleet were to be uniform, simultaneous, and executed with as much precision as speed. Captains who surrendered their ships would be guillotined, as would those who failed to execute an order signalled by the admiral or even those who failed to repeat signals made to them. Special signals were developed so that any French captain could be instantly dismissed and replaced at sea. And captains must attack without pause and without thought of the cost in lives:

> The captain and officers of ships-of-the-line of the Republic who have struck the flag of the nation [surrendered] to enemy vessels, whatever their number, unless their ship has been damaged to the point where it runs the risk of sinking and there is no time left to save the crew, will be declared traitors to their country and punished with death.

With its traditional culture erased; with any hint of individualism suspect; with a poorly found, meanly fed, scantily provisioned and inadequately equipped force; and with a sense of failure somehow implicit in the strictness of such controls, the French fleet fell apart. Fleets do not work unless fed, clothed, equipped and encouraged. They require, in other words, both a sense of their own dignity and a conviction that they are the agents of freedom. The anarchic and impassioned qualities which fuelled the rampaging French armies sweeping all before them in Europe, living off the land, bringing spontaneity and shock to the level of high military art: none of these things can sustain a navy which depends, in its deeper levels, on the far more rationalist, organisational virtues of steadiness of supply and practice, on orderly coherence and a sense of unquestioned mutual reliance. Only when that foundation is set can the famous spontaneities of Nelsonian battle find a role. Nelson could act with Napoleonic aggression and violence in battle only because the Royal Navy had preserved systems which were completely immune to those modern subversive methods.

The direction of French naval affairs under the

Directoire and the Consulate made no improvement: chaotic inflation, a lack of consistency and intermittent supply crippled the French navy. Bonaparte systematised much of the chaos, creating maritime prefectures and appointing at the head of the Department of the Marine an energetic and dynamic engineer, M. Forfait, and to his Council of State, Charles Claret, Comte de Fleurieu, France's foremost geographer, who had been tutor to the Dauphin and a powerful voice in the naval administration before the Revolution. At his imperial coronation in 1804, he had awarded to each ship of the navy an eagle and a flag on which the ship's name was inscribed in gold. Three officers, three petty officers and four sailors had been invited to the coronation to receive their honours.

For all that, so much long-term damage had been done to the body of the French navy and its morale that it would take as long to repair the damage as it had taken to wreak it. When Britain declared war again on France in May 1803, Bonaparte recognised it as a deathblow for the French navy. 'Peace,' he said, 'is necessary to restore a navy, – peace to fill our arsenals empty of materials, and peace because only then is the one exercise-ground for the fleets – the sea itself – open to them.' The French fleet at Trafalgar was limping on to the battlefield.

On this light and gentle morning off the southwest coast of Spain, the three fleets were moving slowly towards their meeting, each a barometer of the almost diagrammatically opposed societies which had created them. Pre-revolutionary Spain was still stuck in the immobilities of the pre-modern world, its population having risen from 8 million in 1700 to no more than 11.5 million a century later, an increase of forty-four per cent; revolutionary France, deeply unsettled by the radical transformations and retransformations of the previous 15 years, was still the central power block of Europe, with a population of 29 million. But that figure concealed a lack of drive and vigour at the most basic biological and social level. France was growing even more slowly than Spain. Over the previous century, the number of French had risen by only 7 million, a growth rate of just over thirty per cent. The failure of the ancien regime in 1789 was the result not of any great demographic pressure coming up from the expanding classes below it, but of the stiffness and incompetence of the ruling class itself. The French Revolution was a failure of government, and the state of Villeneuve's fleet was a reflection of that.

England was different. It had just emerged from a century of unprecedentedly dynamic acceleration and change. Between 1680 and 1820, the growth rate of the English population had been twice the rate of Europe as a whole. England had boomed. Men and women earning wages from businesses did not have to wait, as the poor peasants in Spain and France did, for the old man to die and leave the farm. People could marry younger, have more children, and then continue to live as long as they ever had. Disease was coming under control. Plague never entered 18th-century England (as it did both France and Spain) and by the 1760s smallpox in England had been virtually eradicated by inoculation.

As the population doubled, the value of the work done in England tripled. After 1780, it accelerated again, to an annual growth rate of two per cent, the underlying trend rate ever since. In the century after 1700, there was a sixty per cent increase in agricultural output, more than double the increase over the previous two centuries. It was the burgeoning time. People had plenty of food, children survived the first killing years of life and old men lived on.

England, by 1805, was in this way post-revolutionary. By almost any social or economic measure you might want to choose, England was leaving Europe behind: in the growth of its middle class; in the number of people living in towns and cities; in the size of its government and the level and amount of tax raised; in the ability of both government and individuals to borrow. England in 1805 looked far more like the modern than the pre-modern world. By 1800, well over a third of all people were working in commerce or industry, equalling the number working on the land. Barely one in ten Europeans lived in towns; in 1800, a quarter of the English did. By 1815, that proportion would have risen to a third. There were a million Londoners by 1811, an unprecedentedly vast agglomeration of human beings, a mass of humanity which amazed and appalled its inhabitants, as though it were some sublime effusion of the earth itself; towns in northern England were already black from the smoke of their 'manufactories'. There were no internal trade barriers and Britain was the largest free-trade area in Europe.

The 18th-century English were acknowledged throughout Europe for their violence, shooting highwaymen and seducing 17-year-olds, swearing and farting in public, congratulating themselves on their lack of the effeminate refinements which the French affected. One young English nobleman returned from Paris wearing a wig made of very finely spun iron wire. He became famous for it, a measure of what the English were not. Robert Walpole, the Prime Minister, ate apples in the chamber of the House of Commons to demonstrate his ordinariness. It was not unknown to be shot at in London. Horace Walpole, the Prime Minister's nephew, had to dodge pistol shots in Hyde Park. 'Anything that looks like a fight,' one French traveller, Henri Misson, wrote home, a little scandalised, 'an Englishman considers delicious.'

They liked to bet on anything. The craze for cricket, which swept the country, was largely fuelled by gambling on the outcome of matches, or even on the turn of a single ball. Twenty thousand people came to see Kent play Hampshire in 1772. Lord Sackville batted for a Kent side captained by Rumney, his head gardener. The delights of risk and chance were high on the list of English pleasures. Between its medieval and its 19th-century proprieties, the English spirit of the 18th century had become astonishingly mobile. They were no longer bound to the land. They had made the great escape from the essentially static patterns of a rural agrarian world and moved into the accelerated, modern rhythms of the commercial, the urban, the industrial and the sudden. 'Nobody is provincial in this country,' Louis Simond, a Swiss-American visitor in the first years of the 19th century wrote.

> You meet nowhere with those persons who never were out of their native place, and whose habits are wholly local – nobody above poverty who has not visited London once in his life; and most of those who can do so, visit it once a year. To go up to town from 100 or 200 miles distance, is a thing done on a sudden, and without any previous deliberation. In France the people of the provinces used to make their will before they undertook such an expedition.

They were, by European standards, strikingly literate. By 1790 there were 14 London morning papers and another in the evening. The first Sunday paper began production in 1799. Papers were read at breakfast and as a result an English tradition had already begun: conversation at breakfast was never 'of a lively nature'. They were clean and well fed. The Duc de Rochefoucauld considered the English the cleanest people in Europe. They were also immensely sociable, milling through the streets in crowds. 'I have twice been going to stop my coach in Piccadilly thinking there was a mob,' Horace Walpole wrote, 'and it was only nymphs and swains, sauntering and trudging.' It was a hard-drinking country. There were 16,000 drink shops in London; William Pitt, who had been administered daily glasses of port as a sickly child, was by the 1790s a four-bottles-a-day man (although the port was not so alcoholic and the bottles smaller than ours.) People horded into taverns, where, according to Dr Johnson, 'the true felicity of human life' was to be found. They loved a show. The theatre in Drury Lane held over 3,600 people. George III would read little but *King Lear* as his own madness came on. Boxers were media stars: Jim Belcher, Dutch Sam, Bill Stevens 'The Nailer', Tom Crib and Daniel Mendoza all wrote their boxing memoirs and were feted in the streets. One London show featured Bruising Peg, a woman gladiator, accompanied by Macomo the Nubian lion tamer. In Charlotte Street in London there was a brothel staffed by flagellants. It was the first great age of the hunt, the aristocracy of England pursuing hounds across hedgerows in precisely the way, 150 years later, they would take up skiing.

This is the other side of the French and Spanish view of the English as rapacious, amoral go-getters. It was, needless to say, only obliquely related to the English view of themselves. They saw themselves as the apostles and champions of freedom, set against the various benighted tyrannies, whether revolutionary or Catholic, which had Europe in their grip. The poet laureate, Henry James Pye, who was only given that title because he was a supporter of the Prime Minister, William Pitt, celebrated the English vision of modern Englishness in his 1798 poem *Naucratia: or Naval Dominion*. As a good Tory, gazing out over his acres from the beautiful Palladian villa which he built at Faringdon in Oxfordshire, as loyal MP for Berkshire and a vengeful police magistrate for Westminster, said to be 'destitute alike of poetic feeling or power of expression', he had embraced the civilising beauties of Britain's business mission:

By love of opulence and science led,
Now commerce wide her peaceful empire spread,
And seas, obedient to the pilot's art,
But join'd the regions which they seem'd to part,
Free intercourse disarm'd the barbarous mind
Tam'd hate, and humaniz'd mankind.

The British warships were not usurping the freedom of the seas; they were establishing it, a maritime, commerce-extending force of Roman good. 'Opulence' had yet to acquire its derogatory modern note. Wealth was still unequivocally marvellous. Edmund Burke loved to describe the British House of Commons as 'filled with everything illustrious in rank, in descent, in hereditary and in acquired opulence, in cultivated talents, in military, civil, naval, and political distinction, that the country can afford.' How delicious life was! By the end of the century, a profoundly satisfying complacency had come to settle on British consciousness and the eminently respectable Pye effortlessly embodied it. Not unlike the King he adulated, Henry Pye was the sort of person for whom the Battle of Trafalgar was fought.

If smugness was widespread, even the self-congratulation of *Naucratia* does not quite match the breath-taking complacency of some other contemporary propaganda. An anonymous song, published in about 1801, was to be sung in the voice of 'The Blind Sailor':

A splinter knocked my nose off,
'My bowsprit's gone!' I cries
'Yet well it kept their blows off,
Thank God 'twas not my eyes.'
Scarce with these words I outed,
Glad for my eyes and limbs,

A splinter burst and douted[1]
Both my two precious glims.[2]
I'm blind and I'm a cripple,
Yet cheerful would I sing
Were my disasters triple,
'Cause why? 'twas for my King.'

However grotesque that kind of statist propaganda might now seem now – and did seem then, to those radicals in England opposed to the war and its savage carelessness with poor men's lives – there is nevertheless an important point about the degree to which England was prepared, throughout the period from 1689 until 1815, to subscribe to war. Over that period, the country had been at war for more than half the time. The only long gap was the 16 years of Robert Walpole's consciously peace-seeking administration from 1713 until 1729. Throughout the long 18th century, Britain was either at war, preparing for war or paying off the enormous costs of war. At least three-quarters of all government expenditure during the century had gone on fighting or on paying off the debts which fighting had incurred. In 1793, at a time when the annual tax revenue rarely exceeded £20 million, the national debt stood at £242.9 million. Pitt and his successors taxed and borrowed without hesitation to fight the French. By 1802, when the navy was costing £7 million a year, three times as much was being spent each year on subsidies to Britain's allies on the European continent. Between 1793 and the end of the war in 1815, the British government raised in taxes, and borrowed from the English people, a total of £1.5 billion, a figure which can safely be multiplied by 60 for its modern equivalent. By the end of the war, the national debt had risen to £745 million, or somewhere near

1 Put out
2 eyes

thirty years' government revenue. Pitt and his successors, in other words, put the country in hock, the most radical national gamble of all, pouring money into ships and allies as though their life depended on it, which it did.

This is the second critical difference between Britain and her enemies in the Napoleonic wars: not only were the English riding a big, bucking commercial boom; they were happy to be taxed on their profits. What they didn't give the government in tax, they lent it in return for government bonds. The two were connected. Uniquely in Europe, the British government was able to borrow so much from its own people because it was efficient enough at collecting tax to make sure that the annual interest was paid on the loan. It was a particularly English form of consensual government finance, without which the fleet at Trafalgar would have been as poorly equipped as its enemies'. On this consensual basis the British were able to raise far more in tax throughout the 18th century than the French, while still persuading themselves that they were the freest people on the planet.

British government finance was not without its crises but an extraordinary mutuality in the financial relationship of people and government lay behind the British naval victories in their 18th-century wars. And there is a further element to it, which makes the relationship between the British navy and the commercial classes in Britain particularly intimate and mutually sustaining. The navy was largely paid for by indirect taxes on a huge variety of goods and luxuries, from windows to servants, hair powder, non-working horses, carriages and playing cards, as well as by excise duties levied on imports. The bulk of the tax burden, in other words, fell on the new middle classes as consumers. But the existence of the navy, very much as the great Henry James Pye described it in *Naucratia*, guaranteed and promoted the creation of a world commercial empire. A navy funded by the middle class and largely officered by the middle class created an empire in which the middle classes thrived. Between 1792 and 1800, the commerce of Great Britain on the seas which its navy controlled increased by an astonishing seven per cent year on year, rising from £44.5 million in 1792 to £73.7 million in 1800. Excise revenues rolled into the British Treasury. 'If we compare this year of war with former years of peace,' Pitt told the House of Commons in February 1801,

> we shall in the produce of our revenue and in the extent of our commerce behold a spectacle at once paradoxical, inexplicable and astonishing. We have increased our external and internal commerce to a greater pitch than ever it was before; and we may look to the present as the proudest year that has ever occurred for this country.

Trafalgar, a battle fought by trade, for trade and in some ways *as* trade, might be seen as the first great bourgeois victory of European history, and its heroes as the first great heroes of the British middle class.

There is an important qualification to be made here. The idea of a fleet commanded by members of the British middle class has an implication of settled propriety. But that is an anachronism and something much rawer has to be put in its place. The rampant energy of 18th-century England is founded on the idea of dynamic change. By 1805, the bourgeoisie were only on the cusp of acquiring the strait-laced solidity and evangelical worthiness by which they would come to define themselves in the century that followed. The Georgian bourgeoisie was wilder than that. Tumultuousness, extravagance and flightiness were given full rein alongside tight-fistedness and cold ambition. Add to that background the knowledge that the 1790s had been a desperate time in Britain. A series of bad harvests had meant that the cost of poor relief had gone up to over £4 million a year, almost three times what it had been in the 1770s. The revolutionary events in France had issued a violent challenge to the status quo in England, and 1790s Britain felt like a system in crisis, as the armies of revolutionary France had brushed aside the old order in Europe. It was a time of immense strain. From a brief moment of peace in November 1801 Pitt looked back on it, as if on a traumatic crossing of a wild sea:

> We have the satisfaction of knowing that we have survived the violence of the revolutionary fever, and we have seen the extent of its principles abated. We have seen Jacobinism deprived of its fascination; we have seen it stripped of the name and pretext of liberty; it has shown itself to be capable only of destroying, not of building, and that it must necessarily end in military despotism.

* * *

These are the initial elements of Trafalgar: antique Spanish stiffness; French post-revolutionary uncertainty; and British commercial, bourgeois dynamism, portraying itself to itself as defending the ancient honour of England against the flashy, subversive allure of pretended revolutionary freedom. Or to put it another way: a Spanish navy acting to a pre-modern code of chivalric honour; a French navy surviving as a dysfunctional amalgam of aristocratic hauteur, Enlightenment expertise and revolutionary ideological fervour; and a British navy actively creating a global commercial network but thinking of itself as the guardian of ancient freedoms.

In the Royal Navy, a man's seniors, at least at the level of the officer class, never used 'obedience' as a term of approval. Enterprise was what was required and a man was invariably recommended for his 'zeal'. Zeal was the amalgam of energy, commitment, what we would call 'hunger', an enterprising spirit that wants to land the deal, or in these circumstances, to put the competitor out of business. It was a mechanism that worked within the navy as a whole, within fleets and within ships. Zeal is what Nelson was commended for, above all qualities, by his Commander-in-Chief in the Mediterranean, Earl St Vincent. 'Your Lordship has given so many proofs of transcendent Zeal in the service of your King and country,' the old flatterer wrote, 'that we have only to pray for the preservation of your invaluable life to insure everything that can be achieved by mortal man.'

Emerging from a society in which neither revolutionary equality nor ossified rank was the guiding principle, but a sort of bourgeois capitalist middle ground between those two, something the 18th century would have called the acquisition and retention of *Place* became the motor behind the zeal. They all wanted and needed to win. '*Place*,' Adam Smith wrote in the *Theory of Moral Sentiments*, 'that great object which divides the wives of aldermen, is the end of half the labours of human life; and is the cause of all the tumult and bustle, all the rapine and injustice, which avarice and ambition have introduced into this world.' Of course, in *The Wealth of Nations* published in 1777, Smith identified this individual 'emulation to excel' as the mechanism by which social good was achieved. That idea became the British and American orthodoxy. 'It is not from the benevolence of the butcher, the brewer, or the baker, that we expect our dinner,' Smith wrote, 'but from the regard to their own interest. We address ourselves not to their humanity, but their self-love.'

This legitimising and release of a surging hunger to excel, to achieve and to satisfy the self, was a critical part of the British frame of mind in 1805. Nelson had made his instructions to his captains quite clear. He would bring the fleets to battle, but once there, they were to rely on their own zeal. He would create the market, but once it was created he would depend on their enterprise. His captains were to see themselves as the entrepreneurs of battle. In Nelson's secret memorandum, written on board *Victory* on 9 October 1805, a fortnight before the battle and circulated to his captains, he makes this explicit. He describes how they are to attack in the columns in which they have been sailing, but

> Something must be left to chance; nothing is sure in a Sea Fight beyond all others. Shot will carry away the masts and yards of friends as well as foes . . . Captains are to look to their particular Line as their rallying point. But, in case Signals can neither be seen or perfectly understood, no Captain can do very wrong if he places his ship alongside that of an Enemy.

That is the essence of Trafalgar: the liberation of individual energies to ensure victory. The battle is founded on a clear commercial analogy. Trafalgar worked according to the basic principle enunciated by Adam Smith that the individual's uncompromising pursuit of the end that will satisfy him will also serve the general good. What is good for one is good for all and a fleet which promotes and relies on individual zeal will be more likely to achieve a productive end than one controlled by a single deciding government or admiral.

While the French fleet was acting to an authoritarian pattern (Napoleon had forbidden Villeneuve to tell his captains at any stage what the grand strategy might be) and the Spanish to an aristocratic one, the British mentality and tactics were bourgeois and market-liberal to the core. Edmund Burke, the great anti-revolutionary orator, and defender of English gradualism, had put into a single sentence the factors underlying this drive. 'The laws of commerce,' Burke had told the House of Commons, 'are the laws of nature, and consequently the laws of God.' There was no arguing with them.

As these 47,000 men are moving inexorably towards battle, with the wind on their cheeks wafting them towards the fight, it seems clear that the new, commercial, self-motivating and wage-based conception of the self which the changes in Britain had created over the previous century was the key factor lying behind the extraordinary winning power of the British Royal Navy. Compared with the fixed peasant/aristocratic mentalities of the Spanish crews and the uncomfortable mix of ancient and modern in the French, it was the commercial form of English life that made them into better fighters and killers. Nelson's fleet carried a capitalist charge.

Soon after eight o'clock that morning, with the two columns of the British fleet slowly growing on the western horizon, Villeneuve was faced with a decision. The Combined Fleet, still making efforts to get into line of battle, with many ships still out of place and out of order, were heading southeast for the Strait of Gibraltar. The French frigate *Hermione*, on station to the west, made another signal to Villeneuve: 'The enemy number twenty-seven sail of the line'. From his own quarter-deck on the *Bucentaure*, he still could not see them but this was more than he had reckoned. He knew, from interrogating the neutral merchantmen that had made their way into Cadiz, that the British fleet contained several three-deckers, all of them heavyweight punchers, and despite his own numerical superiority, 33 to 27, he now calculated that in the weight of firepower, not to speak in seamanly skills, the British were superior. His leading ships had already cleared Cape Trafalgar, and would now have been able to turn downwind for the Strait, but his fleet as a whole, stretched over some eight miles of sea, would not in the light airs reach that point before the British caught them. Without the van of the fleet to support them, they would be pinned against the shoals off Cape Trafalgar and either killed in battle or drowned in the huge Atlantic surf they could see breaking on the rocks and sands to leeward. A battle was inevitable. A storm was in the offing. It would be better to have the port of Cadiz to run to than those murderous shoals. Should he head on for the Strait, as his orders from the Emperor himself required? Or should he turn and keep Cadiz under his lee bow, in case disaster struck? He was already crushingly aware that Napoleon no longer trusted him as a commander in battle. Admiral Rosily was en route from Paris, only delayed in Madrid because a broken carriage spring had interrupted his journey, with orders to relieve Villeneuve of his command and replace him. Villeneuve had already written to his friend Denis Decrès, the Minister of Marine in Paris, that he knew himself and his fleet to be the 'laughing-stock of Europe'. He was in 'the abyss of unhappiness'.

It is a mark of his seamanship, and of his moral courage in standing up to the Emperor, that soon after eight o'clock Villeneuve gave the order for the entire fleet to reverse direction, by taking their sterns through the wind (wearing ship) and then to head on a port tack northwards for Cadiz. But this was no run for cover. The British fleet in headlong chase had every sail set but the Combined Fleet was under topsails, staysails and topgallants only, trying slowly and clumsily to form up in good order, but nevertheless waiting for the attack to reach them. The main topsails were hauled tight to the wind, so that their luffs were shivering and not driving the ships as hard as they might. British officers watching through telescopes were aware of this and appreciated it. As he watched them, Nelson 'frequently remarked that they put a good face upon it; but always quickly added, "I'll give them such a dressing as they never had before," regretting at the same time the vicinity of the land.' There was honour in the way they were standing up for battle. No English officer ever suggested that their enemy was not courageous.

But the manoeuvre involved the first Franco-Spanish failure of the day. Villeneuve's plan had been to hold a squadron of twelve powerful ships, under the command of Admiral Gravina, in reserve. His intention was for this squadron to remain to windward of the main fleet as battle was joined and, when it became clear on which part the bulk of Nelson's divisions were descending, for Gravina to commit his force to that part of the battle. At the crucial point, the *Schwerpunkt*, the hard place, as Clausewitz would call it, the defending force would then be able at least to equalise the numbers of ships engaged. This never happened. Early in the morning, as the fleet reversed direction and turned northwards, Gravina's squadron had become mixed in with the rear of the Combined Fleet. Their identity as a separate squadron was muddled away and Gravina's ships would enter the battle, one by one, as they came up to the series of mêlées which developed in the centre of the fleet.

At the very beginning, Villeneuve lost his ability to reshape the battle. His fleet waited in a state of victimhood. By about ten o'clock, they ended up in a shallow crescent, about eight miles long, partly bunched together, partly overlapping, and with vulnerable gaps opening in places through which an enemy could drive. Every eyeglass on every British ship watched those gaps. That was where battle would be joined.

2

ORDER AND ANXIETY

October 21st 1805
8.30 am to 9.30 am

Distance between fleets: 6.5 miles–5.9 miles
Victory's heading and speed: 034°–067° at 2.5 knots

Order is Heav'n's first Law
ALEXANDER POPE, *Essay on Man*, 1734

As the British ships made their slow progress to the eastward, the crews were struck by the beauty of the spectacle they were creating. In the log of the *Mars,* Thomas Cook, her master, described what the men were about this morning: 'making Ship perfectly clear for Action'. The clarity before battle was a form of perfection. It was the beauty of order and arrangement, each part of each ship designed for its task, each related to and dependent on all others, a network of interaction. Forget for a minute that these are killing machines. Years later, Midshipman Hercules Robinson of the *Euryalus* reminisced:

> There is now before me the beautiful misty sun-shiny morning of the 21st October. The delight of us all at the idea of a wearisome blockade, about to terminate with a fair stand-up fight, of which we knew the

result. The noble fleet, with royals and studding sails on both sides, bands playing, officers in full dress, and the ships covered with ensigns, hanging in various places where they could never be struck.

According to John Brown, a seaman on *Victory*, 'the French and Spanish Fleets was like a great wood on our lee bow which cheered the hearts of every British tar in the *Victory* like lions anxious to be at it.' Nelson, again and again, commented to the frigate captains he had summoned on board *Victory* how much the enemy were standing up for a fight, not running and scattering to all corners. The scene looked as these moments were intended to look: a clash of organisations in which men, ships, fleets, naval systems and countries were to be put to the test.

The *Euryalus* had been in close to the mouth of Cadiz harbour on the preceding days, looking for the slightest sign of enemy preparation. Midshipman Robinson remembered how

> The morning of the 19th of October saw us so close to Cadiz as to see the ripple of the beach and catch the morning fragrance which came out of the land, and then as the sun rose over the Trocadero with what joy we saw the fleet inside let fall and hoist their topsails and one after another slowly emerge from the harbour mouth.

His captain, Henry Blackwood, had written on the 20th to his wife in England:

> What do you think, my own dearest love? At this moment the Enemy are coming out, and as if determined to have a fair fight. You see also, my Harriet, I have time to write to you, and to assure you that to the last moment of my breath I shall be as much attached to you as man can be, which I am sure you will credit. It is very odd how I have been dreaming

> all night of my carrying home dispatches. God send so much good luck! The day is fine; the sight of course, beautiful. . . . God bless you. No more at present.

Captain Edward Codrington on the *Orion* wrote smilingly to his wife:

> We have now a nice air, which fills our flying kites and drives us along at four knots an hour . . . How would your heart beat for me, dearest Jane, did you but know that we are under every stitch of sail we can set, steering for the enemy.

Codrington missed Jane with a passion, writing to her that he was 'full of hope that Lord Nelson's declaration would be verified; viz. that we should have a good battle and go home to eat our Christmas dinner.' On the *Belleisle*, Lieutenant Paul Nicolas described how

> I was awakened by the cheers of the crew and by their rushing up the hatchways to get a glimpse of the hostile fleet. The delight manifested exceeded anything I ever witnessed, surpassing even those gratulations when our native cliffs are descried after a long period of distant service.

They were seeing battle as home, as the moment of perfection, with the sweet-smelling scents of Iberia wafting across the stretch of sea at which they had arrived, and the Atlantic breakers beyond it creaming on to the sand.

Over this very stretch of sea, 18 months before, Samuel Taylor Coleridge had sailed to Malta in convoy, shepherded by Captain Henry Bayntun in HMS *Leviathan*. For the poet it was a passage of troubled but at times ecstatic happiness, running from opium and hopelessness in England to the warmth of the Mediterranean. His journal of the voyage speaks, in a way no naval officer could, of the beauties which were so clearly felt on the morning of Trafalgar. 'Oh with what envy I have gazed at our commodore,' Coleridge wrote, half in love with ships,

> the Leviathan of 74 guns, the majestic and beautiful creation, sailing right before us, upright, motionless, as a church with its steeple – as though moved by its will, as though its speed were spiritual.

> This morning, Tuesday April 10th, 1804, a fine sharp morning – the Sea rolls rough & high / but the Ships are before us & behind us. I count 35, & the lonely Gulls fish in among the Ships / & what a beautiful object even a single wave is!
>
> Delightful weather, motion, relation of the convoy to each other, all exquisite/ – and I particularly watched the beautiful Surface of the Sea in this gentle Breeze! – every form so transitory, so for the instant, & and yet for that instant so substantial in all its sharp lines, steep surfaces, & hair-deep indentures, just as if it were cut glass, glass cut into ten thousand varieties / & then the network of the wavelets, & the rude circle hole network of the Foam /
>
> And on the gliding Vessel Heaven & Ocean smil'd!

That is a line from one of Wordsworth's poems in *Lyrical Ballads*, in which the female vagrant who speaks is in a wretched condition herself but can nevertheless grasp the beauty in the gliding Vessel before her. That is Coleridge's predicament too, broken himself, but in love with the orderliness of the *Leviathan*'s convoy around him.

On the morning of the 21 October 1805, with the huge bluff ships surging beneath them and the sails slatting in the swells, there was little to do but contemplate the excellence of their own fleet and the prospect of violence to come. In the steady breeze and on the constant course, there was little need to adjust the trim of the sails. The only movement was at the wheel, where the helmsman steered to port as the swell lifted beneath him, to starboard as it dropped the bow in the trough that followed. Men had breakfast. Captains showed their lieutenants Nelson's memorandum, in case they were 'bowled out' in the action and the lieutenants needed to take command. On the poops, their bands played 'Rule Britannia', 'Britons strike home' and 'Hearts of Oak', first written after the triumphant victories of 1759, the Annus Mirabilis of the Seven Years War:

> Come, cheer up my lads,
> It's to glory we steer,
> To add something more
> To this wonderful year.
> To honour we call you,
> As free men, not slaves,
> For who are so free
> As the sons of the waves?

Half the people who sang that were either pressed men or miscreants sent on board as part of a quota from each county, and a sixth of the entire fleet would desert or attempt to desert in the coming year (an average kept up throughout the Napoleonic war). Their average age was under 22. But the power of the British self-image as free men was such that in all probability these men believed what they sang: theirs was an honourable condition of freedom and order.

This profound shipboard orderliness was no chance effect. The ship itself was to be a model of order. Sailmakers were to see that sails were dry when they went into store, to make sure they were aired and to secure them from 'drips, damps and vermin as much as possible.' Proper sentinels were to be posted 'to prevent people's easing themselves in the hold or throwing anything there that may occasion nastiness.' Rather than order, the prevention of disorder was the essence of naval life. Written Admiralty instructions required the boatswain and his mates on each ship 'to be diligent . . . and see . . . that the working of the ship be performed with as little noise and confusion as possible.' The ship, in fact, is to be worked in silence or near-silence. The repeating of orders was thought to be a symptom of slightly inadequate management.

In a world where the orderliness of things seems so close to disorder and disintegration, an almost dance-like form of behaviour, in which the set moves are made with some grace and precision, was a kind of bulwark against chaos, a guarantee of who you were. On these ships, theatricality of language and dress was more than mere display: it was a mark of civility and order, of a distance from the anarchic mob, of precisely the values for which the war against revolutionary-cum-imperial France was being fought. 'Even a momentary dereliction of forms,' one ship's chaplain wrote, 'might prove fatal to the general interest.' St Vincent had insisted that his captains should remain aloof from their men and even from their brother officers. The idea of a captain eating dinner with his lieutenants appalled him. Distance was a method of command. It is the same instinct for order which lies, for example, behind an instruction issued by Lord St Vincent to the Mediterranean fleet in July 1796. The admiral wasn't going to have any hint of casual drawing-room manners, nor the wit of elegant society, about his fleet or flagship:

> The admiral having observed a flippancy in the behaviour of officers when coming upon the Victory's quarterdeck and sometimes in receiving orders from a superior officer and that they do not pull off their hats and some not even touching them, it is his

> positive directions that any officer who shall in future so far forget this essential duty of respect and subordination be admonished publically; and he expects the officers of the Victory will set the example by taking their hats off on such occasions and not touching them with an air of negligence.

St Vincent was insistent that midshipmen should have a uniform 'which distinguish their class to be in the rank of gentleman, and give them better credit and figure in executing the commands of their superior officers.' Decks were to be swept at least twice a day, the dirt thrown overboard, men to change their linen twice a week, to wash frequently, to make sure the heads were clean every morning and evening. The ship was to appear 'clean and neat from without board.' These orders, written in order books, were to be kept on the quarterdeck and open to inspection 'of every person belonging to the ship', sometimes in a canvas case.

Filthy language, the solid staple of life between decks, was nevertheless not to be used within the hearing of officers. 'There is a word which only comes from the mouths of hardened blackguards,' wrote the extremely clean-minded Captain Riou on the *Amazon* in 1799, 'that will not be permitted to pass with impunity.' What that word was can only be guessed at but certainly Captain Griffiths on the *London* in 1795 thought '"Bugger" a horrid expression disgraceful to a British seaman, a scandalous and infamous word.' Not as scandalous as the act itself, which seems to have been committed rarely, and only then down in the unlit spaces in the depths of the ship, on the cable tier, where love, lust or dominance could have its way with least chance of disturbance.

The essence of the order was of course vigilance, and the roots of vigilance reached far down into the souls of the officers themselves. Officers and men lived, critically, on either side of a moral watershed: an officer's self-control was the source of the discipline which he then imposed on the men. The state of a ship and its company was a test of the officer's inner, moral qualities and each ship needed to be, in effect, a diagram of that highly regulated state. It was a difference which meant that the violence done by officers to men was seen as almost unequivocally good; and violence done by men to officers just as unequivocally bad. A man's duty was to obey, an officer's to be right and so, as an aspect of nothing but logic, a man's failure was a cause for punishment and an officer's a cause for dishonour.

Every aspect of the ship was to conform to this image of order. The stores were to be stored 'with economical exactness.' No excuse would be admitted for stores 'not being neatly arranged and ready to hand.' The officer of the watch was

> to be careful that the sails are at all times well hoisted, reefs repaired if required, sheets home, yards braced, trusses, weather braces and bowlines attended to, and the sails in every respect as properly set as if the ship was in a chase.

'Minute attention', 'her exact place', 'a uniform system of discipline': every phrase reinforced the sense that not only was the ship a fighting machine but a microcosm of rational civilisation, surviving in and threatened by a chaotic and hostile world, a zone of chaos to which the ship's company naturally belonged. The terror with which mutiny was viewed, and with which the mildest whisper of mutinous thought was received, was a measure of the tightness with which the line of order was drawn. For the first lieutenant, in effect on test for promotion to captain, the demands of the system could not be more absolute:

> It is impossible he can be too minute in these particulars of his duty. He ought to know everything, see everything and have to do with everything that is to be known, seen or done in the ship.

He was, in other words, to be Enlightenment, Virgilian man, the representative of civilisation, entirely aware, entirely informed, entirely in control and as a result entirely admirable. From the cleanness and regularity of his heart and mind would 'follow credit and comfort to a well disposed ship's company.' There were some deeply traditional aspects to this. Buried deep within the 1805 conception of the naval officer was a Roman and stoical image of distilled order, of an applied and balanced rationality which both constituted and oiled the fleet system itself. A fleet was an act of English civility. Its orderliness was its virtue, rationality its fuel, clarity its purpose, and in those qualities, the English had long congratulated themselves that they were different from foreigners. After the defeat of the Spanish Armada in 1588, a thrilling discovery was reported in London:

> strange and most cruell Whippes which the Spaniards had prepared to whippe and torment English men and women: which were found and taken at the overthrow of certain of the Spanish Shippes.

The implication, of course, is that no such violence would be natural to an Englishman. No, the English were honest, plucky little fighters against wicked European tyrants and many elements of what would come to be seen as the Nelson persona were in fact utterly conventional parts of this English naval self-image. A rough broadsheet song described the virtues of Rear-Admiral Richard Carter, killed against the Dutch at la Hogue in 1692:

> His virtue was not rugged, like the waves,
> Nor did he treat his sailors as his slaves:
> But courteous, easy of access, and free,
> His looks not tempered with severity.

Change the idiom slightly and those are precisely the terms in which Nelson was described a century later.

Needless to say, though, this straining for order, for the idea of the beautiful machine was founded on an overriding sense of anxiety. Naval order was little more than a thin and tense veneer laid over something that was on the boundaries of the chaotic. Rationality was merely a dreamed-of haven in all the oceans of contingency. Order, it turns out, was in many ways little more than a rationalisation of chaos, anxiety and corruption. The great Admiral Vernon had warned in the 1770s that 'our fleets are defrauded with injustice, marred by violence and maintained by cruelty.' The amount of money voted by parliament each year to pay the seamen was not only calculated on a scale unchanged since the days of Oliver Cromwell but the amount voted never corresponded to the number of seamen raised. No audit was ever done to see how the money was spent and enquiry after enquiry in the late 18th century did little to cure the wastage and muddle. Seamen's pay was often years behind, the principal and justifiable cause of the great mutinies of 1797.

It was generally known that the administration of the navy and its dockyards was a mass of deceit and inefficiency. As one contemporary pamphleteer wrote, it was a scene consisting of

> gigantic piles, and moles, and misshapen masses of infamy, where one villainy is the buttress of another; where crime adheres to crime; and fraud ascends

> upon fraud, inserted, roofed, dove-tailed and weather-proofed with official masonry, and the unctuous mortar of collusion. [The navy was] the central temple of peculation: where the god of interest is worshipped under the mystic form of liberality, and the common conscience of guilt is professed under the symbol of mutual charity and conciliation.

Everyone, in other words, was on the make. The great Earl St Vincent had attempted reform and his brief tenure as First Lord of the Admiralty had ended with a savage attack on him, his competency and his methods in the House of Commons by William Pitt himself. His successor as First Lord of the Admiralty, Pitt's closest friend Lord Melville, had been found guilty of at least borrowing from the state purse. When Barham succeeded him, he was at that time still Sir Charles Middleton, 80 years old, a seasoned naval administrator. Middleton accepted the job on one condition, quite explicitly expressed in a letter intended for Pitt's ear but addressed to Melville: he wanted to be a lord. 'I have no other wish towards the admiralty,' he wrote from his elegantly rustic farm set among the orchards and woods at Teston in Kent, 'but to secure the peerage to myself and family. The admiralty has no charms for me, further than to serve and promote these objects. The opportunity that offers at present to secure me the peerage must be obvious to Mr Pitt, and it would be a reflection on good sense to suppose his Majesty would be adverse to bestowing a mark of approbation on my many years services, and coming out again in the decline of life, at the desire of his ministers.' He got the title, became Lord Barham and took the job. Enlightenment London knew all about self-promotion.

In daily detail, life on board a ship-of-the-line was thick with an atmosphere of supervision, anxiety and the endless efforts at maintenance and mending. Order was achieved in a condition of near-anarchy. Take as a pair of complementary documents, a list of boatswain's stores (to be checked, to be tested against theft and loss) and a ship's surgeon's list of what was wrong with the men, and you can read from them exactly what dominated the 1805 man-of-war.

So for example, the boatswain's stores on HMS *Thunderer*, a 74-gun ship, as recorded on 10 October 1805 included 35 gallons of black varnish; eleven large brushes, three small; 90 lbs of ground yellow paint; 863 yards of canvas of eight different grades and another 100 yards 'old' canvas; 5 ensigns, 4 jacks, 8 pendants; 1237 hammocks, 63½ yards of kersey; 1 fish copper kettle, one small fish copper kettle, 1 machine for sweetening water; 1 machine for making cordage and 9,500 feet of spare cordage; 202 iron cringles; six boat grapnels; 7 hatchets; 24 boat hooks and a fish hook; 16 marline spikes; 78 sail needles and 12 sail making palms; 68 thimbles; 56 leather buckets; 1½ tons of vinegar and 2½ barrels of tar; 68 spare sails and 72 spare blocks; a 32-ft barge, a 31-foot-long boat, a 28-ft pinnace, two 25-ft deal cutters and a ten-foot four-oared boat, plus all their oars. The ship itself had a pair of giant sweeps with which to propel it in a calm. There were two 70-fathom seine nets, and a mass of fishing gear for albacore, dolphin and bonito, plus some shark-fishing gear fitted with a chain. There was a mackerel line but no turtle nets. The *Thunderer* carried a Dutch ensign, as well as a French and a Spanish one; a Dutch, Spanish and French jack and a Dutch, Spanish and French pendant, all of which could be used to disguise her identity or to trick the enemy. The stores themselves are a record of vigilance and danger, of damage foreseen and emergency accounted for. It is a world of shattered spars and blown-out sails, men and objects lost overboard, worn sheets and frayed halyards, blocks split and lost, hammocks torn, lift tackles gone, lanyards broken. It feels nearly comfortless.

Alongside it, one can place the list of complaints with which a ship's surgeon would have to deal, the human impact of this strained life in the damp, dangerous world of a man-of-war: ulcer of frenum of the penis; drunk falling from deck on keelson; hands caught in block; catarrh; rheumatism; diarrhoea; contusion; colic; falling while hauling on the braces, causing venereal hernia; fall while taking down the hammocks, producing dislocated shoulder; letting an adze slip while repairing a cutter and the blade cutting into his Achilles tendon; slipping and falling into tender (a boy aged 16); fractured humerus falling on deck in a wind; rheumatism in the knees; tonsillitis; inflamed glands in groin; 'fell on deck with four or five men over him in a gale'; stabbed in forehead when ashore; fell out of his hammock on to deck; falling down drunk; a fall into the waist; ankles swollen; epilepsy, (the prospect of which aloft was terrifying); guts – griping, discharge of blood, faeces scanty and white; severe pain in loins; right hand dragged into a block, ends of fingers fractured; sole of left foot punctured by a scrape. More often than not men took several days before they reported they were hurt. One was said to complain simply of 'Hypochondriasis'. Others, for whom the strain was too much, are described merely as 'hectic' or 'withdrawn'. 'Mania' afflicted all categories of men on board.

It is remarkable, in the light of the deeply demanding conditions in which it operated for years at a time, that the navy of 1805 achieved what it aimed for. Deep orderliness was a quality which struck visitor after visitor to the fleet. Part of a diary survives kept by an anonymous tutor to a 15-year-old midshipman called Frederick Gilly cruising on board HMS *Gibraltar* enforcing the blockade off L'Orient in 1811. The tutor was catastrophically seasick but, like Coleridge, was entranced by the very things which most navy men would not bother to have noticed. Coleridge had gazed for hours at 'the sails sometimes *sunshiny*, sometimes *snowy*: sometimes shade-coloured, sometimes dingy'. The tutor, despite his seasickness,

> found a pleasure totally new and indescribable in attending to the execution of orders. What most attracted my notice was the silence which prevailed; not a word was spoke but by the officers commanding, which not only showed the fine order to which the ship's company had been reduced, but also the alacrity with which everything might be done in case of emergency . . .
>
> At 11 o'clock all the men are mustered and inspected at their divisions by the captain and officers. All hands are expected to appear dressed in clean linen and their best clothes, consisting in the summer of blue jackets and white trousers.

This is not the usual picture of the rough and ready, brutalised workforce of a British man-of-war, but this journal, naively enthusiastic as it might be, was written for no purpose but the tutor's own. On Friday 9 August 1811, he recorded that

> When several ships are in company it is a very interesting sight to observe the manner in which anything is conducted, as for instance getting under weigh, coming to anchor, loosing and furling sails etc. The signal is first of all given from the admiral's or commodore's ship and then all begin at the same time and there is no small emulation in making a display of smartness and discipline. If the command be given to furl sails, then the first lieutenant orders the bosun to 'Pipe all hands to furl sails'. They then come on deck and wait for the word. In the meantime the midshipmen stationed in the tops take their places. The next word is 'man the rigging'. This is obeyed by the men ascending the first ratlines of the

shrouds and there staying till the lieutenant sings out 'Away aloft'. When they have got into the tops they wait again for the last word, 'Lay out and take in – reefs.'(According to the number of reefs out when the sails were loose.) The whole fleet acts with smartness and dispatch.

That too is what you must imagine on the morning of Trafalgar, as the logs laconically describe the evolutions of the fleet, responding to a shift in the wind by coming on to the other tack, 'wearing ship' by taking her stern through the wind, raising the topgallant yards as the wind drops and more sail is needed, shaking out the reefs in the topsails, setting the steering or studding sails with which to add the slightest extra fraction of a knot in the light airs, setting the royals above the topsails, for that little bit more, and then lowering the ships' boats from the davits and towing them on long lines astern. In their cradles on deck, they would not only have interrupted the line of fire; a shot landing among them would have sprayed the deck with murderous splinters.

A ship, to a stranger a maze of complexity, is to a seaman the infinitely exact working out of a few basic principles. The hull combines two contradictory qualities: quickness through the water for the chase of the enemy; steadiness to provide a platform from which guns could be fired. Greater waterline length provided the first, greater beam the second. The profile of men-of-war, seen from bow or stern, was curved steeply in above the waterline because it was realised that if the guns on the upper decks could be brought nearer to the centreline of the ship, there would be less roll and for a higher proportion of the time the muzzles of the guns would be on target. Two ships alongside each other could be touching at the waterline but forty feet apart at the quarterdeck. The heaviest guns, which fired roundshot weighing 32 pounds each, enormous objects, 9ft 6in long and weighing very nearly three tons, were on the lowest decks, those above getting increasingly lighter, for the same reason. The keel of course was dead straight, made of vast baulks of elm, the bow extremely bluff, because there was more room aboard if the full width of the ship was carried as far forward as possible. The stern sharpened to a point, allowing the water to run smoothly off the lines of the ship, reducing drag. The very structure of their world was shaped to a purpose.

Everything in the hull was for strength. The frames or ribs of the ship were set in pairs along its full width, and carefully jointed so that no joint in any timber lay alongside a joint in another. It was a dense structure. If you stripped away the outer shell, the frames would still occupy two thirds of its outline. The whole structure was held together by iron bolts above the waterline and by bolts made of copper alloy below it. The hull was clenched into tightness. The underwater profile was sheathed in copper to keep it clean of weed, a form of anti-fouling and to deter the ship worm which destroys ship timbers in the tropics.

This immensely solid hull was then bridged internally with the heavy deck beams, huge oak timbers, each one placed beneath a gun, cambered slightly to meet the curve of the deck (cambered so that water would run off it) and fixed with grown-oak knees – cut from the curving part of a tree – which held the beams in place in both the vertical and horizontal plane. Over that was laid the deal deck planking, each plank two inches thick and 12 inches wide. The final element was the hull planking, several layers of it: particularly thick timbers known as wales fixed under each row of gunports, further thickening timbers above and below the wales, a mass of exterior planking, four inches thick, followed by interior planking of the same density, and on top of that, still further timbers known as riders and standards to give yet more internal strength. The construction method is more like that of a tank armoured in oak than a seagoing vessel. A first-rate ship like *Victory* might take ten years to construct. At their thickest, its walls would be three feet thick.

That was only the beginning: steering systems, capstans, anchors and pumps, the captain's great cabin or in the greatest ships the admiral's apartment, the galley, the sick room, the powder magazine – 42,000 lbs of gunpowder in 405 barrels aboard *Victory* – the water storage and the iron ballasting, the pens for the bullocks, pigs, chickens and sheep that were kept on board, the stores for bread, salt meat and the all-important lemons and limes (18,000 for one ship at a single loading) all had to be fitted out for this 850-man war machine to operate.

Above all that, of course, was the rig. Nothing looks more complicated or more idiosyncratic than the maze of lines, canvas and timber that stretch skyward above these ships. *Victory* is 186 feet long on her gundecks, 51 wide at her widest point. The poop is already 55 feet above the keel. The truck on the mainmast, the very highest point of the ship, is another 170 feet above that. Every cubic yard of space above those decks is put to work but in a system whose essence is clear and plain. There are three masts and each carries four square sails: the 'course' at the bottom – the mainsail, whose name means 'the body'; the topsail above it, its name deriving from the time when it was simply the upper of two sails; the 'topgallant' above that, and above that the 'royal'. The bowsprit, protruding 100 feet from the bow, carried four jibs. Between the fore and the mainmast and between the mainmast and the mizzen, still further fore-and-aft staysails – attached to the stays holding up the masts – could be set. Extra studding sails could be hoisted, attached to special booms run out on each side from the yards from which the usual sails hung.

In all, a ship like *Victory* could carry 40 sails, with about 1,000 blocks through which the rigging was led, the whole assemblage weighing about twenty tons and covering an area of more than two acres. Although no element of these extraordinary constructions would have been unfamiliar to anyone alive in 1805 – no special materials; nothing different in the hemp and canvas, iron and timber, blocks and pulleys from those found on land – the man-of-war, as complex as a clock, as large as a prison, as delicate as a kite, as strong as a fortress and as murderous as an army, was undoubtedly the most evolved single mechanism, with the most elaborate ordering of parts, the world had ever seen.

That was the striking fact. One witness after another described the overriding sensation they had on the morning of Trafalgar: the sense of beautiful order; the knowledge of preparedness; of the soundness of hull and spar; of standing and running rigging fully knotted and deeply spliced; of the rope work wormed, served and tarred; of the roundshot in their wooden cups stacked behind the great guns; of the powder cartridges ready far below, the crews in their allocated places; the weekly practice at gunnery known and understood.

The fleet itself, and each ship within it, just as much as a contemporary dockyard or factory, or even the new efficient prisons, was seen by all as an evolving and gyrating machine.

> For every task, from getting up the anchor to unbending the sails, aloft and below, at the mess tub or in the hammock, each task has its man and each man his place. A ship contains a set of *human* machinery, in which every man is a wheel, a band, or a crank, all moving with wonderful regularity and precision to the *will* of the machinist – the all-powerful captain.

Late in September, on arriving back after a short rest in England, Nelson had written to the unsatisfactory and ailing Rear-Admiral John Knight in Gibraltar:

> I was only twenty-five days, from dinner to dinner, absent from the Victory. In our several situations, my dear Admiral, we must all put our shoulders to the wheel, and make the great machine of the Fleet intrusted to our charge go on smoothly.

The phrase 'great machine' had a richer resonance in 1805 than it does today. The Newtonian universe was a machine. Beauty, as Newton had revealed, was systematic. The interlocking, gyrating cogwheeled spheres of the orrery were a model of how things were. No one element could matter more than the system of which it was a part. The universe, in one part of the 18th-century mind, was a uniquely ordered affair, a smoothly clarified machine of exquisitely oiled parts, whose majesty consisted in its rationality. God, it had become clear, did not feel, intuit or imagine. He thought.

As a reflection of that, machines were what grandees loved to visit. The opening of the Albion Steam Mill in March 1786 on the south bank of the Thames in London had been accompanied by a grand masquerade. Dukes, lords and ladies flocked to it. Lords Auckland, Lansdowne and Penrhyn were given tours by Matthew Boulton the great steam machinist and entrepreneur. The East India Company directors were there, as was the President of the Royal Society. A distinguished French Académicien, the Marquis de Coulomb, was caught doing a little industrial espionage on the side. The machine then was still a model of what might be, the image of dynamic exactness, of undeluded inventiveness harnessing natural forces, which not only mimicked the workings of the universe but stepped outside the limits which human muscle had always imposed on human enterprise.

That was at the heart of the machine's allure: it was rational potency, an enlargement of the possibilities of life. When James Boswell had visited Birmingham in 1776, he made a beeline for the works belonging to Boulton at Soho. Boswell stood amazed at the scale and energy of the 'Manufactory' where 700 people were employed (almost exactly the number on a ship-of-the-line) and regretted that Dr Johnson was not there with him

> for it was a scene which I should have been glad to contemplate by his light. The vastness and the contrivance of some of the machinery would have 'matched his mighty mind'. I shall never forget Mr Bolton's expression to me. 'I sell here, sir, what all the world desires to have – POWER.'

It is an analogy that is everywhere in the navy. Lord Barham, First Lord of the Admiralty, a carping, wheedling, occasionally intemperate and unattractive man, who never hesitated to wag the finger, nor remind his superiors of the length, intensity and importance of his labours, who congratulated himself on 'having naturally a methodical turn of mind', saw his job simply as 'keeping the engine moving'. As he wrote to Pitt on 22 May 1805, 'I thought it right to lay these few ideas before you, that, if possible, the whole machine should be made to move a little brisker, so as to afford us some prospect of success. We may flatter ourselves, from what has passed, that our skill in the management of ships and the activity and bravery of our seamen will bear us out; it is a fallacy, which will manifest itself in a few months if we are not furnished with men for our ships.'

Work, business, the oiling of the machine, and the keeping of the wheels turning, the provision of men by the press gangs, of timber, tar, and flax, from America, the Baltic and the Far East: that was Barham's task. In the making of its ropes, the Royal Navy was thought to consume 14,935 tons of hemp a year. For its sails 95,585 bolts of canvas were required. Barham ensured that teak-built battleships were commissioned in Bombay, and both light frigates and ships-of-the-line from the Russians in the White Sea in Archangel. Supplies of English oak were running desperately thin, as they were all over Europe. Large loads of central and eastern European oak, carted to Baltic ports and then trans-shipped to England, were found on arrival to be useless. The navy surveyors were told they 'must cordially agree to substituting elm, fir, beech and any other timber for oak, where it can be used.' England must be scoured, as Barham had written in a memo entitled *Forethought and Preparation* and 'Country gentlemen, and others who have small quantities to sell must be canvassed.' He was keen to show anyone who would listen 'the advantages of forethought and preparation in every kind of business and more particularly in naval matters. By such means an enemy is overpowered before he can prepare himself.' His task was 'to take the whole business upon myself until the machine was set agoing.' Whoever decides the disposition of forces 'must be a perfect master of arrangement. Without this, he must be in continual perplexity.'

Orderliness was in the air. Over 200 English grammars had been published in the second half of the 18th century, by which the wild sprouts of the language were to be disciplined and trained. The water closet with a ball-cock to control the inrush of water into the cistern had been invented in 1778. Public hangings at Tyburn in the west end of London had been done away with in 1783. Branding of criminals had been abolished. The Ordnance Survey, by which every inch of the British Isles was to be precisely triangulated, surveyed and mapped, had been founded in 1793. Income tax had been imposed by Pitt for the first time in 1798. Deduction at source had followed two years later. The first National Census had been conducted in 1801. A year later Thomas Telford had spanned the Thames in one leap with the new London Bridge. In 1803 Luke Howard had named the clouds for the first time. The numbering of London houses became compulsory in 1805. In January 1806, on station off the coast of South America, Captain Francis Beaufort developed the first version of the Beaufort scale by which, ever since, wind has been calibrated in precise increments.

The entire value system of a figure such as Barham was based not on the Nelsonian virtues of dash, inspiration and the heroic but on understanding, reason, clarity and order. Barham's cousin and predecessor at the Admiralty Lord Melville had declared that his purpose was 'to know with perfect accuracy the real state of the British navy as it now stands, with reference as well to the immediate calls upon it, as with a view to its progressive improvement to meet future contingencies. It is my duty to communicate the result of my investigation, for the information of his Majesty and his confidential servants.' Latinate, explicit, attentive, prospective, urgent: this language forms the essential bedrock on which the fleets of 1805, the victory at Trafalgar and the 19th-century idea of the English hero were all laid.

It was, at some intuitive level, an appreciation of the fleet which had penetrated deep into English national consciousness. The navy was beautiful, substantial, orderly and English. Wordsworth would stand on the Dorset shore and stare, as his sister Dorothy wrote to their brother, 'at the West India fleet sailing in all its glory.' William Cobbett, as a boy, had felt his entire sense of being shift into another plane when, in the 1770s,

> from the top of Portsdown, I, for the first time, beheld the sea, and no sooner did I behold it than I wished to be a sailor. But it was not the sea alone that I saw: the grand fleet was riding at anchor at Spithead. I had heard of the wooden walls of Old England: I had formed my ideas of a ship, and of a fleet; but what I now beheld, so far surpassed what I had ever been able to form a conception of, that I stood lost between astonishment and admiration. I had heard talk of all the glorious deeds of our admirals and sailors [which] good and true Englishmen never fail to relate to their children about a hundred times a year. The sight of the fleet brought all these into my mind in confused order, it is true, but with irresistible force. My heart was inflated with national pride. The sailors were my countrymen; the fleet belonged to my country, and surely I had my part in it, and in all its honours . . .

The beauty and power which so struck the young Cobbett also lay behind the great sequence of sea-pieces which JMW Turner was painting in London in the first decade of the 19th century. To see them, thousands of people crowded every year into the 70-foot-long gallery the painter had attached to his house in Harley Street. He had opened it to the public for free, both to promote himself and as a service to the nation. In all of these early sea-paintings, again and again, the roughness of the sea, its turbulence and incipient anarchy, is set against the very opposite: the impassive, dark, stable shapes of the men-of-war anchored within it, the moment of solidity in a world of thrashing light, indifferent to anything which the sea, or trouble itself, could throw at them.

These works by the young Turner are the great English conservative images of the age. They are anti-Romantic pictures. Europe itself is in turmoil; the settled ways of things have been thrown into a stir; and at times alone, at times as the controlling node in a network of alliances across the continent, England, for the English, remains the bastion of reliability and strength. That is what the great black blocks of Turner's ships embody. He rarely, in these years, paints the men-of-war in motion, let alone in action. That is not their role. They are the wooden walls, the irreducible strength of England standing impervious to the chaos which revolutionary France threatened from across the channel.

The fleet at Trafalgar represented fifteen per cent of the British armed strength at sea, no more than the fighting tip of an organisation spread across the whole of the eastern Atlantic. That was the deep and underlying order on which British defence relied. Lord Barham wrote to the King on the eve of Trafalgar describing 'the present disposition of that part of your majesty's fleet now in commission.' The accumulated strength was rolled off with some pride: there were blockading fleets off French and Spanish ports, a home defence fleet in the Downs off the Kent coast, ships-of-the-line off Ireland and the Dutch coast, squadrons of frigates between Ireland and Brittany, between Brittany and the north Spanish coast, south along the Spanish coast to Capes St Vincent and Trafalgar, and on into the Mediterranean, some 180 ships-of-the-line in all and twice that number of frigates. Further ships, in port, were preparing to relieve those on station. Men were being pressed to man them, supplies imported to equip them.

Perhaps Barham, aware of the fragility of George III's mind, was consciously portraying a situation of extraordinary coherence and regularity, evidence of Barham's own foresight and preparedness over the previous 12 months. It was certainly, in this ideal form, a system designed to reassure a king. The task facing Barham was the same as the one that had faced British strategists for centuries. On the Atlantic shores of Europe, the British navy faced the French army. Strength in two different spheres confronted each other. It was a war, as Napoleon famously said, between an elephant and a whale. If France was to defeat her ancient enemy, she needed to invade England across the narrow seas of the Straits of Dover. In response, England needed to control those seas so as to prevent the invasion occurring. The single aim for British naval policy was to control the all-important access to the western approaches of the English Channel.

Napoleon wanted to destroy Britain, whose government was funding the continental alliances against him. 'There are in Europe many good generals but they see too many things at once,' he had said. 'I see only one thing, namely the enemy's main body. I try to crush it, confident that secondary matters will then settle themselves.' The central matter was the invasion of England, or at least its destruction as a world power. 'Bah!' Marshal Masséna was said to have remarked years later when asked about the conquest of Britain. 'Conquer it? No one even dreamt of it. It was just a question of ruining it; of leaving it in a condition that no one would even have wanted to possess it.' Napoleon thought that once in England he could destroy it in three weeks: 'Invade, enter London, wreck the shipyards and demolish the arsenals of Portsmouth and Plymouth.' Then he could march on Vienna. His army for the task, when fully arrayed, stretched nine miles along the sands of Boulogne.

The heart of the problem for the French is that France has few good deep-water ports. Unlike England, which in the harbours of Falmouth, Plymouth and Portsmouth, and in the capacious anchorages of the Nore (in the estuary of the Medway, just south of the Thames) the Downs (just east of Dover) and Spithead (off the Isle of Wight) has room for several world-dominating battle-fleets; France on its Atlantic and Channel coasts has only Brest, and to a lesser extent Rochefort; and on its Mediterranean coast, Toulon. Extravagant attempts before the Revolution to construct a fleet-holding harbour at Cherbourg in Normandy had been abandoned for lack of money.

That geography had governed the naval strategy of the European powers throughout the 18th century. The British need was to pin the French inside their ports; the French to escape the blockades imposed upon them, unite and come in force to dominate the Channel where an invasion could be made. The line connecting Brest to Toulon, via the Strait of Gibraltar, was the battleground on which the naval contest between the great European powers was fought out. Cape Trafalgar is on that line, at one of its hinges, just west of the Strait of Gibraltar, and just south of the great southern Spanish port of Cadiz.

Those were the unchangeable facts. There were of course many more wings and complexities to them: the eastern Mediterranean and the role of the Turks and the Russians there; the position of Egypt as the gateway to India; in the North Sea the role of the Dutch and Danes, and of the Russians in the Baltic; the need for the British to protect Ireland on their Atlantic flank; the inviting vulnerability of the French and British possessions in the Caribbean; the power added to the French naval position by the Spanish coming into the war against the British in January 1805, adding – on the all-important Brest-Toulon route – the outstanding deep-water harbours at Vigo, Ferrol and Cadiz.

Despite those many added complexities, the essence of the strategic situation remained constant. The British Channel Fleet, under Admiral Cornwallis, held the French clamped into Brest; the British Mediterranean Fleet, commanded by Nelson, held the French clamped into Toulon.

The third British fleet, commanded by Admiral Keith, and based at the Downs, controlled the Channel and the North Sea. The British had a lockhold on any French maritime ambitions.

Napoleon's brilliantly lateral idea was to break open the British grip by applying to these maritime circumstances a strategy which he employed on land, with an unbroken string of profoundly bloody successes – he is thought to have been responsible for the death of some 1.5 million Frenchmen and uncounted others – over 30 times between 1796 and 1815. The *manoeuvre sur la derrière* was not his invention – it was the favoured method of Frederick the Great – but Napoleon made it his own.

There was nothing conservative about Napoleon's attitude to war. Large ambitions involved high risks, and the essence of the risky Napoleonic plan, which went through many changes and permutations, was this: both the Toulon fleet under Villeneuve and the fleet at Rochefort on the French Atlantic coast, under Ganteaume, would slip out past the blockading British. That was quite possible: both had done it before. An easterly over the Atlantic coast of France would drive the British out to sea and allow the French in Rochefort to emerge. A northerly in Provence would have the same effect for the Toulon fleet. Villeneuve would make for the Strait of Gibraltar, the Spanish fleets at Cadiz and Cartagena would join him, the Rochefort squadron would drive south and west, and this huge accumulation of firepower – each man-of-war carried the weight of artillery that usually accompanied an entire land army – would be hidden in the immensities of the Atlantic Ocean. The rendezvous would be in the West Indies, from where they would return in force, gather more Spanish ships from Ferrol, push up to Brest, drive off the English Channel Fleet and with the French Brest fleet now accompanying them, would sweep the Channel (Napoleon's phrase – *balayer la Manche*), push on to control the Straits of Dover and enable the invasion flotilla to cross.

The plan relied on the absorbent secrecy of the Atlantic and the desperate slowness of communications across it. The enemy could know nothing. He would be thrown back on to guesswork. A state of acute anxiety would be induced in him. There would be no telling where the French forces were, how they had dispersed or where they might recombine. Napoleon had hints published in the *Moniteur*, the government news organ, that India was the target, as it had been notionally in 1798. As he had done often enough on land, and was to do often again, the long trans-Atlantic feint to the Caribbean was to draw the defending forces out to it, leaving the main target – England itself – horribly exposed. The re-assembling fleets, in the plan Napoleon made, were to cut straight back from the Caribbean to the English Channel, and take up a position between the Straits of Dover and the British fleets pursuing them. Napoleon's veterans, 150,000 of them, would pour across the Channel, England would be ruined and as Napoleon told his soldiers 'six centuries of insult would be avenged and freedom would be given to the seas.'

Wellington thought that 'The whole art of war consists in getting at what lies on the other side of the hill, or, in other words, in deciding what we do not know from what we do.' Napoleon's *manoeuvre sur la derrière* was the opposite of that: using the vastness of the ocean itself as a cloak (his term was 'the curtain of manoeuvre') behind which to concentrate his forces for the attack. The whole secret of Napoleonic war on land was the deceit and confusion brought about by dispersal, sudden appearance in the rear of the enemy, his flank turned, followed by rapid concentration and delivery of the blow. It is what he brought about in the Austerlitz campaign in the autumn of 1805 and it is what he planned for the Battle of the Atlantic too.

The account survives by Denis Decrès, the Minister of Marine, of the moment when he told Villeneuve of the scheme. It was in Boulogne in August 1804. 'Sire,' Decrès wrote to Napoleon, 'Vice-Admiral Villeneuve and Rear-Admiral Missiessy [of the Brest fleet] are here. I have laid before the former the great project. Villeneuve listened to it coldly and remained silent for some moments. Then, with a very calm smile, he said to me "I expected something of that sort." Going on, he said' – quoting Racine –

Mais pour être approuvés,
De semblables projets ont besoin
d'être achevés.

'To meet with approval, such plans need to have succeeded.' It was a pivotal moment and a diagnostic remark: the French admiral, a product of the pre-revolutionary French royal navy, is not taken up by the blaze of inspiration in which the Napoleonic plan was conceived; nor rushes to salute the genius of the Emperor, but remains cautious, controlled, knowing and rational, the reaction of a practised and ordered mind. Nevertheless, and inevitably, the imperial vision prevailed. Villeneuve responded to the inducements dangled before him: once promoted vice-admiral and appointed Grand Officier of the Légion d'Honneur, he became, as Decrès described him, *un homme tout nouveau*. It was, Villeneuve had told Decrès, the prospect of glory which had changed his mind. He would 'deliver himself entire' to the project.

These were the sources of the drama that had then unfolded over the spring and summer of 1805: Napoleon's radical military vision; a French navy out of sympathy with that vision (and a Spanish navy even more so) but doing the best to fulfil the imperial orders; the British Establishment and its naval servants intent on bringing the French fleet to battle. For all sides, it was a period of acute anxiety. If you read the file of correspondence received by the Lords Commissioners of the Admiralty from the captains and flag officers who were part of the command structure of the Mediterranean Fleet in 1805, the beautifully organised pages are thick with worry and trouble, with the sense of incipient failure and inadequate resources, with the desperate mismatch between the sort of coherence which the tradition expected and the realities of sea and war.

Villeneuve broke out of Toulon on 30 March 1805 but in the persistent and disturbing fog of non- or partial-communication, Nelson missed him. His blockade had been set too loosely and Villeneuve escaped to the south along the Mediterranean coast of Spain. French spies in Paris got the news to London, where it soon appeared in the newspapers, with the added (true) detail that a combined French and Spanish fleet was bound for the West Indies. But it would take at least a month to get any such information to Nelson off Toulon. Within a week, Nelson heard that they had got out. But where to? For the best part of a month, Nelson failed to guess that Villeneuve and the Toulon fleet were heading for the Atlantic. Instead, he pursued him eastwards towards Egypt. Endlessly, besieged by worry, Nelson searched for him, or for news of him, desperate not to leave the eastern Mediterranean and Egypt unprotected, not even imagining the complexities of Napoleon's Atlantic strategy. English agents in Madrid, Cadiz, Ferrol and Cartagena scurried for news, but to no avail. 'I wish it were in my power to furnish you with more satisfactory intelligence,' one of them wrote, 'but the object of the Enemies Expeditions have been hitherto kept a profound Secret.' Only on 16 April did Nelson hear that Villeneuve had been seen off the southeastern tip of Spain nine days earlier, and had probably passed through the Strait of Gibraltar the next day. Nelson was horrified: 'If this account is true, much mischief may be apprehended. It kills me, the very thought.'

Other British officers, on guard along the peripheries of the European mainland, were equally susceptible to the possibility of failure destroying their careers. Any hint of inadequacy in battle was to invite a hailstorm of loathing from a well-informed public at home. Rear-Admiral Sir John Orde had been stationed off Cape Trafalgar with a small squadron as the French Mediterranean fleet joined Gravina with the Spanish from Cadiz and set off for the Caribbean. Hugely outnumbered, Orde had made no attempt to stop them. Summoned home, in disgrace, to strike his flag, he was never employed as an admiral again and was subject to virulent loathing from the public, particularly merchants in the City of London who considered their trade put at risk by his behaviour.

The possible rewards of naval life might have been huge, but the penalties – in public humiliation if nothing else – were appalling. Even when Nelson finally guessed and then heard the truth, it took weeks for his news to reach the Admiralty. Nelson's dispatch written on 5 May from off Cape St Vincent, finally announcing that Villeneuve had left the Mediterranean, was received in London only on 3 June, more than two months after Villeneuve had left Toulon. Even then it was unclear if the French were headed for the Caribbean or Ireland. All Barham could do in London was station curtains of warships across the entire width of the western approaches of the English Channel, from Cape Clear in southwest Ireland, across to Scilly off Land's End, to Ushant off the western tip of Brittany and then down to Rochefort and Cape Finisterre at the northwest tip of Spain. With an invisible enemy, the only possible option was to wait, armed and ready. This was the received strategy, but it was one based, essentially, on a condition of ignorance.

Added to the problems of a hidden enemy were the sheer uncertainties of navigation. Great improvements had been made in the course of the 18th century in the instruments and theories by which a ship could calculate its position at sea but still it was as much art as science. It was all very well to know the theory by which noon sun sights could establish your latitude, but they were no good when the sky remained cloudy for weeks at a time, and when maps and charts were far from the reliable documents they are today. The magnetic variation of the earth itself, which disrupts the workings of a ship's compass differently in different parts of the ocean, could only be guessed at. The log lines, which measured a ship's speed through the water, were often found to be inaccurately measured out and subject to wide operator error. Besides, all that such a line could measure was speed through the water. It could not take account of the many unknown currents in the sea by which speed over the ground was radically affected. Taking a log-line measurement when the weather was bad and the seas high was an exercise more in guesswork than in science. The navigator had to rely as much on a far older and more intuitive level of understanding of the sea – its colour, even its smell, the nature of the seabed which soundings brought up on the end of the lead line, or even the behaviour of seabirds. For a great deal of the time, Nelson's fleet had to guess as much where they were as where the enemy was.

The strain told on everyone. Nelson finally left for the West Indies on 11 May. Villeneuve was now a month ahead of him. No one in England, despite the many varied reports about enemy fleets in Ireland, off Ferrol, approaching the Channel, had any idea where either Villeneuve or Nelson had got to. On passage, Nelson began to draft a plan of the battle he hoped for, encouraging his captains and their crews to race the French across the Atlantic, urging his ships to shave two weeks off the French fleet's lead. On 4 June, he finally arrived in Carlisle Bay, Barbados and immediately wrote to William Marsden, Secretary of the Admiralty: 'I am anxious in the extreme to get at their 18 sail of the line.' It was, as Nelson calls it, 'a laudable anxiety of mind', but the nervous exhaustion is palpable. Letter after letter from the Caribbean is full of this urgency and worry: 'My heart is almost broke,' 'the misery I am feeling', 'all is hurry'.

The French fleets failed to meet up in the Caribbean but Villeneuve, partly through some false information received by Nelson, kept one step ahead of him and on 5 June headed north and back for Europe. Nelson was exhausted, longing for home and England 'to try and repair a very shattered Constitution.' 'My very shattered frame,' he wrote to his friend and agent Alexander Davison, 'will require rest, and that is all that I ask for.' Not yet though. He had to set out back across the Atlantic, in pursuit of the French: 'By carrying every Sail and using my utmost efforts I shall hope to close with them before they get to either Cadiz or Toulon to accomplish which most desirable object nothing shall be wanting on the part Sir of your most obedient servant. Nelson + Bronte'.

There is strain and exertion in every word. All he needed was proximity. Get close to them, and he felt he could rely on the destructive power of the fleet under his command. Every rag in every ship was hauled to the mast but he never caught them and never guessed at what the grand Napoleonic scheme might be. Villeneuve was heading, as his orders required, for Ferrol in northwest Spain, but Nelson was still thinking of the Mediterranean, and he headed for the Strait of Gibraltar. By 18 July, after a round trip of 6,686 miles, Cape Spartel, on the Moroccan side of the Strait, was sighted from the *Victory*, but no enemy in sight, 'nor any information about them; how sorrowful this makes me, but I cannot help myself'. They had given him the slip.

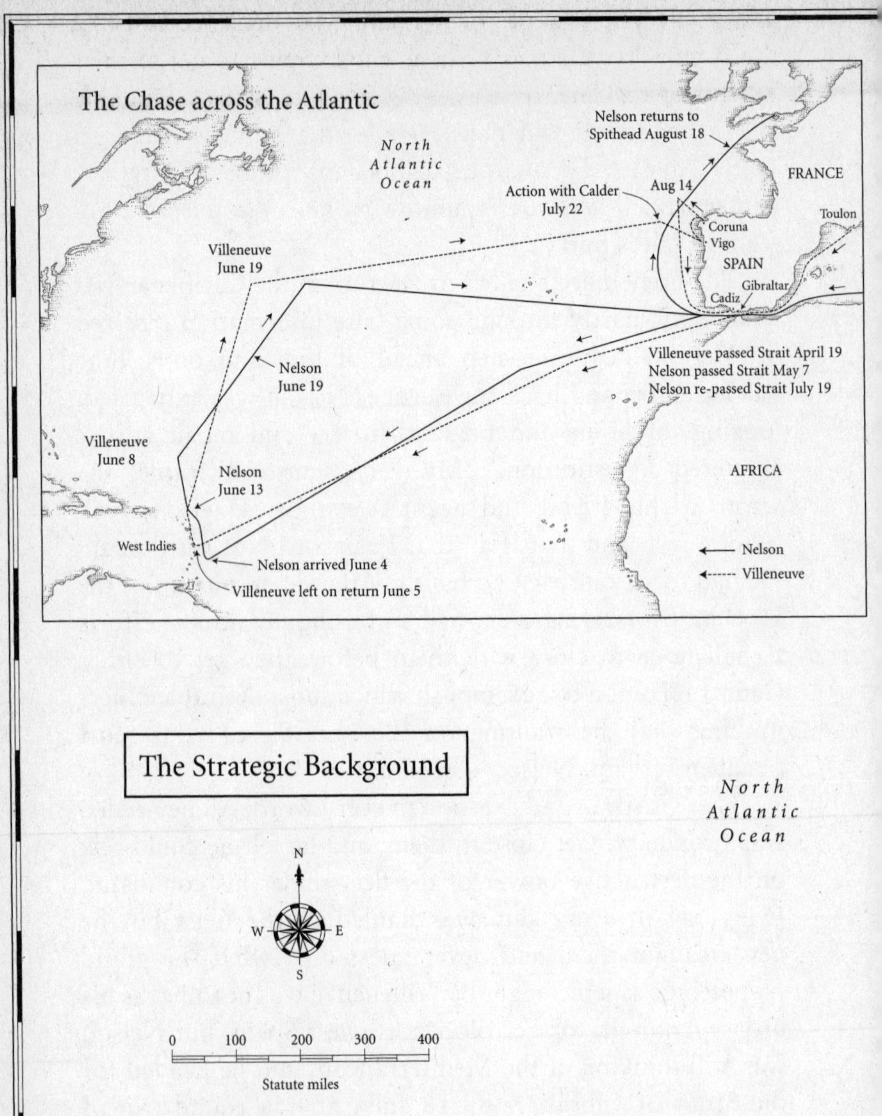
The Chase across the Atlantic
North Atlantic Ocean
Nelson returns to Spithead August 18
FRANCE
Action with Calder July 22
Aug 14
Toulon
Coruna
Vigo
SPAIN
Villeneuve June 19
Gibraltar
Cadiz
Villeneuve passed Strait April 19
Nelson passed Strait May 7
Nelson re-passed Strait July 19
Nelson June 19
Villeneuve June 8
AFRICA
Nelson June 13
West Indies
Nelson
Nelson arrived June 4
Villeneuve
Villeneuve left on return June 5
The Strategic Background
North Atlantic Ocean
N
W
E
S
0
100
200
300
400
Statute miles

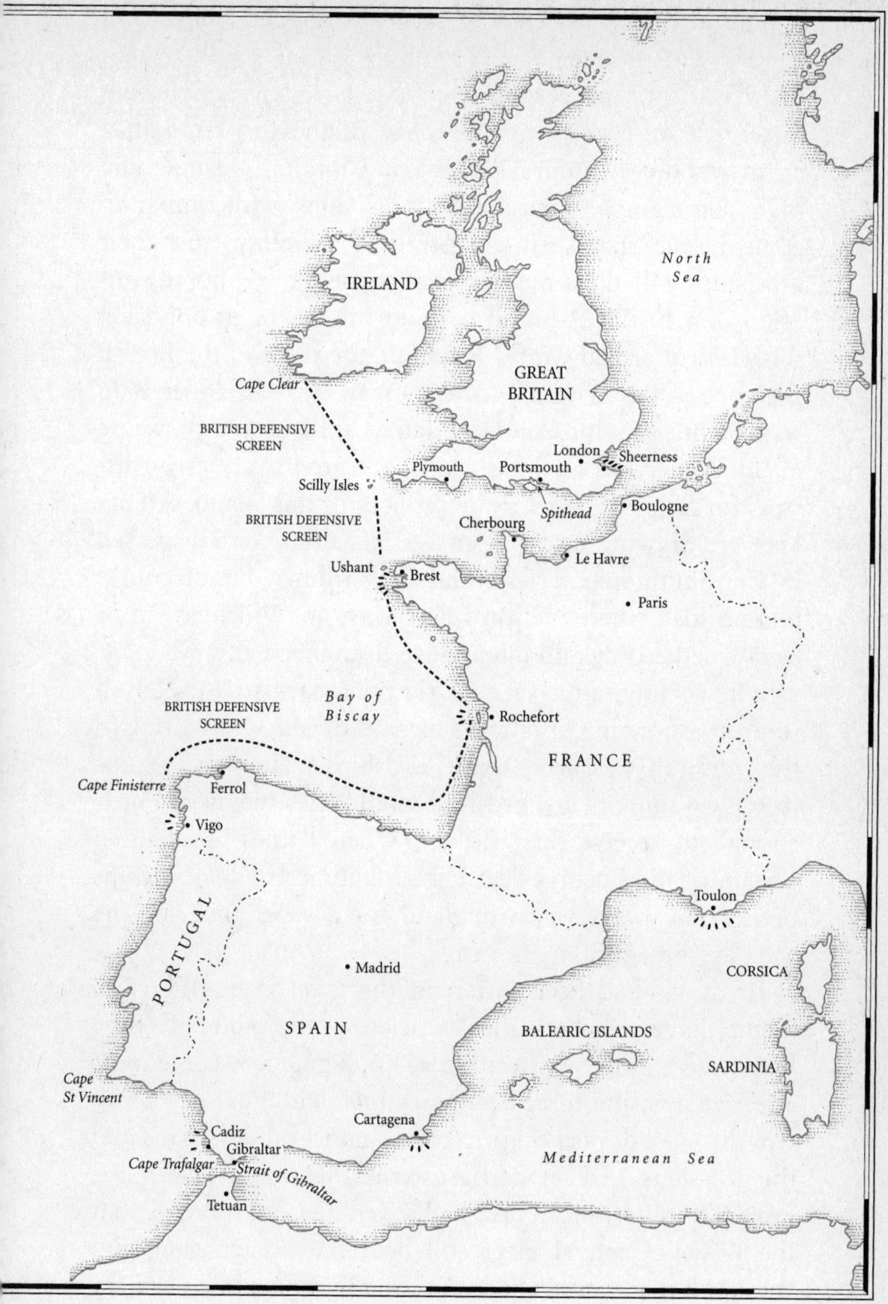
North Sea
IRELAND
GREAT BRITAIN
Cape Clear
BRITISH DEFENSIVE SCREEN
London
Sheerness
Plymouth
Portsmouth
Scilly Isles
Spithead
Boulogne
BRITISH DEFENSIVE SCREEN
Cherbourg
Le Havre
Ushant
Brest
Paris
Bay of Biscay
BRITISH DEFENSIVE SCREEN
Rochefort
FRANCE
Cape Finisterre
Ferrol
Vigo
PORTUGAL
Toulon
Madrid
CORSICA
SPAIN
BALEARIC ISLANDS
SARDINIA
Cape St Vincent
Cadiz
Cartagena
Gibraltar
Cape Trafalgar
Strait of Gibraltar
Mediterranean Sea
Tetuan

Any complacent sense of system that might have prevailed among the armchairs of London was totally absent from the fleet. Throughout the anxious summer, the feeling at sea was of a desperate stretched thinness to the British naval resource. Admiral Knight at Gibraltar – something of a complainer – felt he had no ships with which to confront the Spanish in the Strait: 'I therefore trust their Lordships will allow me to repeat to them the exposed situation of a British Admiral without the means of opposing this Host of armed Craft.' In Malta, the pivot of the British presence in the eastern Mediterranean, Sir Alexander Ball, with Samuel Taylor Coleridge acting as his secretary, wrote in full anxiety on 24 June 1805. 'We are in very great distress for Ships of war for the services of this island. Affairs here are drawing fast to a crisis.' His ships were dispersed in Constantinople, Trieste and off Sardinia. He of course had no idea where Nelson's fleet was, nor Villeneuve's; or even whether England might have been invaded.

On 19 July, after very nearly two years at sea, Nelson stepped ashore in Gibraltar. The next day he was writing to the Admiralty, assuring their Lordships 'that I am anxious to act as I think their Lordships would wish me, were I near enough to receive their orders. When I know something certain of the Enemys fleet I shall embrace their Lordships permission to return to England for a short time for the reestablishment of my health.'

If things had been different, the great events of 1805 might have reached their crisis at the end of July. Napoleon's army was waiting at Boulogne. It was the most effective invasion force ever assembled and would go on to win the most devastating victories against the Austrians and the Russians at Ulm and Austerlitz. The strategy of the French Mediterranean fleet had foxed Nelson. It is true that the British Channel Fleet still held the French shut into Brest. All that was needed was for Villeneuve to collect the

Spanish ships from Ferrol and the French squadron from Rochefort and to drive north to the Channel. The Brest fleet would emerge and in overwhelming numbers they would come to dominate the Channel as Napoleon had envisaged.

On 22 July, 100 miles west of Cape Finisterre, Villeneuve fell in with a British fleet under Sir Robert Calder and in fog and with a greasy swell sliding under them, met in an inconclusive battle for which Calder was pilloried in the British press. Nelson headed north from Gibraltar on 15 August. He left most of his ships with the Channel Fleet and in *Victory* went home to England, the arms of Emma Hamilton and rest. Any idea that the events of the preceding months had been governed by order and rationality would have summoned from him a hollow laugh. All was contingency, guesswork and desperation. He was reading in the newspapers, which he picked up from the Channel Fleet, of Calder's half-hearted engagement off Finisterre. As he wrote to his friend Thomas Fremantle:

> Who can, my dear Fremantle, command all the success which our Country may wish? We have fought together and therefore know well what it is. I have had the best disposed Fleet of friends, but who can say what will be the event of a Battle? And it most sincerely grieves me, that in any of the papers it should be insinuated that Lord Nelson should have done better. I should have fought the Enemy, so did my friend Calder; but who can say that he will be more successful than another?

Napoleon wrote to Villeneuve, to tell him that 'the Destiny of France' lay in his hands. After the action with Calder's fleet, he went first into Vigo and then Coruña. He wrote to Decrès about the rotten condition of his fleet. The *Bucentaure* had been struck by lightning. His ships were floating hospitals. Masts, sails and rigging were inadequate. His captains were brave but inefficient. His fleet was in disorder. On 11 August, full of apprehension, he left Coruña, but two days later, frightened by false intelligence of a British fleet to the north, he gave the order to turn south. On 22 August he entered Cadiz, where he had remained ever since, sunk in shame. On the same day, Napoleon had written him a letter from the camp at Boulogne, addressed to Villeneuve in Brest, where he was expected to arrive at any minute.

> Vice-Admiral, Make a start. Lose not a moment and come into the Channel, bringing our united squadrons, and England is ours. We are all ready; everything is embarked. Be here but for twenty-four hours and all is ended.

Villeneuve failed the test of nerve which Napoleon had set him, but he failed it on rational grounds. His inadequate fleet would have been smashed by the sea-hardened ships of the British Channel Fleet and of Nelson's Mediterranean Fleet which were waiting for him off the Breton coast. Trafalgar would have occurred in August 1805, a thousand miles further north and the British would for ever after have celebrated the great victory of Ushant.

As it was, Villeneuve and his 33 ships were now shut into Cadiz by the small English squadron of between four and six ships-of-the-line under Collingwood, which had been cruising off the port since June. For months, they had been craning their ears to discover what was going on in Cadiz. And even now, reinforced on 30 August by Sir Robert Calder with 19 sail-of-the-line, there was no sense of the anxiety being over. Far from it. Fishing boats were stopped and boarded. Neutral American merchantmen were searched and their captains interrogated. Among the papers of Captain Bayntun of the *Leviathan* is the *Atlas Maritimo de España*, published in Madrid 1789, in its handmade sailcoth cover, sewn by a sailor on the *Leviathan*, and many of the pages deeply water-stained. The chart of Cadiz Bay is covered in Bayntun's notes and lines, the anxious care of a blockading captain drawing in the bearings on the church at Chipion near St Lucar and the Cadiz lighthouse, working out the leading marks and the bearings on various fortifications around the city, carefully annotating and translating the table of soundings for the sand, gravel, rock and mud shoals south of the city. Even 200 years later, in a muniment room in England, it is a document drenched in anxiety.

All year long they had listened to the gossip coming out of Cadiz and all of it was transmitted back to London. The Spanish fleet was watering and taking on provisions. Admiral Gravina had been appointed to command. The Spanish crews had received five months' pay. It was now said that Villeneuve 'was likely to lose his head for his conduct, and it was supposed he would be sent a prisoner to Paris.' The Combined Fleet was reported bound to the Mediterranean. Couriers were seen leaving for Madrid and Paris at ten o'clock at night. Gravina was going to strike his flag, disgusted, the report said, with the conduct of the French.

In early September a spy somehow got to Collingwood a complete breakdown of the ships in Cadiz, including precise information on their captains and the number of guns per ship. On 19 September the entire Combined Fleet was said to be stored and complete with provisions, but in want of sailors. There followed 'a general press on shore, and a strict search of French, and Spanish Deserters on board all the merchant Ships of every nation.' Battle would soon follow.

In the British fleet, this constant vigilance and anxiety exacted its price. A Lieutenant Wharton, in HMS *Bellerophon* on station off Ushant with the Channel Fleet under

Admiral Cornwallis, longs to go home. He has just heard that his father has died and his affairs are 'in a very confused state'. He gives his request to his captain John Cooke, who sends it to the admiral, who sends it to the Admiralty. A minute in response, by Marsden, is written as usual on the corner of the letter: 'The expence of the Service does not permit Lt Whartons request to be complied with.' No relief; he must stick to the task.

On 18 August, Lieutenant Pasco, flag lieutenant on *Victory*, was suffering from rheumatism and 'my weak state of health'. Pasco wrote to Hardy, Hardy to Nelson, and Nelson to the Admiralty requesting that Pasco go ashore. The doctor on the flagship, William Beatty, recommended 14 days 'Country Air, Exercise and change of diet'. Captain Hardy himself had been 'for many months afflicted with very severe rheumatic complaints attended with maciation and privation of rest and obstinately resisting the efficacy of medicine', for which Beatty recommends

> relaxation of some weeks, from the duties of Service, change of air, and Regimen, exercise on horseback, or in a carriage, together with the frequent use of the Tepid Bath.

Sir Richard Bickerton had 'confirmed affection of the liver'; Rear-Admiral Lord Northesk wants to go home 'having urgent business in England'; Captain Morrison of the *Revenge* wants to go home: 'A Rupture of some years Standing has lately become worse. I do not find my Health equal to the Duties of my profession.' Admiral Knight in Gibraltar had become too ill to do anything. On the *Achille* on 21 September, different officers were suffering from repeated liver pain and visceral obstruction, ulcered leg and consumption. Lieutenant Will Davies on *Spartiate* was suffering from 'rapid Constitutional Decay, privation of appetite and general debility'.

By early October, John Wemyss, captain of the Royal Marines on board the *Bellerophon* wrote to his captain John Cooke:

> Sir,
>
> I beg leave to represent to you that Domestic Concerns of a most Urgent and particular Nature, render my immediate presence in England indispensably necessary to my private Interests, and induce me to request you would have the goodness to use your influence with the Commander in Chief, to permit me to proceed thither, either by appointing some Officer included in the late Promotion to serve on board the Bellerophon in my room, or granting me such leave of absence as his lordship may deem proper. From my situation on the List of Captains and having some time ago completed a Tour of Sea Duty, and not having during the last thirteen years troubled my Lords Commissioners of the Admiralty for an indulgence, I trust will, in his Lordships Conscience, have due weight –
>
> I have the Honor to be
> Your most Obedient and
> Humble Servant
> John Wemyss
> Capt Royal Marines

A month and a half later, on 16 November, after Trafalgar had come and gone, when Cooke was dead and Wemyss recovering from a dreadful wound, Barham wrote baldly:

> 'Aqunt Lord Collingwood that Capt Wemyss's request cannot be complied with.'

The ships themselves were as worn as their officers. By early October, Nelson had returned from England to join the fleet off Cadiz. He sent a list to the Admiralty of the state in which he found the ships: *Victory* was fit for service; *Canopus* would be better docked before the winter; *Spencer* was fit for service, *Superbe* 'must be docked for her movement' – the shifting of timbers in heavy weather – *Belleisle* needs docking, *Donegal* 'needs docking but not so much as *Belleisle*.'

The inefficiencies of men, ships and supplies, the annoyance with others, the conscious display to superiors, the squabbles about prizes, prize money and the sums due to flag officers who may or may not have been absent from the station, the tendency to disobey orders, the sheer illness and exhaustion of many of the officers under this strain, the extreme tautness of the naval screen stretched around the European periphery from the Baltic to the Aegean, the vast army ranged opposite the British coast at Boulogne, the threat to the British possessions in the Caribbean, the slowness of communications, which meant that a conversation could take three months, the overriding anxiety about where the enemy fleets and squadrons were and how they were to be prevented from achieving the concentration they need to establish superiority in the Channel: all of this is the human and technical reality underlying the idea of an orderly fleet which they all held as the model of perfection in their mind. Alert they listen all the time for the truth straining at the horizon to identify the ships they see. On 12 September, Collingwood wrote to the Admiralty: 'The intelligence I get of the Enemy is vague, and sometimes contradictory.' It reads at this distance like a plea for understanding.

There was undoubtedly high tension in the exactness. On the morning of Trafalgar, for the first time in his life, Nelson forgot to wear his sword; it was found in his quarters after the battle. All around him on the *Victory*, the anxiety was running at a high level. Nelson, Hardy and the frigate captains who were with them toured the various decks of the ship. Nelson urged the men not to fire unless they knew the shot would tell and 'expressed himself highly satisfied with the arrangements.' There were then discussions over the danger to Nelson himself. Hardy, Nelson's secretary, the ship's chaplain and others discussed the possibility of persuading Nelson to conceal the stars on his coat. None dared raise the question with him, as it was known with what contempt he would treat it. The great officer needed to maintain a heroic bearing. He should, in the aristocratic mould, 'appear and be', which meant that he should wear his stars.

Instead, Blackwood raised the question with the admiral as to which ship should lead his column into the battle. The first ship would take an immense quantity of fire. On tactical grounds alone, the flagship should not be exposed to such fire. Nelson loved and admired Blackwood and accepted his advice. The *Téméraire* was sailing abreast of the flagship, so close that Nelson thought he might shout instructions over to her, that she should go ahead of the *Victory*, to take the brunt of the Combined Fleet's defence. But Captain Harvey of the *Téméraire* could not hear and so Blackwood was sent in one of *Victory*'s boats to deliver the orders. The *Neptune*, one ship further back, was given the same orders by flag signals.

The discussion is anxious, clipped, excited. Nelson's subordinates scarcely dare approach him. Even as Blackwood is away, Nelson, without countermanding them, goes back on the orders and urges the *Victory* forward, asking Hardy to have still more sail set so that the *Téméraire* could not pass. Lieutenant John Yule, who was in command on the flagship's forecastle, seeing that the starboard lower studding sail

> was improperly set, caused it to be taken in for the purpose of setting it afresh. The instant this was done, Lord Nelson ran forward and rated the Lieutenant severely for having, as he supposed, begun to shorten sail without the Captain's orders. The studding-sail was quickly replaced; and Victory, as the gallant chief intended, continued to lead the column.

That is not the action or behaviour of the calm man. A Calder or a Villeneuve might have done the orderly thing, and allowed the *Téméraire* and the *Neptune* to go ahead. But Nelson's battle agitation was governing him. 'Lord Nelson's anxiety to close with the enemy became very apparent,' Henry Blackwood wrote afterwards. That too is another reason that battle was longed for: as a place in which the anxiety was over, a place paradoxically of ultimate order and calm.

3

HONOUR

October 21st 1805
9.30 am to 11.30 am

Distance between the fleets: 5.9 miles – 2 miles
Victory's heading and speed: 067° – 101° at 3 knots

Honour: nobleness of mind; scorn of meanness; magnanimity
SAMUEL JOHNSON, *A Dictionary of the English Language*, 1755

As the sun rose, and with all preparations made on all ships, there was little to do but think of home. The fleets were still more than five miles apart and the maximum range for even the heaviest guns was 2,000 yards. There would be no battle, no death and no resolution before midday. In the *Bellerophon*, the men chalked 'Victory or Death' on the barrels of their guns. In the *Bucentaure*, the French flagship, the eagle which Napoleon had granted to the ship was paraded from deck to deck accompanied by the admiral. *Vive l'Empereur! Vive l'Amiral!* the sailors cheered as it passed. In the Spanish ships, the crews assembled for prayers and absolution. On the *San Juan Nepocumeno*, the captain, Don Cosme Churruca – a 45-year-old, highly educated disciplinarian and scholar, a hidalgo of the highest class, *El Gran Churruca* – spoke to the men. 'In the name of the God of Battles, I promise eternal happiness to all those who die today doing their duty.' Anyone who did not, he went on, would either be 'shot immediately or, if he escapes my eyes or those of the valiant officers I have the honour to command, bitter remorse will follow the wretch for the rest of his days, in misery and disgrace.' He did not tell them what he had written to a friend before leaving Cadiz: 'If you hear that my ship has been taken, you can say that I am dead.' Nor the advice he had given to his nephew, then a volunteer on the *San Juan*: 'Write to your friends that you are going into a battle that will be desperate and bloody. Tell them also that they may be certain of this – that I, for my part, will meet my death there. Let them know that rather than surrender my ship I shall sink her. It is the last duty that an officer owes to his king and country.' Honour for the Spaniard was a matter more of death than of victory.

On board this morning, Churruca told his second-in-command, 'The fleet is doomed. The French admiral does not understand his business. He has compromised us all.' They could look out to the west and see their fate approaching. The captain stood on his quarterdeck with his telescope fixed to his eye, trained on the masts of the *Bucentaure*, waiting for Villeneuve to respond to the threat which the two approaching columns of the British fleet posed. The British plan was becoming clear. Nelson would throw the weight of his attack on the centre and rear of the Combined Fleet. In the light winds, once the attack had begun, the French and Spanish van would not be able to turn in time to bring their force to bear. Arriving in force, the British would outnumber the centre and rear of the Franco-Spanish fleet. As Churruca understood, there was a perfectly clear tactical move Villeneuve could have decided on as the two British columns approached which would have made the British position much more vulnerable. All Villeneuve had to do was order his van to wear round and double on the rear squadron. That way they could envelop the British as they attacked. But no signal came and Churruca finally lowered his telescope and walked across the quarterdeck, saying to himself, '*Perdidos, perdidos, perdidos.*' Why Villeneuve did not make this signal until far too late and why the Combined van did not take it upon themselves to turn back towards the battle are the two great conundrums of Trafalgar. It may, as Churruca thought, have been mere indecisiveness on the part of Villeneuve. It may have been a reluctance on the part of Dumanoir, the admiral commanding the van, to make an independent decision, without orders from his Commander-in-Chief. This fatal mistake may, in other words, have been a failure of morale on one side and a failure of initiative on the other. In that double weakness lay the roots of the British victory.

Nemesis was on the western horizon. What was it like on the British commander's quarterdeck? No word-by-word record survives of Nelson's behaviour on the morning of Trafalgar, as it does of his tragic end during the afternoon, but an extraordinarily illuminating account of Nelson's behaviour in pursuit of the enemy, also when hard on the chase of the French, survives from five years earlier. Scarcely any document describes more exactly the man he was.

Nelson was in command of a small squadron in the central Mediterranean, on board his flagship the *Foudroyant*, with his friend Captain Sir Edward Berry on the quarterdeck beside him. They found themselves in the same stretch of sea as a French squadron, under Rear-Admiral Perrée, whose flagship *Le Généreux* had been one of the very few French ships-of-the-line to have escaped from the Battle of the Nile. The account was published by one of his lieutenants, George Parsons.

'Ah! An enemy, Mr Stains. I pray God it may be Le Genereux. The signal for a general chase, Sir Ed'ard, (the Nelsonian pronunciation of Edward) make the Foudroyant fly!'

Thus spoke the heroic Nelson; and every exertion that emulation could inspire was used to crowd the squadron with canvas, the Northumberland taking the lead, with the flagship close on her quarter.

'This will not do Sir Ed'ard; it is certainly Le Genereux, and to my flagship she can alone surrender. Sir Ed'ard we must and shall beat the Northumberland.'

'I will do the utmost, my lord; get the engines to work on the sails – hang butts of water to the stays – pipe the hammocks down, and each man place shot in them – slack the stays, knock up the wedges and give the masts play – start off the water, Mr James, and pump the ship.'

Nelson is competitive, goading, and extraordinarily hungry for conflict. Berry's orders are all designed to get extra speed out of the ship and prepare her for battle. 'Engines' are pumps with which to wet the sails, since damp sails set fairer and will not catch fire in a fight; water butts on the deck are further fire precautions; shot placed in the windward hammock netting on deck helps balance the ship and a level ship sails faster; the slackened stays and masts given play both allow more sail to be set; pumping the ship and draining the water butts lightens the load.

The Foudroyant is drawing a-head, and at last takes the lead in the chase. 'The Admiral is working his fin (the stump of his right arm), do not cross his hawse I advise you.'

The advice was good, for at that moment Nelson opened furiously on the quartermaster at the conn [wheel]. 'I'll knock you off your perch, you rascal, if you are so inattentive. Sir Ed'ard, send your best quartermaster to the weather wheel.'

'A strange sail a-head of the chase!' called the look-out man.

'Youngster, to the mast-head. What! Going without your glass, and be d–d to you? Let me know what she is immediately.'

'A sloop of war or frigate, my lord,' shouted the young signal-midshipman.

'Demand her number.'

'The Success, my lord.'

'Captain Peard; signal to cut off the flying enemy – great odds, though – thirty two small guns to eighty large ones.'

An order which in itself is the mark of a ruthless commander: to set a 32-gun frigate against a ship of the line rated at 74 guns, with extra upper deck armament, was to set a poodle on a bear.

'The Success has hove-to athwart-hawse of the Genereux, and is firing her larboard broadside. The Frenchman has hoisted his tricolour, with a rear-admiral's flag.'

'Bravo – Success, *at her again*!'

'She has wore round my lord, and firing her starboard broadside. It has winged her my lord – her flying kites [her lightest sails] are flying away all together. The enemy is close on the Success, who must receive her tremendous broadside.' The Genereux opens her fire on her little enemy, and every person stands aghast, afraid of the consequences. The smoke clears away, and there is the Success, crippled it is true, but bull-dog like, bearing up after the enemy.

'The signal for the Success to discontinue the action, and come under my stern,' said Lord Nelson; 'she has done well for her size. Try a shot from the lower deck at her, Sir Ed'ard.'

'It goes over her.'

'Beat to quarters and fire coolly at her masts and yards.'

It might often have been the case that the French aimed for the rigging and the British for the hull, but that was never a universal rule. Where a chasing ship wanted to halt or slow the progress of the enemy, destroying the masts and yards, the source of any motive power, was the obvious option.

> Le Genereux at this moment opened her fire on us; and as a shot passed through the mizzen stay sail [i.e. immediately above the quarterdeck], Lord Nelson, patting one of the youngsters on the head, asked him jocularly how he relished the music; and observing something like alarm depicted on his countenance, consoled him with the information that Charles XII [the great 18th-century Swedish warrior king] ran away from the first shot he heard, though afterwards he was called 'The Great', and deservedly, from his bravery. 'I, therefore,' said Lord Nelson, 'hope much from you in future.'
>
> Here the Northumberland opened her fire, and down came the tri-coloured ensign, amid the thunder of our united cannon.

Even in this tiny fragment, his method of command can be seen to run across all the strings: intemperate, charming, theatrical, anxious, impetuous, educative, curt, considerate, indifferent to death and danger, inspirational to those around him and above all fixed on attack and victory.

Rising and falling in the wake of the British flagship in the weather column, behind the *Téméraire,* was the *Neptune*, 98 guns, one of the big and heavy three-deckers which, with the other two, formed the battering ram at the head of

Nelson's windward line. The *Neptune* was not a good sailer but capable of dominating and destroying any craft she fell in with, firing plunging shots down through the decks of her victims. She was force, not elegance. The *Neptune* had been part of the British Channel Fleet and for many months had suffered the long, wearing tedium of holding the French locked into their ports. One of the boys on that station, the eleven-year-old Bernard Coleridge, had written to his father and mother:

> Indeed we live on beef which has been ten or eleven years in corn and on biscuit which makes your throat cold in eating it owing to the maggots which are very cold when you eat them, like calves-foot jelly or blomonge being very fat indeed. Indeed, I do like this life very much, but I cannot help laughing heartily when I think of sculling about the old cyder-tub in the pond, and Mary Anne Cosserat capsizing into the pond just by the mulberry bush. I hope I shall learn not to swear, and by God's assistance I hope I shall not.

Every ship at Trafalgar, in all ranks, quarters and stations, carried its freight of homesickness. The *Neptune*'s captain was Thomas Fremantle, who had his copy of Pope's *Iliad* in his library on board. There was no doubt that he too was longing for home, quite as much as any powder-monkey. A battle is not only the aggression at the point of contact; it is a meeting of hinterlands. Fremantle's anger, violence, anxiety, tenderness, professionalism and sheer ambition – all constituents of his honour – were also some of the vital factors in battle.

He was not quite 40 years old, and one of Nelson's favourites. As Nelson had been blockading Toulon, he had written to his old friend in the Channel. 'I Trust, my dear Fremantle, in God and English valour. We are enough in

England if true to ourselves.' It was the sort of encouragement at which Nelson had no equal. His words, which carry subtly heroic undertones, echoing the famous speech of Henry V in front of Harfleur, transform the king's exhortations into a kind of complicit togetherness: '*We* are enough in England if true to ourselves'. That is the Nelson charm in action, a form of combined balm and stimulus for any officer suffering the sapping and demoralising conditions of a blockading fleet.

Off Brest, Fremantle had been forced to stay in his quarters for four days, his head swathed in bandages, his eyes burning from an acute inflammation. To hold the tedium at bay, he took to brewing spruce beer, smoking 'segars' in his cabin and reading *Family Secrets,* a book of wonderfully consoling pornographic stories given him by the ship's purser. His wife rapidly sent out a set of Shakespeare to fill the gap and some of Cobbett's diatribes against the wickedness of the French. In thanking her, Fremantle described how his goat had fallen down a hatchway and died, depriving him of his daily glass of milk. He asked her to send him out some toothpaste with the next set of letters. The air of his private correspondence is more exhausted than heroic. Nelson's undoubted role was as a goad to honour, to lift these men to a higher conception of themselves and of their duty.

Like most officers, Fremantle had been at sea since he was twelve and he was in some ways fed up with the life he had led for almost 30 years. The strain and the tedium, the impositions of duty, were of a kind unknown to those who stayed ashore. In the summer of 1803, the last time he had been at home, he had not wanted to leave England again. 'He really goes to sea quite *à contre coeur*,' his wife had written in her diary, 'as he was now so comfortably settled here.' He had wept at dinner on the evening before he left and had to leave the room to conceal his tears.

Despite this intense emotionality – and Englishmen in 1805 had more immediate access to their emotions than at any time before or since – Fremantle was no Nelson. He was, at least on the surface, and unlike the admiral, a strong, tough, stocky man, with an intimidating rather than a persuasive presence, but was certainly capable, when required, of a kind of charm. In the summer of 1796, as a 30-year-old captain in Nelson's Mediterranean squadron, he had been ordered to take on board his frigate, the *Inconstant*, then at anchor off Leghorn, an English family, the Wynnes, who were threatened by the French armies then sweeping down into Italy. Fremantle was already the hero of a famous action against a French 84-gun ship, the *Ça Ira,* when quite alone in the *Inconstant*, with 38 guns; he had tacked to and fro behind her, bringing first one broadside to bear, then the other, on the French man-of-war's stern, like a boxer with his jabs, all the time staying out of reach of the French ship's massive broadsides, any one of which would have sunk the *Inconstant* in a few minutes. Nelson loved him, one of the few captains he referred to as 'one of my darling children', as much for Fremantle's capacity to apply unbridled violence as for any softer human qualities. He was a member of the Band of Brothers.

Among the Wynnes was 18-year-old Betsey. The *Inconstant*'s captain was 'not handsome', she decided,

> but there is something pleasing in his countenance and his fiery black eyes are quite captivating. He is good-natured, gay and lively, in short he seems to possess all the amiable qualities that are required to win everybody's heart the moment one sees him.

That is a picture of enlightened civility, of a man whose frigate struck even the young Betsey as clean and sweet-smelling, who made a practice of having the guns cleared away and holding candlelit dances on his quarterdeck, even within range of the French batteries on the Italian shore. During one of these dances, a round from one of the French cannon passed clean over the quarterdeck and on into the sea beyond the ship. No one but the naval officers even noticed. Fremantle's dark eyes sparkled, and he embodied a word and a moral quality which recurs again and again in this late-Enlightenment world: he was 'amiable' – a man to be liked and loved, in whom the bonds of society seemed happily alive. But this was his party-face, his charm. Profound and ferocious anxieties lay behind Fremantle's smiles.

He was the product of precisely the middling class and indeterminate situation which yielded the great majority of successful British naval officers. He was the third son of a Buckinghamshire gentleman, with a bit of land from a family with a sense of its own standing. That standing might be seamlessly transmitted to the eldest son, but in 18th-century England, a third son needed to shift for himself. Fremantle, self-motivating and aggressive, did precisely that.

He was not easy. He could often, as Betsey Wynne described in her diary, be in 'quite a fever'. He was angry from time to time and he was far from emotionally or financially secure. Within a few days of the Wynnes arriving on board the *Inconstant*, Betsey fell in love with him and he with her. But Fremantle had rapidly to confess something to Mr Wynne: 'his fortune at present was not sufficient for him to maintain a family.' Only the money he would get from his share of enemy prizes could propel him into the category of a gentleman who could sustain the state of marriage.

Social and financial insecurity, which are deeply connected to the question of honour, had a shaping effect on the officer corps of the British fleet at Trafalgar. They were men on edge, not certain of the place they held in the hierarchy for which they were fighting, with enormous rewards in money and status dangling before their eyes, but the equal and opposite possibility of failure, ignominy and poverty if chance did not favour them or their connections did not steer them into the path of the great rewards. The quartet of honour, money, aggression and success formed a tight little knot at the centre of their lives, the source at times of an almost overwhelming anxiety.

Fremantle's skill and aggression, and the patronage of Earl St Vincent, had guaranteed that he soon got the prizes that made him rich enough to marry Betsey Wynne. (Her father, at the earliest opportunity, had a plain conversation with St Vincent, asking him to send his prospective son-in-law on a profitable cruise. St Vincent had complied, sending him to prey for weeks at a time on the juiciest Mediterranean shipping lanes.) But the character traits of an uncertain and ambitious man do not disappear even with success. After they were married, and in private, Betsey's diary continues to find her husband difficult, and edgy: 'Fremantle attacked me for some nonsense or other. I am too inanimate. I see that very little is required to make him uneasy.' With fellow officers, he could be violently assertive. When the general in command of the army detachment in Porto Ferrajo in Corsica said he would fit out his own privateers, Fremantle told him that he would order the navy to attack and retake any prizes which the general's craft managed to capture. No negotiations or mutual accommodation: pure aggression would provide the solution. It was one of the qualities in an officer which Nelson treasured.

Fremantle was severely and painfully wounded in the right arm during the same catastrophic attack on Tenerife in the Canaries where Nelson lost his right arm in 1797, and the wound kept Fremantle at home. While Nelson led the Mediterranean Fleet to its triumphs at the Nile, Fremantle festered ashore. Betsey bought a 'piano forte' in Portsmouth to comfort her husband as his arm healed. They had a Miss Fortnum to tea 'whose father keeps a grocer's shop in London.' They went to see the French prisoners in Porchester Castle and bought 'a Guillotine neatly done in bone'. They moved to London but it was rarely the favourite place of naval officers, and the Fremantles soon left their small house off Curzon Street for the balm of rural, low-land, cow-filled, welcoming Buckinghamshire.

They found a place, as Betsey described it, 'about two miles from the turnpike road in the village of Swanburn, very agreeably situated on a hill. There is three little fields with the house and a good kitchen garden.' The price was 1,000 guineas, Fremantle offered 900 guineas from the prize money St Vincent had enabled him to win and, on the day after the Battle of the Nile, the offer was accepted. It was an emblematic moment: a navy that was funded by taxes on consumer goods had allowed an impoverished younger son of the minor English gentry to capture from merchants of other, competing nations the prize money which allowed him to set up as a country gentleman in the county of his birth. It is a central aspect of Trafalgar that the officers who fought so hard and uncompromisingly to win it were fighting, in the end, to establish themselves as members of a comfortable, pastorally-minded rural gentry. The road of battle led unerringly to the country house.

It is possible, fascinatingly, to reconstruct exactly the world the Fremantles now arranged for themselves. An inventory of the Trafalgar captain's house and library at Swanbourne survives, describing everything in precise detail. It is, on its surface, and in its accoutrements, a graceful and elegant existence. The striking orderliness of the *Inconstant*, of the ship-of-the-line the *Ganges* to which he was appointed in 1800, and of the *Neptune* which he commanded at Trafalgar, extends to the elegance of his house. Any hint of the gripping anxieties at sea lies buried in his other documents. At home, Captain and Mrs Fremantle have everything that civilisation can provide. There are tall looking-glasses over the marble chimneypieces in the dining room and drawing room. Elegant cane chairs stand around the walls, and other softer furniture is covered in chintz which matches the curtains. There is the 'piano forte', a music stool and stand, a card table, and in the hall a billiard table. There is enough silver for 24 to come to dinner, and a particularly treasured, and specifically mentioned, butter trowel. Turkey carpets are on the floors and green Moroccan curtains hang before the windows. The kitchen has a cheese toaster, a chocolate pot and a coffee pot as well as '1 Large Beef salting pan & 2 Tongue salting pans'. Striped pink chintz furniture decorates the bedrooms and a large yellow and black covered sofa with 'five hair cushions and 2 feather ditto' fills the 'Sopha Room'. In the nursery there is a 'Mahogany Horse' for Thomas, Emma and the baby Charles, who, Betsey thinks 'a pretty child but Fremantle calls him an ugly dog.' In the attic are four gingham-decorated garrets for the servants.

The Fremantles are not philistines. Among the pictures, there are of course portraits of Sir Thomas himself, of his wife, father and grandfather, of Nelson, of the Eddystone Lighthouse, Windsor Castle and a painting of the *Inconstant* humbling the *Ça Ira*. But there is another finer strain, a head called simply *L'Amabilité*, three moonlit and snowy Romantic landscapes by Biagio Rebecca, a copy of *Socrates in search of a Wise Man* by Rembrandt, a Gainsborough landscape and, confronting Sir Thomas himself in the dining room, a large picture of 'Buona Parte'.

His books describe his mind. There are the volumes of the working navy man: Meare's *Voyage* and Guthrie's *Geography*, *Extracts from Treaties* and *Admiralty Statutes*, the invaluable *Ship Master's Assistant*, *Ready Observer* and *Elements of Navigation*. Unsurprisingly, he has poked a little into the affairs of his enemies. *Gréement des Vaisseaux* [the Rigging of Ships] sits in the Buckinghamshire shelves alongside *Le Petit Neptune François*, a *French Marine Vocabulary*, a *Tactique de Signaux*, a Spanish grammar and a Spanish Naval List.

These are the working parts of the library, but it is far from all. For those long and dreary weeks on blockade, he has eleven volumes of the *Novelist Magazine* as well as Philidon *On Chess,* five volumes of Rabelais, the nine of Shakespeare, the complete, unnumbered *Oeuvres de Molière*, eighteen volumes of Swift, six of Voltaire, five of Rousseau, six of Sterne and the volumes of Pope which included the *Iliad*. He might have turned with some relief to the sexy and scandalous story of the *Life of the Duchess of Kingston*, the most famous bigamist of the century, or to the excitements of Horace Walpole's gothic thriller *The Castle of Otranto*.

But also preserved in his papers, alongside this carefully cultivated, chintz-lined image of order and propriety, of the gentleman at home, is the record of another incident, which throws a different light on the nature of the man and of the role of anxiety and honour in the shaping of Trafalgar. At Swanbourne, in July 1802, during the peace of Amiens, when Fremantle along with the majority of naval officers was ashore in England – like many naval officers, he was standing for parliament – he had received the following letter in the post from London:

> July 16 1802 Adelphi
>
> Sir,
>
> I have mentioned to all my Friends, that your conduct to me, when First Lieut^{t} of H:M:S: Ganges, was unlike a Gentleman, unmanly, Base and dishonorable.
>
> You pledged your word and honor, never to

take an advantage of me, and then went and told yr Gallant Adml, who commanded the Fleet, an infamous falsity, & succeeded in your Views in attaining my removal.

Ask any of my friends what balsam will heal the wounds you have inflicted, & they or myself will say, you ought to meet me in the Field, like a Man of Honor.

My mind has long been purpos'd to make every sacrifice; and if I do not receive some satisfaction; I will publish a statement of faith, & have the World to judge, who has acted dishonorable. I shall conclude by saying, I would rather expire on a Scaffold than have my Liberty and feelings trampled on, by a dirty Tyrant.

I remain Sir, with marked Contempt; for your having persecuted

&c &c. &c
Henry Rice

That must have come as some shock to the Fremantle household, but it would be difficult to find a more concentrated capsule of what it meant to be a British naval officer in the early 19th century: manliness, honour, gentlemanliness, Liberty, opposition to tyranny, the Field as the place of honourable action, and all of these set in a frame of intense emotionality. Fremantle must have replied, in a letter now lost, that to engage in any kind of duel would be an inconvenient use of his time. Rice responded on 30 July 'that it will not be inconvenient to me, to go two thirds of the way, to any part of England, or France.'

Rice was not to be brushed off and the case was soon in the hands of the lawyers. The story that emerged hinged on the acute status anxiety among British naval officers, and on the twin concepts of 'Honour' and the 'Gentleman' to which that status was pinned. 'Knob' had been the naval slang for an officer since at least the mid-16th century, but that term – part vulgar, part ridiculing, in part merely an abbreviation for 'noble' – was by 1805 a source of worry for those to whom it was applied. No longer were the officers knobs by birth, as they had been in the 16th century. If they were knobs at all, they were knobs because of inner qualities which needed to be outwardly recognized and repeatedly confirmed. They were both the servants and products of a mobile, commercial society and their position in what can be called 'the status market' was constantly under threat. As Burke had written in a letter to a friend in 1795, 'Somebody has said, that a king may make a nobleman, but he cannot make a gentleman.' A gentleman could not be appointed to that position; he had to live as a gentleman himself.

The Rules of Discipline and Good Government to be Observed on Board His Majesty's Ships of War, made it clear in Article I that captains were 'to show in themselves a good example of honour and virtue to their officers and men.' Underlying that instruction is the sense that both those labels, of such overriding importance, were both terrifyingly vulnerable to 'unmanly, base and dishonorable' behaviour. Because honour was both defined and besieged by the possibilities of dishonour which surrounded and threatened it, the moral category which 'honour' enshrined was fragility itself. Honour always teetered on the lip of its own failure; you could never be sure that you belonged within its dignifying embrace. The doing of one's duty is what gave you access to the realms of honour. It was what England expected of you. And honour was the goddess Nelson would address some six hours later, at the end of his life and his battle, as his last breaths left him on the *Victory*'s blood-soaked orlop deck. 'Thank God I have done my duty,' he muttered again and again, and in those seven words spoke for his age and class. He had not fallen out of the gilded net. Honour and duty would remain identified with him for the rest of time.

That is the context which can explain Lieutenant Rice's agony. The central incident had happened on 30 October 1800. The *Ganges* had been mooring at the great naval anchorage of Spithead outside Portsmouth, but it was not going well:

> the people at the capstern [up in the bows] were hallowing and making a very great noise, an open breach of all order and discipline, which Captain Francis [of the Marines] was endeavouring to suppress by ordering them as loud as he could speak through a speaking trumpet, to stand fast heaving in order that he might discover the ringleaders of such unusual tumult.

Lieutenant Rice told them to continue, at which Captain Fremantle, a hundred feet further aft on his quarterdeck, lost his temper. 'He sent for Lieutenant Rice on the quarter deck, asked him with some warmth how he could suffer the men to make such a noise at their duty . . . To which Lt Rice, in a careless and disrespectful manner, with his hands in his pockets, answered in these words "I did not tell them to do so."' It was probably a misunderstanding, a mishearing along the length of the ship, among all the hubbub. But Rice's hands in pockets was a crime against the all-important symbolic hierarchy on which the ship's working depended. He behaved, Fremantle said, 'in a manner wholly unbecoming an inferior to a superior officer.'

The relationship rapidly began to plummet. The men had been paid; there was money, drink and sex between the decks, with a carefully counted 112 Portsmouth women on board. But now the women were to be sent ashore in the ship's boats and Rice was in charge of the transfer. Here, though, poor man, he made another mistake and somehow allowed the midshipman who was in charge of the boat that took the women ashore (not a boy, but a mature seaman who had come up from the ranks) to stay ashore himself all night with three of the boat crew, all of whom were qualified as able seamen. A ship could scarcely afford to lose four such valuable men and Fremantle used 'gross language' to Lieutenant Rice about this. Two days later, once the ship had weighed anchor and moved down the Channel, Rice wrote to the First Lord of the Admiralty to complain.

> 1 Nov 1800
> To Lord St Vincent from HMS *Ganges* Torbay
>
> My Lord
> It gives me inexpressible concern to inform Your Lordship that I have recently been most undeservedly abused by my Captain for a mistake in giving orders he damned my blood said I deserved to be hanged and if I did so again he would hang me.

The row deepened and tensed. Fremantle sent Rice a note via the purser, Mr Alcott:

> Tell Mr Rice I have no wish to hurt him that I am as anxious to have the Business made up as he possibly can be & if he will write to Earl St Vincent and say his Letter were premature I will meet him in as handsome and honorable manner as ever I met any officer.

Fremantle was clearly as anxious as Rice about his own standing in the eyes of his superiors. Naval careers could collapse on the basis of a single bad report, a single false decision, and Fremantle urgently needed the impression of his first lieutenant's letter to be cancelled. Rice then made the condition of his doing so an apology from his captain. Mr Alcott trundled back and forth between them. Fremantle sent a message to say he wouldn't apologize first, but invited Lieutenant Rice to dinner with him ashore. Rice accepted and they met for dinner at an inn in Torquay. But at dinner Fremantle made no apology. Instead he said to his first lieutenant, 'You could not suppose what I sayd in my passion was meant. I may say the same thing before a month to any other officer. And unless my tongue is cut out I cannot help it.'

As Rice told his lawyer, 'This sort of apology was so repugnant to his feelings as an Officer and a Gentleman that he refused to dine with the said Thomas Francis Freemantle [sic].' There was no reconciliation possible, Lieutenant Rice declared, 'while Captain Fremantle entertains such sentiments with respect to propriety of Language.'

Over the weeks that followed, as the *Ganges* took up her role as part of the blockading fleet off Brest, Fremantle inexorably took his revenge on Rice. He made him keep the same watches as the junior lieutenants, another status humiliation for the first lieutenant. He told Rice in front of the other officers 'not to chatter to him but to give his orders like a seaman and an officer.' He told him not to be 'impertinent'. At different times, he said to Rice, in front of others on the quarterdeck, 'You always talk nonsense;' 'You might as well be in your hammock;' 'You are no use to me.' Each one of these remarks was stored up and nurtured in the brine of the poor man's heart, his standing being eaten away by the rage of an intemperate captain. Rice was then suspended and told by Fremantle that he was to consider himself 'a prisoner'. Rice queried the judgement and was told 'if he did not understand the meaning of the word he might look into the Dictionary for it.'

After they had returned to England, Rice, still in a frenzy of hurt, piled up the affidavits from the senior officers who had known him. He had 'always conducted himself as a Gentleman'; 'the said Henry Rice was always invariably ready to do his utmost'; he was 'an Officer blessed with a well tempered courage equally incapable of either giving or receiving an Insult'; 'a Gentleman particularly beloved and esteemed by all'; Rice 'at all times manifested that zeal which is so indispensable in the character of a British officer.' He was 'most mild and amiable'; 'I thought him a young man of aimiable manners, zealous and desirous of what he could to please me.'

Fremantle, on his side, attempted the same, but with rather less clear-cut results. He preserved in his papers a letter from Luke J Nagle, late surgeon of the *Ganges,* an old friend who was with him again on the *Neptune* at Trafalgar:

> Your temper to those who know you is at times warm but as to Malice or Ill Will to any officer who saild with you in the Ganges, I am positive it never entered into your Breast. As your study always was to make it comfortable to Officers and Men.

Even Luke Nagle couldn't quite give Fremantle a full-blooded endorsement. The captain was clearly a bully, running an exceptionally tight ship, ferocious to those around him and capable of being more than short with any rather gentle young man who did not do quite as required. But he was the captain and had his contacts. The Lords Commissioners of the Admiralty were soon instructing their solicitors to prosecute Rice for having issued a challenge, which was a technical breach of the peace.

Rice, in a rage, then wrote to Fremantle from Fitcham Grove, Leatherhead:

> Sir,
> Your claiming the protection of the Admiralty reminds me of a little, dirty, sniveling boy at School, running to the Master, when threatened to be chastised, for low, mean, conduct –
>
> You know my opinion & as you have not the feelings of a Gentleman, it is unnecessary saying more on this subject.

With crushing inevitability, Fremantle won and Rice was forced to make a public climb-down, writing an open letter in April 1803, finally confronting the sin of addressing his commanding officer with his hands in his pockets:

> I did not sufficiently consider that naval subordination so essential to the public Service, might suffer by such an example.
>
> It never was my wish, or intention to bring into question Captain Freemantle's [sic] general merits as an officer. I acted from my own feelings as a gentleman.

Although he was still unable to spell his captain's name, Rice was guilty of little more than speaking to him as any man might speak to another. His career, though, as they would have said at the time, was 'broke'. He was not here at Trafalgar; Fremantle was. Fremantle went on to become a Vice-Admiral of the Blue, a Knight Grand Cross of both the Order of the Bath and of the Order of St Michael and St George, a baron of the Austrian States, a Knight of Maria Theresa and of St Ferdinand and Merit, the founder of a naval dynasty, one of the acknowledged heroes from the age of heroes, dripping with what they called 'honours'. Rice, though, nurturing his wounded gentlemanliness and his damaged amiability, sinks from view. He is too sweet to be a hero. The iron, on which honour in the end relies, is not in his soul. On the south wall of the chancel of Exeter Cathedral in Devon, there is a plaque:

Sacred to the memory of

Lieutenant Henry Rice RN
late of Tooting in the county of Surrey.

He died
October 17th 1808
aged 31

That's all: no more elevated rank, no honours, no glory. The cause of his death is unknown.

Rice's degree of tenderness and vulnerability is not an aberration. His interest in preserving his honour unharmed is one of the central motors of the fleet at Trafalgar. A body of officers coming from an uncertain and ill-defined social position needs to rely on the idea of their honour to establish their place in the social hierarchy. Anyone either above or below that tender middle ground can be more relaxed about it. The securely placed aristocrat can behave as he will, in the knowledge that his status is unlosable. The wage-earning or labouring poor can be equally certain that the position of gentleman is almost unavailable to them. But when, if you defined yourself as a gentleman, you had nothing else, as so many of them did not, honour was what you had. It was membership of a moral community, which is why the use of language was so critical. Your membership was defined by the respect with which other people treated you. Fremantle, in his ugly spitting 'warmth', expelled Rice from the community to which he needed to belong. In those circumstances, risking one's life in a duel was a perfectly rational choice, because the treatment to which Rice had already been subjected had effectively destroyed him as a man of honour.

Honour had mutated through the 18th century. Its Latin etymology is clear: *honor* means 'esteem', the standing in which you are held by others. It is a public virtue, virtually inseparable from 'reputation'. Inevitably, in a hierarchical society, 'reputation' acquired a social dimension. A man of honour was a man with the sort of reputation which men of the upper classes should have. Or as Lord Stanhope put it in 1705:

> What is Honour, but a greatness of mind which scorns to descend to an ill and base thing?

George, Lord Lyttelton, a friend of Alexander Pope and slightly ramshackle politician, a famously scruffy man of unimpeachable integrity, expressed it even more unequivocally in 1764. Honour, Lyttelton said, was

> something distinct from mere probity, and . . . supposes in gentlemen a stronger abhorrence of perfidy, falsehood, and cowardice and a more elevated and delicate sense of the dignity of virtue, than are usually found in vulgar minds.

The idea of an honourable member of the working class is a 19th-century invention. It would have been a contradiction in terms to the 18th century. Seamen called senior officers 'Your Honour' as a matter of habit, and St Vincent, writing as First Lord of the Admiralty, to Henry Addington, the Prime Minister, would address him as 'Your Honour', as a friendly joke, treating him in a chummy and self-deprecating way, as a senior shipmate.

Among younger minds, though, by the time of Trafalgar, there had been a subtle shift. Honour had gone inward and had begun to lose its social quality. Honour, around 1800, came to define a man simply as a man among men, without reference to his standing in society. It became very nearly equivalent to sincerity or integrity. So Wordsworth in 1809 could ask 'Say, What is Honour?' and answer his own question:

> 'Tis the finest sense
> Of justice which the human mind can frame.

In the same year, Coleridge, writing in his periodical *The Friend*, with the massive and half-penetrable grandiloquence to which he had become prone, put it still higher:

> Honor implies a reverence for the invisible and super-sensual in our nature.

Honour, by the first decade of the 19th century, had become otherworldly and immaterial, set apart from material concerns. It was now very nearly an aspect of saintliness, no longer social but both psychological and metaphysical. Heroism was unthinkable without it and in the light of this new concept of honour, the stage was set for the event which, more than any other, came to identify Trafalgar in British national consciousness: the beatification of the hero in the ultimately honourable act of self-sacrifice.

Fremantle may not have understood what the great men of the navy consistently understood, that 'The Honour of an officer may be compared to the chastity of a woman, and when once wounded may never be recovered.' Those are the words of Earl St Vincent. Honour, in this context, is not a choice but a compulsion, the sine qua non of an effectively aggressive fighting navy. Nothing could raise the level of anxiety in Nelson, as among all these officers, more steeply or more quickly than the idea that his honour was in question. In 1795, a rumour had begun to circulate in the western Mediterranean, and then back in Britain, that the squadron under Nelson's command had made a formal arrangement to connive with, and profit from, merchant ships running the blockade of the Italian coast, which he was meant to be enforcing. The rumour reached the ears of Lord Grenville, the Foreign Secretary, who wrote to Francis Drake, the British Minister in Genoa wondering what truth there was in it. Nelson responded like a she-wolf in front of her threatened pups:

> Having received from Mr Drake a copy of your Lordship's letter to him of October, enclosing a paper highly reflecting on the honour of myself and others of His Majesty's Officers employed on this coast under my orders, it well becomes me, as far as in my power lies, to wipe away this ignominious stain on our characters.

> I do therefore in behalf of my self and much-injured brethren demand that the person, whoever he may be, that wrote or gave that paper to your Lordship do fully and expressly bring home his charge; which as he states that this agreement is made by numbers of people on both sides, there can be no difficulty in doing. We dare him, My Lord, to the proof . . .
>
> Perhaps I ought to stop my letter here; but I feel too much to rest easy for a moment when the honour of Navy and our country is struck at through us . . .

On and on Nelson goes, raging with indignation at the slur, defending his captains as men who were 'more alert and more anxious for the good and honour of their King and Country [than] can scarcely ever fall to the lot of any Commanding Officer . . .' Nothing of course can endear a leader to the men he leads more than that kind of impassioned defence. And Nelson put his own case equally forcefully and with equally passionate indignation. He had fought 'in more than one hundred and forty skirmishes and battles, at sea and on shore; have lost an eye and otherwise blood, in fighting the Enemies of my King and Country; and God knows, instead of riches, my little fortune has been diminished in the Service . . . and when instead of all my fancied approbation, to receive an accusation of a most traitorous nature – it has been almost too much for me to bear.'

The critical difference from Fremantle, of course, is that Nelson includes his 'brethren' within the community of honour. 'My darling children' are the honourable men with whom he identifies. Often, and not only from the pen of Nelson, it seems as if the real enemy is not the French or Spanish but the self-indulgent, effeminate and affected people at home in England, who take up an interest in the doings of the navy from time to time, but who know nothing of it, and who all too easily condemn behaviour they have no means of judging.

The people Nelson loved, apart of course from Emma Hamilton, were his captains. In some ways he treated Emma as though she were one. 'If there were more Emmas,' he once told her, in a remark deeply coloured by the combination of love and self-love which drew people towards Nelson as if to the centre of a whirlpool, 'there would be more Nelsons.' And as for the captains, he told one immensely grand Spanish diplomat, 'I can assure you, Sir, that the word of every captain of a British man-of-war is equal, not only to mine, but to that of any person in Europe, however elevated his rank.' That too is a diagnostic thought: rank is dissolved in the community of honour. The radically entrepreneurial world of which this honour class is a part, cares nothing for rank and everything for duty, which meant the radical and uncompromising imposition of violent will on the enemy, with the view to killing his people and either destroying or capturing his ships. There is a straightforward chain of connection and implication. The naval officer is a gentleman and acts with honour because he does his duty in bringing about the annihilation of the enemy. Someone like Henry Rice cannot comply with this model, cannot mobilise and activate its various constituent parts. With more of an instinctive grasp of the anatomy of honour than anyone else in the world in 1805, Nelson could and did.

Battle was the place where honour was validated. That alone can explain something about the fleet at Trafalgar which seems strange to the modern world: the hunger for the fight. Battle was the moment in which a man could be for ever identified as honourable, where the fragility of the status was expunged and the possibility of 'hero' pinned to his breast, not to speak of the accompanying prize money being pushed into his pocket. Leaving aside for a moment its obvious terrors and suffering, battle was not the place of agony but the moment at which the agony was over. To be denied it was to be denied the great resolution of the naval officer's life.

In some, the hunger for battle was to be disappointed. When Nelson had rejoined the fleet off Trafalgar on 27 September, he had found it in 'very fair condition and good humour' but 'getting short in their water and provisions'. He had brought reinforcements with him from England and so could afford to send ships into Gibraltar for stores and to Tetuan in Morocco for water. The first detachment to leave was made up of six ships-of-the-line, commanded by Rear-Admiral Thomas Louis in the *Canopus*, one of the 98-gun ships captured from the French at the Battle of the Nile. Louis had been at the Nile with Nelson and the captain of his flagship was 31-year-old Francis Austen, Jane Austen's brother.

The story of Captain Austen's life is also strikingly emblematic of the age. He had been a wild and 'saucy' boy, whose sister described him as 'fearless of danger, braving pain' with 'warmth, nay insolence of spirit.' He too, like Nelson, was a vicar's son, and well down the family hierarchy, the fifth of six sons. These were the men whose need for honour, not as an option in life but a guarantee of who they were, drove the British fleet.

He had grown into a hectic, impatient man and when, sitting in the great cabin on *Victory*, Nelson proposed to Captain Austen and Admiral Louis that they should go into Gibraltar, both reacted with despair. 'You are sending us away, my Lord,' Louis said, '– the Enemy will come out, and we shall have no share in the battle.' Nelson replied – this is Austen's account, the memory still passionately alive 40 years later –

> The Enemy *will* come out, and we shall fight them; but there will be time for you to get back first. I look

upon *Canopus* as my right hand (she was his second astern in the Line of Battle); and I send you first to insure your being here to help beat them.

This was off-the-peg Nelson charm. The position of being Nelson's right hand was both a poignant compliment (he'd had no right hand of his own since the whole of the lower arm was amputated in the Canaries) and an often-repeated one. Nelson must have guessed that the news of six ships-of-the-line being absent from the British fleet would have encouraged Villeneuve to make his move.

That is exactly what happened and Admiral Louis and Captain Austen missed the battle which would have secured them a place on the roll of honour. They were not the only ones. William Hoste, captain of the *Amphion*, had been sent by Nelson on a diplomatic mission to the Dey of Algiers. He missed the battle and afterwards, in despair, wrote to his father: 'Not to have been in it, is enough to make one mad . . . I am low indeed, and nothing but a good Action with a French or Spanish frigate will set me up again.'

These conceptions of honour are part classical, part bourgeois, part Romantic. The modern, entrepreneurial man saw himself standing in the long tradition that stemmed from the armed citizens of ancient Rome, and beyond that to the Homeric heroes. What he did was honourable because he served both the state and his higher self. That was the repeated test, seen quite explicitly in these terms, to which the honour-seeking officers of the Royal Navy submitted again and again.

Early in 1804, Lieutenant George Hardinge, for example, then aged 22, was in command of HMS *Scorpion*, a sloop, in the North Sea. His class background could stand for all the great officers of the navy. He was the son of a Durham vicar, but the adopted son of his uncle, who was Attorney General to the Queen, and who sent George to Eton. As a very young man, he had been in the *Foudroyant*, part of Nelson's Mediterranean squadron, at their dramatic capture of the *Guillaume Tell* off Malta in March 1800. Now he had his own command, cruising off the port of Vlie on the Dutch coast. Having spotted 'a couple of the enemy's Brigs at anchor in the Roads', he 'determined upon a dash at the outermost one in the boats.' Another British sloop, the *Beaver*, came up and the two captains decided to join forces for the night attack. What happened is a model in miniature of Nelsonian war. 'At half past nine in the evening', he wrote to his uncle, addressing him as 'My dearest friend,'

> we began the enterprise, in three boats from the *Scorpion* and in two from the *Beaver*. We had near 60 men, including Officers, headed by your humble Servant in the foremost boat. As we rowed with tide and flood, we arrived along-side the enemy at half past eleven. I had the good fortune or (as by some it has been considered) the Honour, to be the first man who boarded her. She was prepared for us, with Board Nettings up, and with all the other customary implements of defence. But the noise, the alarm, &c so intimidated her crew, that many of them ran below in a panic, leaving to us the painful duty of combating those whom we respected most.
>
> The decks were slippery in consequence of rain; so that in grappling with my first opponent, a mate of the watch, I fell, but recovered my position & fought him upon equal terms, and killed him. I then engaged the Captain, as brave a man as any service ever boasted; he had almost killed one of my Seamen. To my shame be it spoken, he disarmed me! And was

> on the point of killing me – when a seaman of mine came up, rescued me at the peril of his own life, and enabled me to recover my sword. – At this time all the men had come from the boats, and were in possession of the deck: two were going to fall upon the Captain at once – I ran up – held them back – and then adjured him to accept Quarter. With inflexible heroism he disdained the gift, kept us at bay, and compelled us to kill him; he fell covered with honourable wounds.
>
> To the end of my existence I shall regret the Captain. He was a perfect Hero; and if his crew had been like him, critical indeed would have been our peril . . . In two days after the Captain's death, he was buried with all the Naval Honours in my power to bestow upon him: during the ceremony of his interment, the English colours disappeared, and the Dutch were hoisted in their place. All the Dutch Officers were liberated [not the men] – one of them pronounced an éloge on the Hero they had lost – and we fired three volleys over him as he descended into the deep.

For this action, Hardinge was promoted Captain, received post rank and was given a sword by Lloyd's to the value of 300 guineas. A Nelson in the making? Perhaps: the necessary combination is there of aggression, sweetness, courage and an almost painful conception of honour. But he too is forgotten by history, killed in action off Sri Lanka in 1808 and buried in Colombo.

The word to describe such a man is 'chivalrous' and by 1805 it is perfectly clear that honour had acquired another layer. The officers of the British navy saw themselves as heirs, strange as this might sound, to the knights of the Middle Ages. Their sense of honour was stoked by the rich, antiquarian fuel of chivalry. It is that medievalism which lies behind the most famous moment on the morning of Trafalgar.

The medieval inheritance was present, of course, in the officers of all three nations at the battle, but it takes on a peculiarly potent and mythic quality among the British. Chivalry, and the utterly unhistorical idea that the English were above all nations its champions, was in the air. It was to chivalry that Edmund Burke most famously appealed after the French Revolution in response to the 'fresh ruins of France, which shock our feelings wherever we can turn our eyes.' The arrival in France of sterile, nude, anti-traditionalist principles of mechanistic, rational government meant, for Burke, that

> the age of chivalry is gone. –That of sophisters, oeconomists, and calculators, has succeeded and the glory of Europe is extinguished for ever. Never, never more, shall we behold that generous loyalty to rank and sex, that proud submission, that dignified obedience, that subordination of the heart, which kept alive, even in servitude itself, the spirit of an exalted freedom. The unbought grace of life, the chief defence of nations, the nurse of manly sentiment and heroic enterprize is gone! It is gone, that sensibility of principle, that chastity of honour, which felt a stain like a wound, which inspired courage while it mitigated ferocity, which ennobled whatever it touched, and under which vice itself lost half its evil by losing all its grossness.

These marvellous, Romantic words implied, of course, that in Britain these dignities survived. England was not the rapacious usurper of the global seas; it was a medieval jewel, Arthurian in its purity. Burke's fantasy of the nature of Englishness had found a fertile seed-bed in a country already turning towards the reassurance of the medieval. This was the first age of the antique and the aesthetics of 1805 were dominated by the moral value of the old. George III had commissioned the architect James Wyatt to re-medievalise 17th-century parts of Windsor Castle. At Kew, on the Thames, an enormous, new brick castle was begun for him, also by Wyatt. It remained unfinished until it was blown up in the 1820s as yet another unwarrantable royal extravagance. In 1788, the American painter Benjamin West created sequences of heroic medieval scenes for the King. George appointed Richard Hurd, the author of the antiquarian *Moral and Political Discourses*, as tutor to his son, the Prince of Wales. 'Affability, courtesy, generosity, veracity,' Hurd had written, 'these were the qualifications most pretended to by men of arms, in the days of pure and uncorrupted chivalry.' Perhaps in response, the Prince Regent, in 1811, would have himself painted by PE Stroehling as the Black Prince, his reproduction-armour ballooning out over acres of princely stomach and royal thigh. It may have looked too ridiculous; the portrait has vanished.

The 18th century had considered the Middle Ages stupid rather than noble. In 1761, David Hume had called the crusades 'the most signal and durable monument of human folly that has yet appeared in any age or nation.' But by 1805, that scepticism had almost entirely disappeared. On St George's Day in 1805, 25 Knights of the Garter, the most distinguished knightly order of medieval England, founded by Edward III, were installed at Windsor Castle in the most elaborate ceremony seen there since a previous phase of revivalism in the early 17th century. Banquets for the knights and for the assembled lords and ladies were held in different parts of the Castle. A baron of beef was roasted and served on a dish specially made for the occasion. 'It was His Majesty's particular wish,' it was said, 'that as many of the old customs should be kept up as possible.'

There was more to this than fancy dress and slabs of beef. To an astonishing degree, chivalric medievalism penetrated the Royal Navy. Earl St Vincent, writing to Emma Hamilton in 1798, explaining to her why Nelson and not he was commanding the British squadron charged with the 'succour of their Sicilian majesties', informs her that even though he is 'bound by my oath of chivalry to protect all who are persecuted and distressed' he is sadly 'forbid to quit my post before Cadiz'. He is 'happy however to have a knight of superior prowess in my train who is charged with this enterprize, and will soon make his appearance, at the head of as gallant a band as ever drew sword or trailed pike.' St Vincent signed himself off as Emma's 'true knight and devoted servant'.

This may well be the old admiral flirting outrageously with the most beautiful woman in Europe, but it is clear that this medievalist talk did not seem absurd at the time. The Middle Ages, above all else, embodied both honour and a conception of England which went beyond the compromises and tricksy dealing of its modern commercial culture. The all-powerful presence of that new, rampant bourgeois culture of course created the appetite for something which stood outside it. The fantasy of an honourable medieval purity lay conveniently to hand, almost as a form of pastoral, a place where morality was still clear and duty obvious. It seems at times that the navy itself, for all its rapaciousness, tedium and dangers, represented to its officers a place apart from the modern world of getting and spending, a place of innocence, where honour still lived.

Nelson was entranced with the medieval. Again and again he quoted from the battle speeches of *Henry V*, the great 15th-century warrior and self-dramatising man of honour. The very phrase the 'Band of Brothers', which he used to describe the captains who fought with him in the Mediterranean, was drawn from it. And he misquotes

Henry V in a way that measures the role of honour in his own mind. Writing to St Vincent in September 1801, Nelson, already a peer and the holder of three battle medals, says, in the unequivocal way which was his habit and one of the foundations of his charm:

> I feel myself, my dear Lord, as anxious to get a medal, or a step in the Peerage as if I had never got either, – for 'if it be a sin to covet glory, I am the most offending soul alive'.

That, Nelson thinks, is a quotation from the words Shakespeare gave to King Harry. But it is not. As part of the great St Crispin's Day speech to his cousin Westmoreland, Shakespeare in fact wrote:

> But if it be a sin to covert honour,
> I am the most offending soul alive.

Honour and glory have become inseparable and interchangeable in Nelson's mind. Glory is inaccessible without honour; honour is the foundation of the glorious. The speech as a whole, which portrays itself as the thinking of a medieval king, is in fact founded on a new, post-medieval conception of honour. For Shakespeare's Henry, as for Nelson and the other officers in his fleet, honour is not a question of social rank but an amalgam of daring, fame, and manliness. As King Henry says, the man who fought at Agincourt, (no class or social status attached) will

> strip his sleeve and show his scars,
> And say, 'These wounds I had on Crispin's day' . . .
> And Crispin Crispian shall ne'er go by,
> From this day to the ending of the world,
> But we in it shall be remembered;
> We few, we happy few, we band of brothers;
> For he today that sheds his blood with me
> Shall be my brother; be he ne'er so vile

This day shall gentle his condition:
And gentlemen in England now a-bed
Shall think themselves accurs'd they were not here,
And hold their manhoods cheap whiles any speak
That fought with us upon Saint Crispin's day.

That is a speech Nelson undoubtedly knew by heart and it would serve as a guidebook to the place of honour in the British fleet at Trafalgar. It thrives on manliness and companionship. It substitutes valour, or perhaps honour, for rank. As a speech, it is physical, engorged and primitive. There is a latent sexuality in it, circling around the ideas of manliness and manhood, of men who can 'stiffen the sinews and summon up the blood', disparaging those now lying flaccid in bed in England, but celebrating their own potency, imposing themselves and their honour on the world abroad.

One word glows out of it: 'England', the name not of the increasingly efficient, ruthless modern state which paid for the fleet at Trafalgar, which is Britain; but of the pre-existent, half-fantasy kingdom of medieval honour which embodied not the grubby commercial ambitions of the modern country, but the higher ideals to which this fleet aspired. *Henry V* is full of this imagined 'England': 'Now all the youth of England are on fire,' 'And you good yeomen,/Whose limbs were made in England, show us here/The mettle of your pasture.' This England, in a play about the ruthless and at times deeply disturbing pursuit of fiercely destructive and yet honourable ends by war, is what motivates the single most famous moment on the morning of Trafalgar.

Nelson had been below in his cabin. When he returned to the quarter-deck the enemy were little more than two miles away to the east-southeast. Nelson spoke to Lieutenant John Pasco, the flag lieutenant on *Victory*, returned to duty after his bout of sickness. As an old man in the 1840s, Pasco described the scene to Sir Nicholas Harris Nicolas:

> His Lordship came up to me on the poop, and after ordering certain signals to be made, about a quarter to noon, he said, 'Mr Pasco, I wish to say to the fleet, "England confides that every man will do his duty";' and he added, 'you must be quick for I have one more to make, which is for Close Action.' I replied, 'If your Lordship will permit me to substitute the *expects* for *confides* the signal will soon be completed, because the word *expects* is in the vocabulary, and *confides* must be spelt'. His Lordship replied in haste, and with seeming satisfaction, 'That will do, Pasco, make it directly.'

Nelson's instinct for 'confides' rather than 'expects' was right. To 'expect' is to command but to 'confide' is to trust. It is the binding word, it represents the community of honour, and the mythical 'England' to which it appeals is a place where duty is a matter of trust, not of instruction or obedience. But the heart of the idea survived the translation into flags. 'England', not 'Britain'; 'duty', not 'obedience'; and 'every man', not 'every officer and man' as Henry Blackwood remembered it: a summation of Nelson's method of command, founded on inspiration, rigour, and inclusiveness, the three elements of the modern notion of honour.

The working admiral, conscious that time is short, accepted the compromise and the famous signal was made with the flag signalling system developed by Sir Home Popham. 'England', 'expects', 'every', 'man', 'will', 'do' and 'his' all had a designated flag. 'Duty' was spelled out with flags 4, 21, 19 and 24, and, ship by ship, the British fleet – not English: at least a third of the officers and a higher proportion of the men came from Scotland, Wales, Ireland

and abroad – gave three cheers as the message was conveyed. Collingwood at first complained that Nelson was signalling too much. They all knew what to do. But when he was read the meaning of the signal, he too welcomed it. In the violence to come, the necklace of ideas represented by 'England', 'expectation', 'manhood' and 'duty' would sustain a fleet in the horror and grief that would surround them.

4

LOVE

October 21st 1805
11.30 am to 12 midday

Distance between fleets: 2 miles – 1 mile
Victory's heading and speed: 101° at 3 knots

Love: to regard with passionate affection;
to regard with the affection of a friend.
SAMUEL JOHNSON, *A Dictionary of the English Language*, 1755

Three ships behind the *Victory*, just astern of Fremantle in the *Neptune*, was the *Leviathan*, the ship-of-the-line which had shepherded Coleridge's convoy to Malta the year before. The ship was ready for battle. Hammocks had been stowed in the netting alongside the upper decks, soft bulwarks to absorb musket balls. Other nets had been spread above the deck and poop to catch falling debris. Further anti-boarding nets had been rigged up. Cabins had been dismantled to give a clear run from stem to stern on the gundecks. Furniture had been stowed far below in the hold, thrown overboard or hauled up into the rigging. Animals were usually slaughtered, sent down to the hold, or in a crisis also thrown into the sea. Nelson had at times on a chase in the Mediterranean pushed bullocks overboard to lighten the ship and to clear them out of the way. This morning off Cape Trafalgar, *Leviathan*'s goat was explicitly saved from any such fate by her captain, 39-year-old Henry Bayntun.

He too brought a version of England to the battle. Bayntun was an immensely experienced officer, who had spent most of his life since he was in his early teens at sea in the West Indies, a career full of danger and aggression. He is a forgotten figure now but Nelson knew him and trusted him; they had been watching the Toulon fleet for many months together (British sailors called it 'Too-Long') and in pursuit of Villeneuve's fleet in the summer of 1805 they had crossed and re-crossed the Atlantic together. Nelson had defended him against some aspersions from the Admiralty, calling him an 'excellent officer' and 'extremely correct and proper'.

It would be easy enough to consider him, from these facts alone, as little but a hardened warrior. His personal papers are now preserved among the Bedfordshire County Records and from them a subtler picture emerges. They include his annotated copy of *A Treatise on Practical Navigation and Seamanship* by William Nichelson, published in 1792. Nichelson was Master Attendant at Portsmouth and from time to time Bayntun has written 'Note!' in the margins of this standard work. The emphasis of what Bayntun – the son of the Consul-General at Algiers – marked was consistently towards the need for an understanding of the general shared humanity on board a warship. Order was necessary; without order the great machine would not work; but subject to that order, all were men and all should be treated as human beings. 'There is a sort of doctrine,' Nichelson had written,

> which I hope will never gain credit in the service, and which cannot be too much discountenanced or reprobated, which is, that it is possible to be a good Officer without being a good Seaman, which

> I positively deny, it being a flat contradiction of reason and common sense; I believe it to be generally favoured by those Officers who came too late into the service to be initiated into a Seaman's duty; wishing at once to become officers, they were perhaps placed to command, instead of being placed in the tops, or other parts of the ship to be taught a sailor's duty.

Bayntun drew asterisks in the margins next to this passage. It is a measure, for all the distinctions of rank, of the communality in the British man-of-war. The form of organic order on which such a ship relies is in fact dependent on recognising that communality:

> There is a confidence also which the men have in their commander; when they find he is a seaman, the duty is carried on with a good will and a steady chearfulness because they know he is a competent judge of all that can be expected in the performance of their duty.

Only when that sharedness is absent does the system disintegrate. It is not that sailors are the usual run of men. They are not like soldiers, 'since any able bodied landsman will make a soldier, a plowman taken from the plough today, in two or three months may be made a good soldier.' But a seaman 'should be understood to be quite different from all other classes of men, he does not spring up like a *Mushroom*, it requires many years to make him a seaman, with fatigue both of body and mind.'

That is why naval officers needed to be seamen first and officers second: if an officer does not truly know the ways of a ship, he will be deceived and cheated at every turn. And if he doesn't know what to expect, he will punish unfairly: 'how often has it happened, that a whole set of top-men have been flogged because the top-gallant yards have not been got across so soon as other ships?' Nichelson asked, and Bayntun took due note.

Of all the passages he marked, the most heavily starred was this, a sermon on the nature of shared danger, in which Nichelson rises to some rhetorical heights, emphasising the need for the commander to be a man like other men, and for a single social fabric to cover all parts and all manner of men within the ship:

> It is night time, or it is foggy or very hazy weather, that you cannot see the ship's length, which is as bad as if it were night time; under those circumstances the mariner's art, skill and experience are put to the trial, he is loaded with care and anxiety, but this is the time to shew himself a man of experience and true knowledge of his profession, as a Seaman and an Officer, to conduct and govern a ship or ships in such times as those; It is not *hats and periwigs, powdered hair or silk stockings, fribbles or beaux*, that are equal to the task required to be performed at this time, it must be men with heads and brains, the Seaman and the Officer, that must support the man at all times.

These are some of the ideas deep in the pre-conceptions of those on board the British fleet at Trafalgar. It is, for all the severity of its corporal discipline and the essential violence of its methods, a humane world and Henry Bayntun, by the evidence of his own letters was a humane as well as an energetic, resourceful and, in Nelson's word, 'excellent' man.

When appointed to the frigate *Quebec* in the West Indies in 1799, he was, as new captains are, constantly busy perfecting his ship: applying to swap his old-fashioned 6-pounders for the more powerful new man-smashing carronades; changing the way in which the *Quebec* was ballasted; requiring another officer of marines; writing for a new supply of boys from England as well as a new 8-oared deal cutter instead of a heavy barge; replacing the gun carriages which were unserviceable; stowing the bread in 'Iron Bound Casks'; commissioning new casks for the all-important scurvy-preventing lime juice; complaining of the lack of onions. He was, as he needed to be, zeal in action and his commanding officers saw the best in him.

> From Robert Montague, Admiral
> 22 Oct 1801 in Port Royal
>
> I desire to know who you wish to have for a Lieutenant and I also desire you will at all times ask, respecting your Officers appointments without any Ceremony as I am sure you will never wish to promote any person who is not Zealous in the public Service & I shall be happy at all times to evince by my Actions, how extremely high I hold your conduct in Estimation.
>
> There is a little Boy named Thomas on board your Ship whose story excites my Compassion, I wish to see him immediately in order to give him a little Money, which perhaps may be acceptable: the Boat shall bring him back.
>
> I am Sir Your Humble Servant
> Robert Montague, Admiral

When the admiral asked him to inspect the prison and hospital ships in Port Royal in Jamaica, Bayntun was appalled. There was nothing like enough awnings to protect the prisoners when on deck, nor windsails with which to direct breezes down into the foetid spaces below.

Baynton was horrified to find that half of them were naked, that their guards beat them 'with more brutality than is absolutely necessary', that there were no safety ropes to prevent them falling down hatchways and that some of them were so ill fed and emaciated that they were on the point of death.

This is the voice of compassionate humanity confronted with a situation which had probably persisted ever since naval forces had taken prisoners. There were officers who thought ships could be run on kindness, a sin known in the 1805 navy by the significant term 'fraternizing with the people', as though the lower deck was a form of enemy. It was not to be tolerated and Bayntun was not one of them. He flogged when necessary, and at times more than the regulation maximum of 12 lashes to which a ship's captain was limited. Nevertheless, when humanity was called for, he applied it:

> Aug 28 1800
> H.M.S.*Quebec*, Port Royal, Jamaica
>
> Richard Wilton a Seaman of the said Ship was sentenced by a Court martial to receive one Hundred & Fifty Lashes for Desertion. He received Seventy Five Shortly after. But from Youth and Delicacy of Constitution could not at that time receive more. His character in other respects stands fair. Has been confined in Harbour and a prisoner at Large at Sea ever since.

And it is significant that among the papers discovered in the attic of his Bedfordshire house when his descendants sold it in the 1950s were both the log and muster book of the *Leviathan* for 1805. These were documents which by law Bayntun should have surrendered to the Admiralty at the end of a voyage but which he had kept. Out of pride? Or affection? It is impossible to say but they remain poignantly evocative documents.

Both are covered in stained and filthy sailcloth,

made into a loose wrap almost like a fitted bag. The grey, coarse-woven covering is spotted with lamp oil and grease from food. Candle wax is dripped all over the cover on which the name of the ship is written in ink in huge Roman capitals.

The log itself is a coarse, working document, each page bearing not only the entries of the officers of the watch, each succeeding the other, but the signs of the weather, sea-splashed, sun-bleached. This morning – and the reality of the moment is never more insistent – there is an air of excitement, repetition and muddle to it:

> Light airs and cloudy – at daylight observed the Enemy's fleet to Leeward 35 sail; [*corrected to 33*] bore up, made sail pr sig [*ie per signal*] out first reef Topsails [*ie the full depth of the topsails, the main driving sail of a man-of-war, shaken out to catch the wind*] Cleared for action. At [*illegible*] hours [*illegible*] light airs and cloudy weather. All sail set standing down for the Enemy's Fleet; they consisting of 35 [*changed to 33*] Sail of Line 5 Frigates and 2 Brigs Empd clearing ship for action. In company with 26 [*changed to 27*] sail of the Line 4 frigates and a schooner and Cutter.

One can all too easily imagine Admiral Sir Henry Bayntun, as he was to become, at home with his grandchildren in Bedfordshire, reading out to them from the *Leviathan*'s log of his day of glory. The muster book is its companion, bound and lettered in precisely the same way, the long list of the men with whom Henry Bayntun entered the cockpit of battle. The nominal complement of the ship, subjected to a weekly muster, is 640 people. But for the whole of 1805, there are never more than 515 men on board. The *Leviathan*, like every ship in every navy in the world, was undermanned. Some 180 of them were Irish, and of them 116 were listed as 'landmen', or men who had no previous experience of the sea and had been driven on board not by the press gang but by the wages, preferable to the pittance which an Ireland, already moving towards congestion, poverty and starvation, could afford. Apart from them, it was mixture of England, Scotland and a world community: Jamaica, Bermuda, Barbados, men from Bremen, from Norway, a John Ferris from 'Russia', men from Ostend, Rotterdam, Philadelphia, Boston, Maryland, New York, Marblehead, and a man called Domingo, an armourer's mate, from 'Bengall'.

Every officer, it was said in the best ships, knew the name of every man. This was no undifferentiated mass of humanity. Every man was allocated a precise task in handling the ship and another precise task in the station he was to take up for battle. Ships carried precise descriptions of each of member of the crew, useful in case of desertion but also in the daily management of a large concentrated body of young men. It may be a step too far to say that Henry Bayntun's keeping of this precious muster book at home was a sign of love but it is at least a sign of attachment to his men.

That method of command was what his men expected. When a commanding officer fell short of that level of humanity, ships complained to the Admiralty. The company of HMS *Terpsichore* presented a petition in about 1800:

> We are constantly on deck and beat and kicked about by Captain Mackellar and Mr Hall and the Boatswain now carries a stick cut of rawhide, plaited and served over with tarred twine, with which he cuts and slashes all he come near. We your petitioners have been seven years in this ship and always behaved ourselves as loyal and true-hearted subjects both by sea and land, under Admirals St Vincent and Nelson.

It was in part a question of simple dignity. The men of HMS *Centaur*, lying in Plymouth harbour, complained in 1812:

> We the humble petitioners, the crew of His majesty's ship the *Centaur* beg leave to inform you of doleful complaints. The first act of White's cruelty was break up the hogsty and suffer the swine to range the main deck to the annoyance of the crew . . .
> In exposing the private parts of a man's body to public view and flogging on the posterior instead of the back; in terming damned useless trash and degrading us beneath brutes.
> We therefore beseech you to extend your lenity to us and disperse us throughout the navy,
> The divine blessing will be on you for it.

Of course, one can't be too dewy-eyed about this. The degree of punishment, compulsion, anger and maltreatment of men on board the Trafalgar fleet would be considered barbaric today. In the days before the battle, in ship after ship, punishments had been given. On *Victory*, according to the log kept by the master, Thomas Atkinson, on the 5th of October 6 men had been given 36 lashes each for drunkenness; on the 8th another 7, the same punishment for the same crime; on the 19th another 10, again the same number of lashes for the same crime. In the battle, the flagship would suffer some terrible casualties: 54 killed, 25 dangerously wounded, 12 badly wounded and 42 slightly wounded – one in six men killed or hurt by enemy fire. But in the aftermath of battle, there was no let-up. The habits of punishment continued. On 29 October, barely a week after the guns had ceased firing, and after the most dreadful storm that many of the sailors had ever encountered, Atkinson's log would record:

> Steering for Gibraltar. Fresh breezes and Cloudy. Out 1st Reef Topsails. Departed this life Mr Palmer Mid^{n} [one of the Trafalgar wounded]. Punished Jno Matthews, Richd Collins, Wm Stanford, Jno Mallard [or Walland], Chas Waters & Mich^{l} Griffiths Seamen with 36 lashes each for Contempt & Disobedience of Orders.

There could be no sentimentality about this. The destruction of the French and Spanish Fleets could not mean the end of imposed discipline.

Thomas Hardy, Nelson's beloved captain, was more severe than most in the discipline he imposed on his crew. In the course of 1804 on the Mediterranean station, according to the evidence of *Victory*'s log, some 380 dozen lashes had been meted out to the men who made the flagship work, about 4,500 lashes in all. Drunkenness was by far the commonest offence, but all crimes that were punished with the lash could be classified as threats to order. Contempt, disobedience, insolence, neglect of duty and sleeping at one's post were all the offences of people who were not fulfilling their place in the regulated structure on which the fleet relied. Only five instances of theft – a crime not against the ship but against fellow members of the crew – are recorded against over 150 acts of insubordination. For very exceptional offences, including desertion, use of mutinous language or buggery, punishments of several hundreds of lashes would be given.

To some at the time it seemed barbaric, and there exists a rare description of what it was like to be beaten in this way:

> I felt an astounding sensation between the shoulders under my neck, which went to my toe-nails in one direction and my finger-nails in another, and stung me to the heart as if a knife had gone through my

> body . . . He came on a second time a few inches lower, and then I thought the former stroke sweet and agreeable compared with that one. I felt my flesh quiver in every nerve from the scalp of my head to my toe-nails. The time between each stroke seemed so long as to be agonizing, and yet the next came too soon . . . What with the blood from my tongue and my lips which I had also bitten, and the blood from my lungs or some other internal part ruptured by the writhing agony, I was almost choked and became almost black in the face.

Sickening as that is, and no doubt reflective of one reality, it nevertheless sounds like propaganda. Seamen in 1805 did not write 'What with the blood from my tongue . . .' nor would they have called a heart-rending pain in their gut 'some other internal part ruptured by the writhing agony' Neither of those expressions are the authentic voice of the lower deck. When you look harder, at genuinely contemporary documents, something different emerges: both a more phlegmatic attitude to suffering and an extraordinary sense that the revolution in feelings which had overtaken the gentry in the 18th century had yet to penetrate the social levels below them. Just as in Jane Austen's novels members of the working class do not exist in the same exquisite universe of feelings inhabited by their social betters, there is a sense on board the Nelsonian ship-of-the-line that ordinary seamen, a little like slaves or farmed animals, were somehow beneath the level at which consideration for their feelings was relevant.

The Rev. Edward Mangin, a temporary and admittedly disenchanted Irish chaplain on HMS *Gloucester*, blockading the Dutch in the uncomfortable broken, shallow waters of the North Sea in 1812, considered the world of a fighting fleet a place where 'every object [was] at variance with the sensibilities of a rational and enlightened mind', full of 'preparations the most complex and ingenious for the purposes of plundering and murdering [one's] fellow creatures.' Each man-of-war, Mangin thought, was nothing but 'a prison, within whose narrow limits were to be found Constraint, Disease, Ignorance, Insensibility, Tyranny, Sameness, Dirt and Foul air: and in addition, the dangers of Ocean, Fire, Mutiny, Pestilence, Battle and Exile.'

Mangin only lasted three months in the navy but it was an educative time. 'Just before we sailed,' he wrote in his journal,

> occurred one of those accidents, which though shocking to me, made little or no impression on my ship-mates, and was not talked of five minutes after it happened. A seaman, employed at the moment, with all the energy and fearless activity peculiar to this class of people, fell from the mainyard of the *Stirling Castle*, 74, lying close to us: he struck, as he dropped, against the main-chains, and was probably killed, for he instantly went down and disappeared.

If it had been an officer or a gentleman to whom this had happened, it is inconceivable that the ship's company would have treated it as 'one of those things'. Later, at sea, Mangin was even more forcibly struck by the emotional and conceptual gap between quarter- and lower decks. A seaman on board the *Gloucester* had been fishing for mackerel when somehow he had fallen overboard. A boat was launched after him as he struggled in the water far behind. Just as his rescuers arrived, he sank, his water-logged coat dragging him down. He was within seconds of death and only saved by the quick-wittedness of one of the boat crew grabbing a boat hook and hooking it under his clothes. He was brought back on board, restored by the doctors and, to Mangin's amazement, the next day was on duty as usual.

This is May 1812 and the man – significantly nameless in the story; Mangin only names officers – had been through one of the central liminal experiences by which the cultivated classes of Europe were then entranced. He had seen death; he had been within death's grasp; he had lived through a moment of revelatory, Gothic intensity and yet he shrugs it off like a dog that has been for a plunge in a river. Mangin is puzzled. The incident

> admits of a question whether bravery in men of the lower classes of society should not rather be termed insensibility: or is it that they have the sensibility of the enlightened, but want expression? The man above mentioned owed his safety to his resolution; . . . yet, it was perfectly impossible to discover that he was in the smallest degree perplexed by the prospect of death, or exhilarated by his preservation.

For the governing classes, the men they subjected to such brutal discipline, to whom strong alcohol and women shipped over in bumboats when in port was a regrettable and in part hideous necessity, seem to have been of a different kind, for whom the 'sensibility of the enlightened' was as alien as loyalty to King George would be to a Frenchman. This sense of a conceptual class division was not confined to the navy. It was generally accepted that men who could not be considered gentlemen were, at least in a political and social sense, of a different kind to those whose concern was order, government, rationality and business. Even John Wilkes, making his radical case, carefully delineates the boundaries of the political:

> The people (I do not mean the illiterate rabble, who have neither capacity for judging of matters of government, nor property to be concerned for) are the *fountain* of authority. What they order is right,

> what they prohibit is wrong. Because the public *business* is their business.

The illiterate rabble were not to have a vote because they could not understand what they were voting on or for. Enlightened captains and flag officers attended with detailed and constant care to the wellbeing of their men, both physical and mental, and the crew of a man-of-war were often referred to simply as 'the people' or by the captain as 'my people' but this term represented concern for the effective and profitable working of a complex organisation, much as a farmer would be interested in the health of his livestock. In some critical sense, these people were not considered people in the same way that the people who walked the quarterdeck were people. Love and honour operated down to a certain social level; below that it was a question of discipline and obedience, lubricated with drink and occasionally interrupted by sex and war.

When, in 'the complex and wonderful machine of which I was an inhabitant' Mangin found that, for some obscure reason, a gentleman was living on the lower deck, it was as if the natural order had been turned upside down. He discovered one seaman on board the *Gloucester*, called Hickey, who

> spoke French fluently, had the manners and address of a gentleman, fenced well, drew with taste, was a good mathematician and arithmetician, wrote a beautiful hand, conversed with a very happy choice of expression, quoted various authors, poets, philosophers and orators; criticised with judgment and novelty of feeling, statuary, architecture and painting – and played the violin finely: he besides impressed every one with respect, by his air of genteel and humble melancholy.

The officers of the *Gloucester* had a total of 500 books on board, which was all very well. But to find a Hickey slinging his hammock between the 32-pounders on the gundecks with between five and six hundred other men, where 'the ports being necessarily closed from evening to morning, the heat, in this cavern of only 6 feet high, and so entirely filled with human bodies, was overpowering', that was simply disturbing.

Of course, this gulf between the classes on board was at least in part, as Mangin guessed, a question of language. They 'wanted expression'. Within a few decades, the English gentleman would become identified with a hopeless stiffness and lack of emotional vocabulary. The working man, for figures like Marx, Ruskin and Morris, became the source of a kind of emotional authenticity which the gentleman lacked. In 1805, the position was precisely reversed. Nothing was more fluent than the affective language of the 1805 officer. It was the seamen who struggled to express their love and affection. When Tom Flynn, coxswain of the *Gloucester*'s first cutter, died on 29 July 1812, he had been lying for days in his cot in the ship's hospital, 'mad, pale as ashes, and convulsed with dying spasms. Four or five of his messmates stood about him, holding lanthorns to his face, dropping silent tears on him, or in the most heart-rending accents calling him "Poor Tom" and "honest messmate"!'

When men from the lower deck needed to express feelings of a more sustained or elaborate kind, they reached with great difficulty, often in ways that remain profoundly moving two centuries later, for the language of gentility. A letter survives in the archives of the National Maritime Museum in Greenwich, addressed to 'Mr George Hancock. Worksop. Nottinghamshire'. It was written on board *Victory*, by John Vincent, a 30-year-old Londoner, who was a quarter gunner on the flagship, He was writing to the father of a friend of his who had died in an accident during the long blockade off Toulon. It is worth quoting in full, as evidence from the other side, of precisely the gap between officers and men which Edward Mangin had seen. In every line one can make out the careful, sombre attempt to address the grief and concern which friend and father shared.

H.M.S. *Victory*
July 24 1805

Mr Hancock
I have rec^d the Letter directed to your son, dated Jan^ry 1st [1805] and as a Messmate of your son's, think myself in duty bound to inform you of your son's unhappy and sudden Death, tho' at present being unknown to you, as a Parent, I feel a Parent's tenderness and affection, it certainly is a tender point to disclose, and will cause a tender and mutual sensation to commiserate his unhappy and untimely end, to you his Parents, his Brothers, Sisters, and acquaintances. On or about the 24th of November last, as we were cruising off Toulon, and at the time little or no Wind, the Day of the Month and time were taken down by me, but by some accident have lost the Memorandum, but hopeing this will reach you safe as a means of Giving you Satisfaction, I specify the time and place, as near as possible my recollection will allow me, tho' fully convinced this unhappy News will cause a grief not easy to be describ'd but by those persons, who experience so close and tender a tie in Nature, as the Agitation of Mind descri'd from a parent to a Child. I hope you will not say I express myself in too fully, tho' it is, a Candid and sincere manner, for I am a father, and possess'd of a Parent's feeling and concern. About half after ten at Night the time before mention'd, having left him about ten minutes or a Quarter of an

Hour, walking on the Larboard Gangway of the ship, but as I was Informed by Persons who were near him, that he being a young Man of a sprightly disposition, was moving himself about in different attitudes, unfortunately press'd the end of one of the rails, which are ship'd upon the Gangway, on purpose to hold the Ship's company's hammocks upright, I believe rather too hard, which upset with him, and not being able to save himself, he unfortunately fell overboard and was Drown'd, tho' every Effort possible was made use of for to save him, but at the time of his falling overboard, he had a great Coat on, which I believe must have been a great annoyance to him, I am very sorry, Sir, that I am the channel of such unwelcome Intelligence, tho' think myself in duty bound to Inform you, and if not too great an intrusion, should wish to be Informed of your receiving this Letter, which will be a great satisfaction to your Ever
Obd[t] Servant
JOHN VINCENT

A winter night in the Mediterranean; the sailors wrapped up in their heavy greatcoats; some of them larking about on the gangways that crossed the waist of the ship from the quarterdeck to the forecastle, perhaps drunk, although Vincent couldn't mention that; and then the sprightly boy going a step too far and disappearing into the dark. It happened in the course of the war tens of thousands of times. It has very roughly been reckoned that an average of about 5,000 men in the Royal Navy died every year: about 400 in enemy action or of their wounds; another 500 in shipwreck: about 2,600 from disease and almost 1,700 from accidents on board. In a war that lasted 22 years, that gives a figure of about 37,000 men who died from accidents on board. Ships were intensely dangerous places but only rarely can there have been a letter such as Vincent's. More often the news would have come in a far colder fashion. This is a letter which the young Henry Bayntun wrote to the Lords Commissioners of the Admiralty from Jamaica in August 1800:

> Gentlemen,
> I beg leave to inform you of the Death of the persons named in the Margin late belonging to His Majesty's Ship under my command who had allotted part of their wages for the maintenance of their families and I have to request you will stop the payment of the same in consequence.
>
> George Cuttler
> Lott. Boyce

That's all: the money from the distant son or father stops coming one day. It is a commercial arrangement: the man is dead and so the navy no longer pays for his services. The stopping of the pay may well have been the only way in which the family of the dead man heard the news. Like hundreds of thousands of others, they will go on the poor relief and all they are left with is the knowledge that the body of their man has been dropped into the ocean, sewn into a hammock, shotted at each end with a 32lb ball.

On either side of the class division, a form of love operated. The British fleet was thick with it. Officers loved officers and men loved men. That closeness did not cross the divide between quarterdeck and lower deck. But without doubt, on the best ships, there was a sense of oneness in a ship's company, a treasuring by the men of a commander they admired; and a nurturing by the commander of the men he relied on. Captains might transfer from one ship to another and take their entire ship's company with them. Elderly midshipmen might look after young gentlemen volunteers, much as family retainers might have attended to them at home.

Certainly, this morning, there is an outpouring of love to those at home. On board HMS *Mars*, Captain George Duff was already a hero. He had run away to sea when he was nine, had been in 13 engagements before he was 16, and had been placed, on Collingwood's recommendation, in command of the all-important inshore squadron watching the Combined Fleet in Cadiz. It was intended that the *Mars* would lead Collingwood's lee column into battle. There was a heroic look to him: 'a man of fine stature, strong and well made, above six feet in height, and had a manly, open, benevolent countenance,' famous in the fleet as 'an instructor, and father, to the numerous young men who were under his command.' He had his eldest son, 13-year-old Norwich, with him on board the *Mars* as a volunteer and this morning he wrote to his wife, whom he had married fifteen years before, a desperately rushed, ink-blotched letter which was found among his papers when the battle was over.

> Monday Morning 21st Oct.1805
> My Dearest Sophia I have just time to tell you we are just going into action with the Combined, I hope and trust in God that we shall all behave as becomes us, and that I may yet have the happiness of taking my beloved wife and children in my arms. Norwich is quite well and happy I have however ordered him of the Q^{r} Deck Yours ever and most truly Geo: Duff

The quarterdeck was the most dangerous part of the ship in battle, where officers stood desperately conspicuous and with the protection only of the men's hammocks brought up from below and stowed in netting along the gunwale. The quarterdeck was the killing zone. Any father would send his son below hidden behind the thick oak bulwarks of the *Mars*.

And more famously Nelson was writing to Emma Hamilton with the emotionality and immediacy that marked all his letters to her, his love pouring without thought on to the page:

> Victory Oct^r: 19th: 1805
> Noon Cadiz ES.E 16 Leagues
>
> My Dearest beloved Emma the dear friend of my bosom the Signal has been made that the Enemys Combined fleet are coming out of Port. We have very little Wind so that I have no hopes of seeing them before tomorrow May the God of Battles crown my endeavours with success at all events I will take care that my name shall ever be most dear to you and Horatia both of whom I love as much as my own life, and as my last writing before the battle will be to you so I hope in God that I shall live to finish my letter after the Battle May Heaven bless you prays your Nelson + Bronte

Nelson is not an aberrational figure. For him, as for his officers, love, longing, battle, glory, sacrifice, honour, risk, excitement and the terrifying beauty of the moment are all bound up in his words. Love and battle are two parts of the same thing. They seem, in Nelson's heightened language, to be almost interchangeable. Love, in a sense, is what battle is for and the battle is where love becomes most clear. He envisages Emma and Horatia forever cherishing not himself but his 'name'. Henry Blackwood also writes to his wife this morning about his 'name'. Death hangs in the background; the foreground is filled with love and glory.

Love in the 18th century had been seen, essentially, as a social virtue, part of the politeness which distinguished the 18th century from the rough violence and extreme views of the century before. 'Politeness' for the enlightened Englishman did not carry its wooden, post-Romantic and post-revolutionary sense of constraint, inhibition and hypocrisy. The polite was the easy, the open, the courteous, the civilised and the loving. Well dressed and well behaved amicability allowed people of every degree and every condition to mix. The country had lost its martial front. The wearing of swords to public gatherings became unfashionable; towns had their medieval walls demolished and substituted with parks and avenues. This belief in courtesy and the efficacy of charm – at least within the gentlemanly class – was inherited by the best of the Nelsonian officers. It was a belief which despised the old naval tyrants, 'the oppressive and tyrannical characters in the Navy,' as Captain Anselm John Griffiths described them in his *Observation on some Points of Seamanship*, published in 1809. Griffiths went on:

> The man who endeavours to carry all before him by mere dint of his authority and power would appear to me to know little indeed of human nature. Surely there can be no comparison between those who obey from fear and those who do it from inclination, or those who feel that necessary restraint alone is correctly laid on them.

The Royal Navy was, in part, a love structure, for two reasons. Love was one of the marks of a gentleman. 'Amiability' was one of the characteristics which distinguished an enlightened man. Even old Mr Austen advised his son Francis to treat the men of the lower decks with 'a certain kind of love' not because they deserved it but because that was what was expected of him. Love was one of the values for which Trafalgar was fought.

More than that, though, love worked as a tool of battle. It was the twin of courage. At the time of Trafalgar, Coleridge, attempting to remake his life after chronic catastrophes over love and drugs in England, had gone to

Malta, where he was working as the secretary of the Governor, Sir Alexander Ball. Ball had been one of Nelson's band of brothers at the Nile. Now he was administering Malta like a philosopher-king. Coleridge, from his own position of half-broken, self-doubting despair, looked up to Ball as pure hero. From another naval officer in Malta, younger than Ball and just as much a hero-worshipper as Coleridge had become, Coleridge heard a story which seemed to encapsulate everything that mattered most about love and courage. Ball had been the lieutenant in command of a cutting-out expedition in the West Indies, in which a small British force, in open boats, attacked an enemy frigate. The young man who spoke to Coleridge had then been a very junior midshipman, a boy:

> As we were rowing up to the vessel which we were to attack, amid a discharge of musketry, I was overpowered by fear, my knees trembled under me, and I seemed on the point of fainting away. Lieutenant Ball, who saw the condition I was in, placed himself close beside me, and still keeping his countenance directed towards the enemy, took hold of my hand, and pressing it in the most friendly manner, said in a low voice, 'Courage my dear Boy! don't be afraid of yourself! You will recover in a minute or so – I was just the same when I first went out in this way.' Sir, added the officer to me, it was as if an Angel had put a new Soul into me. With the feeling that I was not yet dishonoured, the whole burthen of agony was removed; and from that moment I was as fearless and forward as the oldest of the boat crew, and on our return the Lieutenant spoke highly of me to our Captain.

That moment is the culmination of a culture. Nelson, famously, use to run up the ratlines alongside the junior midshipmen going aloft for the first time, encouraging them upwards, by the example of his ease and grace in the predicament they feared. But Alexander Ball adds even greater dignity to the act. He looks at the enemy not at the midshipman – a gesture which itself preserves the young boy's honour. He holds and presses the midshipman's hand, like a father and a friend. He understands, as a man educated in the knowledge of his own and others' feelings, that it is not the enemy the boy fears, but himself. 'Don't be afraid of yourself! You will recover in a minute or so – I was just the same when I first went out in this way.' This is the community of honour vivified by an act of loving care. It is one of the foundations of the British victory at Trafalgar: glory as an outgrowth of love.

Its absence from a ship or a fleet could be fatal, but the distinctions are fine and subtle here. The boundary between order and tyranny, between a hard, coherent regularity and a tight brutalism was in fact far more narrow, movable and vague than those terms might suggest. The possibility of abuse in the name of good order and professionalism was inherent in the system. There were certainly officers who behaved as tyrants on ships. Captain Robert Corbet of HMS *Nereide* was typical of those in whom the unbending moral test to which he was subjected destroyed his understanding of what a ship's company might be. He bullied his men, repeatedly humiliating them in front of the rest of the ship's company, had them beaten again and again, repeatedly forcing them to do the same task until it was done to his satisfaction, tyrannising the people he wanted to be part of a perfect fighting machine.

Transferred to HMS *Africaine*, his reputation going ahead of him, Corbet soon arrested a marine for insubordination. An anonymous death threat, in the form of a letter thrown on to the quarterdeck, was then sent to the captain. Corbet immediately armed his officers, confronted the crew and read out the letter to the company, telling them that 'it was his fixed determination to be a great deal more severe than he had ever yet been.' The marine was given eight dozen lashes and the ship's purser wrote in his journal: 'If the People had before this entertained any doubts of the Nerve & determined character of their Captain, they must now no doubt have been undeceived.'

Soon afterwards, when the *Africaine* had been horribly mauled by the French off Mauritius, leaving 163 of her 300 men dead and wounded, Corbet himself died of wounds, either shot by his own men – he had refused to surrender as the French destroyed his ship around him – or, it was said, killing himself by removing a tourniquet and bleeding to death, rather than submit to the humiliation of capture.

A high state of order, courage, devotion to duty, unremitting zeal, a sense of honour, a commitment to ferocious battle: why does Corbet not emerge a hero? So much of him – his daring, his extremeness, his ruthlessness, his courage – is like Nelson, and was perhaps modelled on Nelson, but there is nothing Nelsonian about him, because in Nelson, not uniquely, but all-importantly, there was a quality of grace and humanity, within which the necessarily violent aggression found a dignifying frame, and which inspired love in others. Without it, Nelson would have been a Robert Corbet and no one would have heard of him.

The entire network of love, honour, mutual reliance, self-belief and sense of responsibility to an end greater than yourself lies behind the morning of Trafalgar. In his great cabin, already partly dismantled for battle, Nelson had written his famous Trafalgar prayer, in which he prayed for a 'great and glorious Victory' and after it 'for humanity to be the predominant feature in the British fleet.' He then turned to the codicil to his will, bequeathing both Emma and their daughter Horatia to the care of his country. Those were 'the only favours I ask of my King and Country at this moment when I am going to fight their Battle. May God bless my King and Country, and all those who I hold dear. My relations it is needless to mention: they will of course be amply provided for.'

Those few words, at this intensely heightened moment, provide a map of Nelson's and in some ways the naval mind. Nelson was an immensely easy writer, capable of transmitting a wide range of emotion, irony and bitterness to the page. The distance which opens up under the phrase 'their Battle' is no accident. Nor the astonishing coldness in the reference to his relations. These are the last sentences Nelson ever wrote and they describe a radically polarised world. In England, the Establishment of King and Country, which imposes on its servants duties it would never dream of undertaking itself, and a cluster of relations, parasitically demanding the crumbs that fell from the hero's table; and here, off Cape Trafalgar, a different world, a fleet of friends, of co-partners in the realm of risk and glory, to which, by extension, the woman he loved and the daughter they shared, also belonged.

It was a gesture which embodied a profoundly Nelsonian combination of naivety, deep trust and high egotism. In retrospect it is inconceivable that an increasingly strait-laced British Establishment would look after either a scandalous mistress or her illegitimate child, however noble and glorious the lover and father might be.

That is the view of history and was certainly the view from London in 1805. From within the fleet, though, from the world of interconnected lives which the Royal Navy fostered, such a legacy was neither odd nor wrong. The trust by which it worked was founded on their sense of honour and on the habit of mutuality on which a ship relies. The social connections and practice of care within the navy, by which captains took on their young relations and the sons of their friends as midshipmen, might just as well be extended to the two people most loved and adored by their own adored admiral. In the heightened emotional atmosphere before the battle, the request that Britain should look after Horatia Nelson might have seemed little different from Captain Duff sending 13-year-old Norwich Duff away from the quarterdeck, Alexander Ball holding the midshipman's hand, Henry Bayntun asking for the prisoners to be better treated in the Caribbean, from George Duff's hurried and desperate long-distance love for his Sophia in Edinburgh or even from John Vincent's letter to Mr Hancock in Nottinghamshire. Each of those instances was a symptom of sociability and of a naval civilisation which, if anything, went further in its mutual attachments than those Englishmen who stayed on shore and relied on the navy for their security.

From a distance of a good mile away, the first shot from the French and Spanish fleet, aimed high, flew over the flagship. Henry Blackwood recorded his last minutes with Nelson:

> When Lord Nelson found the shot pass over the Victory, he desired Captain Prowse of the Sirius and myself, to go on board our Ships, and in our way to tell all the Captains of Line-of-Battle Ships, that he depended on their exertions; and that if, by the mode of attack prescribed, they found it impracticable to get into Action immediately, they might adopt whatever they thought best, provided it led them quickly and closely alongside an Enemy. He then again desired me to go away; and as we were standing on the front of the poop, I took his hand,

and said, 'I trust, my Lord, that on my return to the Victory, which will be as soon as possible, I shall find your Lordship well, and in possession of twenty prizes.' On which he made this reply, 'God bless you, Blackwood, I shall never speak to you again.'

5

BOLDNESS

October 21st 1805
12 midday to 12.30 pm

Distance between fleets: 1 mile – Contact
Victory's heading and speed: 104° at 3 knots

Boldness: the Power to speak or do what we intend, before others, without fear or disorder

JOHN LOCKE, *Essay on Human Understanding*, 1695

The more southerly of the two British columns, led by Collingwood in the *Royal Sovereign*, was nearer the enemy line and came within range first. The wind was still light, now more westerly and dropping fast, the sea smooth, the sun shining on the newly painted sides of the French and Spanish ships. As soon as the first shots of the French were fired, from the *Fougueux*, the flags on the British fleet were let fly. Jacks and ensigns were lashed to the fore topgallant stay, the main topmast stay and the mizzen shrouds, a multiplicity of signals so that in the battle, when in the still airs smoke would hang in thick clouds around them, friends would have a chance of recognising friends. The multiple flags were a sign both of comradeship and isolation. This was a battle in which all of them, jointly, would be alone.

At the *Victory*'s main topgallant masthead was 'fast-belayed' – not to be taken down unless a man was sent

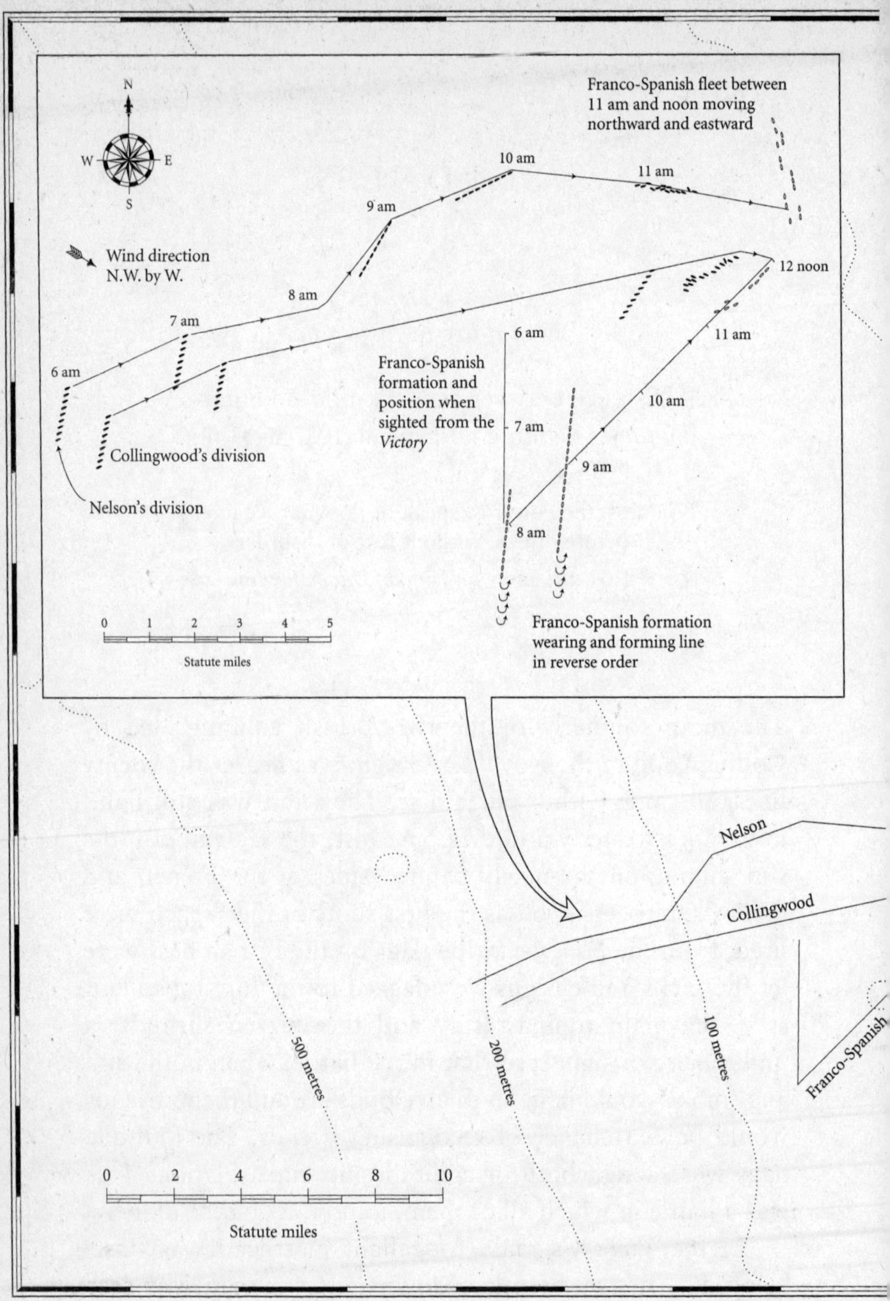

N
W
E
S
Franco-Spanish fleet between
11 am and noon moving
northward and eastward
10 am
11 am
9 am
Wind direction
N.W. by W.
8 am
12 noon
7 am
6 am
11 am
Franco-Spanish
formation and
position when
sighted from the
Victory
10 am
7 am
9 am
Collingwood's division
Nelson's division
8 am
0 1 2 3 4 5
Statute miles
Franco-Spanish formation
wearing and forming line
in reverse order
Nelson
Collingwood
Franco-Spanish
500 metres
200 metres
100 metres
0 2 4 6 8 10
Statute miles

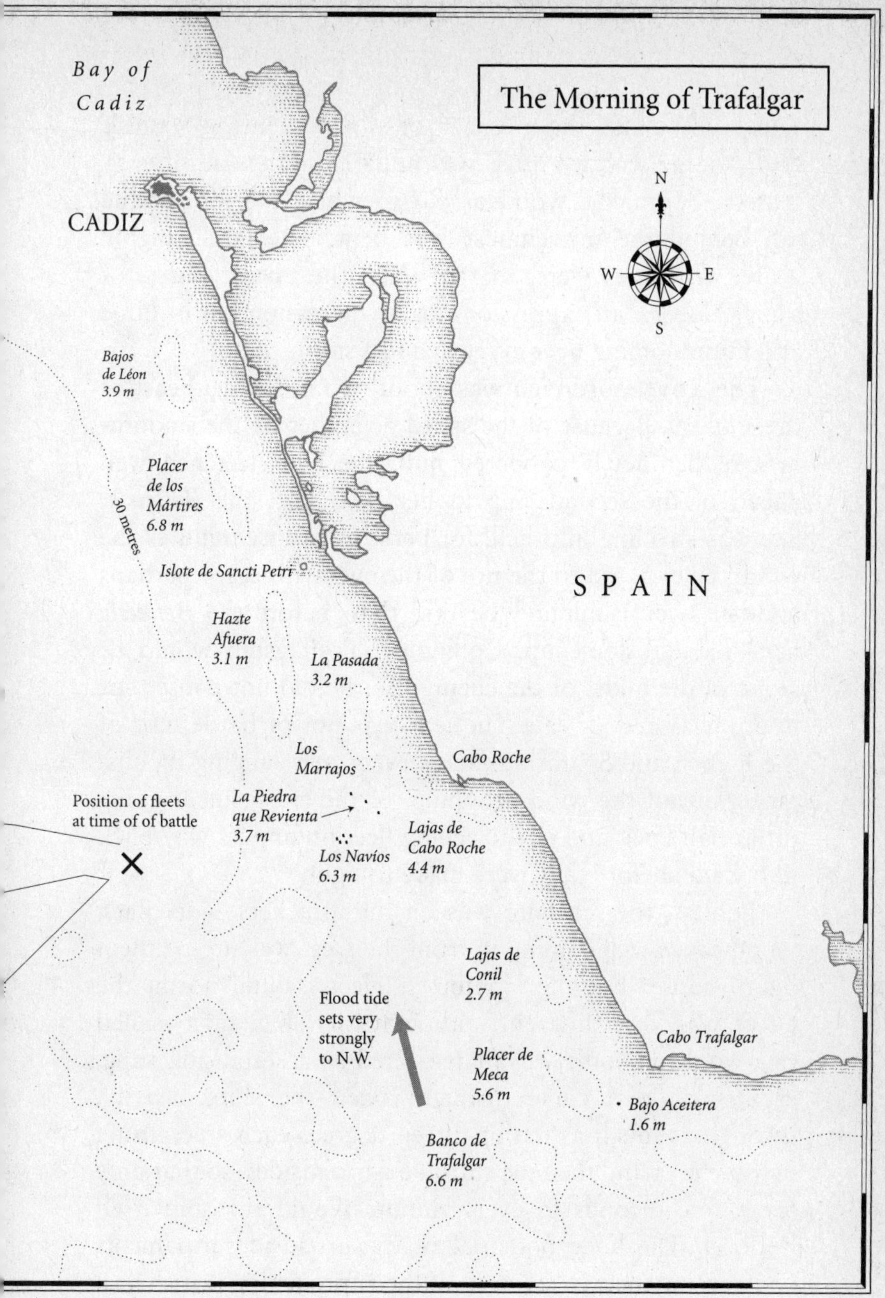
The Morning of Trafalgar
Bay of Cadiz
CADIZ
N
W
E
S
Bajos de Léon 3.9 m
Placer de los Mártires 6.8 m
30 metres
Islote de Sancti Petri
SPAIN
Hazte Afuera 3.1 m
La Pasada 3.2 m
Los Marrajos
Cabo Roche
Position of fleets at time of of battle
La Piedra que Revienta 3.7 m
Lajas de Cabo Roche 4.4 m
Los Navíos 6.3 m
Lajas de Conil 2.7 m
Flood tide sets very strongly to N.W.
Cabo Trafalgar
Placer de Meca 5.6 m
Bajo Aceitera 1.6 m
Banco de Trafalgar 6.6 m

up there to untie it – Nelson's signal No. 16: 'Engage the enemy more closely.' It remained there throughout, until shot away, less an instruction than a philosophy of battle: Touch and Take, the intimacy of violence. In the Spanish fleet, a large wooden cross was hung from the end of each spanker-boom, the wooden spar to which the foot of the sail behind the mizzenmast was bent. The large, highly visible crucifixes were, in that way, the mirror image of signal No. 16, an expression not of aggression but of hope and faith looming over every Spanish stern.

The *Royal Sovereign* was about two miles southeast of the *Victory*. Because of the speed given her by the smoothness of her newly coppered hull, she had stretched well ahead of the second ship in her own line, the *Belleisle*. She was strolling into hell: for perhaps twenty minutes she would be exposed to the fire of the enemy line; for perhaps another twenty minutes beyond that, before the *Belleisle* herself could come up, Collingwood's flagship would be alone in the midst of the enemy. But he did not pause, nor in any way reduce sail. The fear was not of battle, nor of the French and Spanish gunners even then gauging the distance, but of the wind dropping, of the engagement going off at half cock and of the enemy fleet finding its way back into Cadiz before they were made to fight.

Besides, the sea-state was on the attackers' side. Each long heavy swell coming in from the west was urging them on to battle. For the Combined Fleet, sailing north, the effect was very different: although their big, many-sailed rigs would in some ways have acted as a stabilising vane, each swell that came through rolled the ships heavily, through as much as ten or fifteen degrees each side, lifting first the port and then the starboard broadsides, so that only for a few seconds in every minute would the ship itself be level. The huge potential of the broadside armaments confronting the two columns of the approaching British fleet

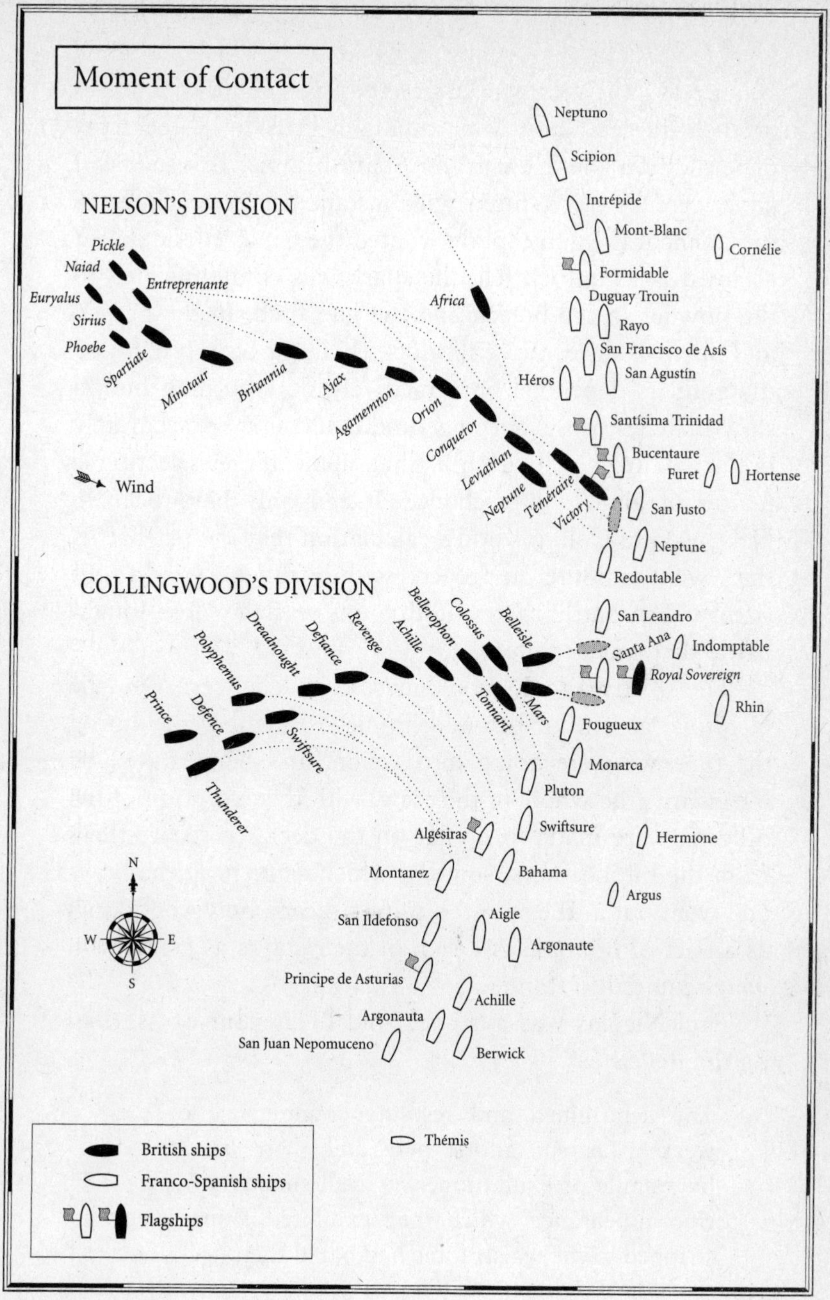
Moment of Contact
NELSON'S DIVISION
Pickle
Naiad
Euryalus
Entreprenante
Sirius
Phoebe
Spartiate
Minotaur
Britannia
Ajax
Agamemnon
Orion
Conqueror
Africa
Leviathan
Neptune
Téméraire
Victory
Wind
Neptuno
Scipion
Intrépide
Mont-Blanc
Cornélie
Formidable
Duguay Trouin
Rayo
San Francisco de Asís
Héros
San Agustín
Santísima Trinidad
Bucentaure
Furet
Hortense
San Justo
Neptune
Redoutable
COLLINGWOOD'S DIVISION
Prince
Polyphemus
Dreadnought
Defiance
Revenge
Achille
Bellerophon
Colossus
Belleisle
Defence
Swiftsure
Thunderer
Tonnant
Mars
San Leandro
Santa Ana
Indomptable
Royal Sovereign
Rhin
Fougueux
Monarca
Pluton
Swiftsure
Algésiras
Hermione
Montanez
Bahama
Argus
San Ildefonso
Aigle
Argonaute
Principe de Asturias
Achille
Argonauta
San Juan Nepomuceno
Berwick
N
W
E
S
Thémis
British ships
Franco-Spanish ships
Flagships

were, in these conditions, and at any distance, very nearly unaimable. The first shots fired at the British columns either fell short into the Atlantic or flew high over the top of their targets. Nor was aiming helped by a technical deficiency on the French and Spanish guns. British naval guns were by 1805 fitted with instant firing mechanisms: the moment the gun captain wanted the gun fired, he pulled a lanyard, a flintlock fell, the spark was communicated to the powder in the breech and the gun fired. In the French and Spanish ships, those flintlocks had not been fitted, and the gunners depended on a relatively slow-burning fuse, a slow-match, whose burning time could not be accurately predicted. In a rolling ship, that made target-selection a matter of almost pure chance. It can only have been in Nelson's and Collingwood's calculation that the pre-battle, the twenty-minute approach within range, would not signify. The battle that would count was the close-fought battle that was to follow.

The British took no unnecessary chances. On the *Neptune*, as one of her midshipmen remembered, 'during the time we were going into action, and being raked by the enemy, the whole of the crew, with the exception of the officers, were made to lie flat on the deck, to secure them from the raking shots, some of which came in at the bows and went out at the stern.' But the officers, however young, as an act of honour, as a sign of their status as gentlemen, were required to stand.

Paul Nicolas was a 16-year-old Lieutenant of Marines on the *Belleisle*:

> The determined and resolute countenance of the weather-beaten sailors, here and there brightened by a smile of exultation, was well suited to the terrific appearance which they exhibited. Some were stripped to the waist; some had bared their necks and

> arms; others had tied a handkerchief round their heads; and all seemed eagerly to await the order to engage. My two brother officers and myself were stationed, with about thirty men at small arms, on the poop, on the front of which I was now standing. An awful silence prevailed in the ship, only interrupted by the commanding voice of Captain Hargood, 'Steady! Starboard a little! Steady so!' echoed by the Master directing the quartermasters at the wheel.

Whatever the perceived inadequacies of the enemy gunners, the sheer density of gunfire would ensure that the British columns were sailing into air filled with death and destruction. It was a moment of revelation at which the young Lieutenant Nicolas came to recognise what was expected of him:

> Seeing that almost every one was lying down, I was half disposed to follow the example and several times stooped for the purpose, but – and I remember the impression well – a certain monitor seemed to whisper 'Stand up and do not shrink from your duty.' Turning round, my much esteemed and gallant senior fixed my attention; the serenity of his countenance and the composure with which he paced the deck, drove more than half my terrors away; and joining him I became somewhat infused with his spirit, which cheered me on to act the part it became me.

The instinct is to flee, or the next best thing, to hide behind the hammocks piled up in the netting on the bulwarks of the ship. But 'a certain monitor' – a Latinate, Enlightenment phrase for what an earlier more religious age would have called 'conscience' and a later, more psycho-analytical one the 'super-ego' – deflects him into the path of duty, which is revealed as a mixture of cool self-possession and in

Nicolas's extraordinary, half-theatrical, half-psychological language of 'to act the part it became me.' The echoes of *Henry V* are so deeply embedded they have become entirely unconscious: to act is now to act; fully to exist is to become the received role. Here, in these phrases, on the lip of extreme violence, can be seen the English hero in the making, a process whose roots go far back into English history.

The early 18th century had not liked the idea of a hero. A hero was unconformable; would not know about delicacy or even courtesy; and threatened rudeness. A hero would break the rules which it was the function of a civilised man to observe and sustain. Heroes were crude, whereas what was required was the polished and the developed. Sir Richard Steele, Gentleman Waiter to Prince George of Denmark, editor of the *Spectator* and one of the great arbiters of early 18th-century taste and understanding, discussed for his readers the most suitable paintings with which to decorate their apartments. 'It is the great use of pictures,' he instructed them,

> to raise in our minds either agreeable ideas of our absent friends; or high images of ancient personages. But the latter design is, methinks, carried on in a very improper way; for to fill a room full of battle pieces, pompous histories of sieges, and a tall hero alone in a crowd of insignificant figures about him, is of no consequence to private men. But to place before our eyes great and illustrious men in those parts and circumstances of life wherein their behaviour may have an effect upon our minds; as being such as we partake with them merely as they were men; such as these I say, may be just and useful ornaments of an elegant apartment.

Heroism in the 18th century, in other words, was vulgar. It was not part of a system, as the third Earl of Shaftesbury described it, in which 'We polish one another and rub off our corners and sides by a kind of amicable collision.' Earlier society had been both stiff and violent. Modern civilisation was both supple and peaceful. Arrogant lords, illiterate squires, fanatical puritans and swashbuckling heroes were all in their own way angular rather than polished, and so were not to be embraced. People had to be taught how to be civilised and they could learn from a flood of books such as F. Nivelon's, *The Rudiments of Genteel Behaviour*, published in 1737 to 'distinguish the polite Gentleman from the rude Rustick'. 'If at any times we must deal in extremes,' John Toland had written in 1711, 'then we prefer the quiet, good-natured hypocrite to the implacable, turbulent zealot of any kind. In plain terms, we are not so fond of any set of notions, as to think them more important than the peace of society.' It was better to lie than to be rude.

Anyone in the swim in mid-18th-century England accepted lying and hypocrisy as both a necessity and the norm. When, for example, in 1746 as a young naval lieutenant so far disappointed in his hopes for command, Lord Augustus Hervey made his way into the higher reaches of London society, looking for promotion, his own cynical *savoir faire* allowed him to understand its manners and mannerisms for what they were:

> I went after dinner to the Duke of Grafton's, where I found the Duke of Newcastle [Chancellor of the Exchequer] dined at a wedding dinner for Lady Caroline Fitzroy, married to Lord Petersham, Lord Harrington's eldest son. [She would soon become famous as the Countess of Harrington, the most promiscuous flirt in London.] The Duke received me with all that civility ministers can put on, and with

> all that falseness natural to his Grace, and seemed astonished that I was not a Captain, when he was the very person in the year 1744 who prevented Lord Winchelsea giving me the *Grampus* sloop . . . I received the Duke's carresses and flatteries as if I believed them good current coin

In response to this need for courtesy and delicacy, wide swathes of English 18th-century life became fragile and dainty, in a way that no age in England, before or since, has managed. It became possible, for the first and only time, for a perfectly serious man to attend ceremonies at court in 'a lavender suit, the waistcoat embroidered with a little silver or of white silk work worked in the tambour, partridge silk stockings, gold buckles, ruffles and lace frill.'

Politeness became a kind of affliction. The Duke of Newcastle who had been so smooth with Hervey acquired the nickname '*Permis*', as he prefaced every remark with the bogus-sycophantic phrase '*Est-il permis?*' This was the man to whom half of England had themselves been crawling, hoping for preferment in church, court, government, army or navy. In some ways, natural human dignity had been sacrificed on the altar of a kind of rococo politeness. A letter addressed to Newcastle in January 1756 concluded:

> That your grace will permit me to subscribe myself with the inviolable duty and attachment to your grace,
>
> My Lord Duke
> Your Grace's
> Most devoted
> Most obliged
> Most obedient
> And ever faithfull
> humble servant
> W. SHARPE.

This was not a culture from which the heroic would emerge. Apartments described as Frenchified (the adjective would also become slang for 'suffering from the clap') and floored in light deal, lit by modern open glazed windows, were furnished not with the big old comfortable chairs of the late 17th and early 18th centuries but little light French chairs, fitted with little swivel wheels on their feet and decorated with French linen festoonings instead of the thick welty damasks which England had once loved. Tables were no longer solid and immovable. They had been replaced by delicate gilded 'scuttling' tables in front of what, as Horace Walpole described it, 'they now call a fireplace, a little low dug hole surrounded by a slip of marble and what does that do for a man? It toasts his shins.' No longer did England have the giant roaring holes in the side of the room in which half trees were burned for hours at a time.

Mrs Caroline Lybbe Powys, a distant relation of the Austens, visited the by-then ancient and untouched late-sixteenth interiors of Hardwick Hall in Derbyshire in 1757:

> Of course it is antique and rendered extremely curious to the present age, as all the furniture is co-eval with the edifice. Our ancestors' taste for substantialness in every piece makes *us* now smile; they too would, could they see our delicateness in the same articles, smile at us, and I am certain, if anyone was to compare three or four hundred years hence a chair from the dining room of Queen Elizabeth's days and of the light French ones of George II, it would never be possible to suppose them to belong to the same race of people, as the one is altogether gigantic, the other quite Liliputian.

Acceptable behaviour had become toy-like and it was not long before the anti-heroic fashion for a delicate sensibility ran out of control. Manliness, or even the ability to survive, had in fact almost entirely deserted those who were suffering from the cult of sensibility. In the Abbey of St Peter and St Paul in Dorchester, there is this poignant epitaph to poor Sarah Fletcher who died in 1799 aged 29:

Reader!
If thou has a heart fam'd for
Tenderness and Pity, Contemplate this Spot.
In which are deposited the Remains
Of a Young Lady, whose artless Beauty,
Innocence of Mind, and gentle Manners,
Once obtained her the Love and
Esteem of all who knew her, But when
Nerves were too delicately spun to
Bear the rude Shakes and Jostlings
Which we meet in this transitory
World, Nature gave way; She sunk
And died a Martyr to Excessive
Sensibility.

Of course, the Cult of Courtesy and Feeling was, at least in part, thought ridiculous even as it was happening – Dr Johnson defined 'Finesse' in his 1755 *Dictionary* as 'an unnecessary word which is creeping into the language' – and never more than when subject to the unforgiving verdict of the Grub Street journalists. No figure loomed more symbolically over the naval mythology of the 18th century than Admiral John Byng. Among navy men, he stood as an example of the honourable naval officer who had been betrayed by a combination of deceitful politicians and a crude, vengeful mob. He had been sent to the Mediterranean with a fleet that was inadequate in size, inadequately manned and inadequately equipped. His task was to relieve the siege which the French were laying to the British garrison in Minorca. On May 20 1755, he engaged their fleet under Admiral de la Galissonière, with the sort of inconclusive results which 18th-century naval battle often produced. His own leading ships were severely mauled by the French; de La Galissonière had adroitly withdrawn to leeward when it looked as if Byng was about to attack him with the centre and rear of the British fleet and Byng soon decided to withdraw himself to the safety of Gibraltar.

Every aspect of what he did, given his inadequate force, had been perfectly reasonable, without being in any way heroic, but as a result the Mediterranean base of Minorca had been lost by the British. The government ministers did their best to blame Byng and the English broadsheet writers rubbed their hands with pleasure. Byng was a gent, not a fighter, and as a result of the popular clamour against him, abetted by the astonishingly corrupt desire among ministers for self-preservation, he was famously shot for cowardice,

And, in Voltaire's famous words, to encourage the others. His death was intended to satisfy a widespread demand for aggressive leadership, not among the cultured and political élite, but among the non-enfranchised populace. At that level, throughout the 18th century, another vision of admirable behaviour persisted. The mob did not want the smooth, conformable man, the slick hypocrite who could so politely manoeuvre his way into the rewards of high politics and high society. They wanted his very opposite, the clever thief, the man who thrived not by using the well oiled wheels of society, but by opposing them and cheating them, by attending only to the wellbeing of his own heroic self. The notion of the hero – alive in England in the 17th century and again in the 19th – had gone underground in the 18th century and flourished there as the criminal king, full of daring, guile, violence when needed, and a flamboyant theatricality, which emerged nowhere more entrancingly than when on the way to the gallows. For conservative supporters of the status quo, such as Henry Fielding, the novelist and magistrate, nothing was more subversive of that order than the behaviour of the show-off thief as he was taken to his judicial execution at Tyburn. The crowd views him as a 'hero' dressed in 'imaginary glory'. He is puffed up with 'Pride' and 'passion'.

> The day appointed by law for the thief's shame is the day of glory in his own opinion. His procession to Tyburn and his last moments there, are all triumphant; attended with the compassion of the meek and the tender-hearted, and with the applause and the admiration and envy of all the bold and hardened. His behaviour in his recent condition, not the crimes, how atrocious soever, which brought him to it, are the subject of contemplation. And if he hath sense enough to temper his boldness with any degree of decency, his death is spoken of by many with honour, by most with pity, and by all with approbation.

This extraordinary passage, written by Fielding in 1751, part of his *Inquiry into the Cause of the Late Increase in Robbers*, might be the template on which the heroic figure of Nelson himself was based. Every single keyword and key phrase of the Nelsonian amalgam is there: hero, pride, passion, 'the day of glory', 'his last moments', 'triumphant', 'the compassion of the meek and the tender-hearted', 'applause', 'admiration', 'envy of all the bold and hardened,' 'his death spoken of by many with honour, by most with pity, and by all with approbation.' It is as if, half a century before, the appetite was there among the mob in the streets en route to Tyburn for the kind of figure which Nelson would provide them in the late 1790s and early 1800s. The public figure of Nelson is modelled not on the Newcastle-Byng template, the big, solid, respectable, prudent and lying establishment, but on the bold, brave, tricky, clever, daring, nimble-minded and nimble-fingered, counter-culture hero of the thief.

The appetite for such a hero was certainly there, but the 18th-century cult of gentlemanly courtesy could not satisfy it. It was fed by a stream of twopenny broadsheets and sixpenny pamphlets, filled with journalistic accounts of criminals in Newgate prison in London. For sale singly or bound in collections for a shilling, by 1760 almost 1,300 of these Newgate prison lives had been published. Men of charm, wit, honour, violence and great professional skill, with a protean ability to appear and disappear, with no social standing, money or education, alert for captures, prizes and victories, ready to risk all for the glory of their triumphs: more connects the image of the naval hero and the thief than divides them. There is, in other words, something in the national hero of 1805 which looks like an adopted and legitimised criminality. Nelson and his band of brothers might be seen as a set of sanctioned villains, living lives that oscillated between intense risk and predatory gain, a role in which a deeply prepared public consciousness welcomed and adored them. And in that role, distinguishing them from the stiff establishment figures with whom the populace in general felt little sympathy, two qualities were central: daring and sincerity.

By 1805, the femininity of the mid-18th century was being left behind. Exaggerated sensibility had started to look absurd. Clothes, for both men and women, had become sober and simple. Their colours were plain; embroidery had shrunk to a minimum. The wig and hair powder had both been dispensed with and men wore their own hair unpowdered, either short in the Roman style or longer and romantically wayward. There is at least some evidence that portrait painters, including Sir William Beechey, when painting Nelson, fluffed up his rather flat reddish-grey hair into much more of a heroic creation than it was. The hero needed big hair. The same treatment was given by Sir Thomas Lawrence to Wellington, whose real hair, as painted by Goya, was insignificant and mousy. In Lawrence's version, Wellington looks as if he has just emerged from the salon into a fresh breeze, the correct setting for a hero. The admirable had moved outside.

A fashion for manliness had begun to take over the culture. You can see it happening before your eyes in *Pride and Prejudice*. Jane Austen had completed the original draft of the novel before 1800 and in it one can see dramatised the shift in values between the 18th and 19th centuries, arranged around the two potential heroes of the book: Mr Bingley and Mr Darcy. Mr Bingley is 18th-century man: handsome, young, agreeable, delightful, fond of dancing, gentlemanlike, pleasant, easy, unaffected and not entirely in control of his destiny. Darcy is fine, tall, handsome, noble, proud, forbidding, disagreeable and subject to no control but his own. It is a strikingly schematic division. Darcy is like a craggy black mountainside – Mrs Bennett calls him 'horrid', the word used to describe the pleasure to be derived from a harsh and sublime landscape; Mr Bingley is a verdant park with bubbling rills. Darcy is 19th-century man, manliness itself, uncompromising, dark and sexy. And it is Darcy, of course, whom the novel ends up loving. Darcy is the coming man, Bingley the old way of doing things. In some ways, Darcy is the template on which the severe and unbending model of Victorian manliness is founded.

The implication of the novel is that there is something better than politeness and that the merely civil is inadequate. Pride and self-possession, even to the extent of rudeness, taciturnity – 'He does not rattle away' – sudden unpredictable behaviour and abrupt judgements had become not a symptom of barbarism but of authenticity, of a truth to a more fiercely defined self which cannot tolerate the hypocrisy on which the previous century was founded. Darcy is 'silent, grave, and indifferent', words in this new moral universe which signal pure approval.

It is not difficult to see in this powerful and spreading ethic and aesthetic a version of the new economic reality. A society based on the fixed and ancient ranks, while dressing its aesthetic sense in patterns derived from the ancients, will like the idea of fixed perfectability, of a static order as the definition of beauty. But British society in 1805, in which the motor and generator of national life was increasingly commercial, a commercial empire and armed forces in which enormous prizes and high prestige could be won, was increasingly impatient with and contemptuous of the stupidities of rank. What mattered was authentic, self-generated worth. The first years of the 19th century were a surprisingly rude and frank moment. St Vincent, when First Lord of the Admiralty, could write to the Marquises of Salisbury and of Douglas in a way no one could have dreamed of doing even 20 years before. Both grandees had written to St Vincent, outraged that employees of theirs should have been taken by the press gang, and asking them to be released:

> 23rd June 1803
> *To the Marquis of Salisbury*
>
> If the Board was to give way to the numerous applications for the discharge of Seamen, the Fleet could never be manned. Let me entreat Your Lordship therefore not to listen to the representations which are made to you on this head.
>
> 23rd June 1803
> *To the Marquis of Douglas*
>
> The Peerage is become so numerous that if Noblemen grant their Badge and Livery for the sole

purpose of protecting Men whose occupation is upon the water from the Impress, it will be impossible to man the Fleet.

With the increasing erosion of the élite by bourgeois culture, something of the street understanding of the hero-thief in the 1750s had become 1805 middle-class mainstream thinking. By the time of Trafalgar, England had not only been long subject to an expensive and threatening war. She was deep into the social transformations which a commercial revolution had worked, and had, as a result, become a more serious place: tense, anxious, interested in material facts. War and commerce had rubbed away the frivolities which a previous age had come to see as normal and natural. A new roughness and harshness was in the air. As Linda Colley has written, there was 'a distinctively *sturm-und-drang* quality about British patrician life in the late eighteenth and early nineteenth centuries.' William Pitt died at the age of forty-seven, a victim of incessant work and compensatory drinking. One minister after another committed suicide, most by cutting their throats. Nineteen members of parliament killed themselves between 1790 and 1820. More than twenty went mad. Both Russian and real roulette became the diversion of the moment. Duelling and gambling enjoyed a resurgence they had not known since the 17th century.

Delight in easy gradients had been replaced by a passion for suddenness. The sudden was integral to the sublime. As the young Burke had described it,

> Whatever, either in sights or sounds, makes the transition from one extreme to the other easy, causes no terror, and consequently can be no cause of greatness. In everything sudden and unexpected, we are apt to start; that is, we have a perception of danger, and our nature rouses us to guard against it.

That rousing of the inner nature was the source of sublime pleasure, and the new delight in the 'great' feelings which suddenness produces had penetrated very deeply into English society. Throughout the summers of the 1790s, the British royal family spent their time at Weymouth on the Dorset coast. At night there was dancing and in the daytime expeditions into the Dorset countryside. Far more exciting, though, was sailing in the bay. A 74-gun ship-of-the-line, the *Magnificent* and, faster and more fun, a frigate, the *Southampton*, stood by every day, one for royal protection, the other for royal pleasure. The favourite game was for the *Magnificent* and the *Southampton* to approach each other under full sail on opposite tacks, with a combined speed of twenty knots or even more and to rush past one another, almost brushing sides. At the moment of climax, when the gunports of the two ships were inches apart, the entire crew of the *Magnificent* would cheer the rapidly passing royals. The experience was said to have 'had a charming effect on the whole party' and at the end of the summer Captain Douglas of the *Southampton* was knighted.

There is a cluster of new ideas here: the beauty in sudden change; the admirableness of the man whose character is authentically his and stands out from his surroundings; the flaccid nature of the courteous quadrille; the possibility of the heroic in the sublime; the delight in roughness rather than high finish. Perhaps the most intriguing question about Trafalgar is how this deep transformation in sensibility and in the sense of what was valuable played itself out in the conduct of naval war.

Eighteenth-century naval war had been based on the line of battle and the line of battle was founded on two unavoidable facts: a ship is longer than it is broad; and it cannot always manoeuvre where required. Its most defended and its most aggressive aspects are along its length;

the most vulnerable its bow and stern where there are no or few guns and the structure is weakest. The essential idea of the line of battle, first used by the English in 1653 against the Dutch, is that the fleet lines up bow to stern, and presents those long armed broadsides to the enemy. This arrangement protects individual ships from both the raking fire of an enemy firing from ahead or astern and the possibility of being outnumbered and 'doubled' – with an enemy on both sides. It also avoids the danger of friendly fire. Ships in line ahead cannot by mistake fire into each other, something which had often happened in the chaotic mêlées of the 16th and 17th centuries. The line of battle, in theory, combines the force of many ships into a single fighting instrument.

But it had its problems. It was most effective as a defensive posture: it minimised one's own risk but it also minimised the potential of damage to the enemy. It was a flock or a shoal of fish, bristling with violence, but concerned to look after itself, hugging itself for protection. In attack, in ships which anyway could not sail closer than 67° to the wind, and only sailed happily with the wind on the quarter, it was cumbersome and stiff. The line had to sail at the speed of the slowest ship and to turn a line without ships losing position, creating dangerous gaps, could only be done slowly and steadily. The ballet of naval warfare was a stately business.

Until the 1780s, when new gun-training tackles were introduced to the British fleet, allowing guns to be trained 45° both ahead and abaft of the beam, the broadside could only be fired at 90° to the direction in which the ship was sailing. To bring the guns of a fleet to bear on a mobile enemy in shifting conditions of wind and sea, with the possibilities of gear failing, ships running into each other or falling off to leeward, was an extraordinarily demanding task, only rarely achieved with anything like conclusive effect. What is called 'decisive action' – in other words one ship battering another for long enough for its crew to be killed or its rig destroyed – usually required broadsides to be fired into the enemy for at least half an hour at a distance of no more than 200 yards, closer if possible. 'Hailing distance' was Nelson's favoured range for the ideal moment at which to open fire.

Inevitably, by the mid-18th century, there was an element of stalemate to line-of-battle fighting. Admirals became concerned above all to preserve their forces to fight another day and not to allow their captains to expose themselves to danger. Exactness was all. Admiral Edward Vernon, in 1740, for example, ordered that 'During the time of engagement every ship is to appoint a proper person to keep an eye upon the admiral and to observe signals.' No free spirits there. Captains needed to obey. In some ways, the ethic and aesthetic of order, propriety and communality which shaped so much of mid-18th-century life, also dictated the behaviour of fleets, the mentality of admirals and the fighting instructions they issued.

Battle as a result remained something of a quadrille. Lord Augustus Hervey, watching from the quarterdeck of a frigate in Admiral Byng's fleet as they manoeuvred against the French outside Port Mahon in Minorca, considered the 'evolutions' of the enemy 'pretty and regular'. Even the terrifying Admiral Boscawen, known to his sailors as 'Old Dreadnought', who when woken as a young captain by the officer of the watch and asked what to do with two large Frenchmen then seen to be bearing down on them, asked famously, standing in his night shirt on the quarterdeck, 'Do? Do? Damn 'em and fight 'em,' – even this termagant could in 1759 (in written instructions they all carried on board) address his captains like a dancing master:

> If at any time while we are engaged with the enemy, the admiral shall judge it proper to come to a closer engagement than at the distance we then are, he will hoist a red and white flag on the flagstaff at the main topmast-head, and fire a gun. Then every ship is to engage the enemy at the same distance the admiral does.
>
> When I think the ship astern of me is at too great a distance, I will make it known to him by putting abroad a pennant at the cross-jack yard-arm, and keep it flying till he is in his station; and if he finds the ship astern of him is at a greater distance than he is from the [flagship] he shall make the same signal at the cross-jack yard-arm, and keep it flying till he thinks that the ship is at a proper distance, and so on to the rear of the line.

This insistence on orderliness and on the stately meeting of equally matched forces began to break down in the last quarter of the 18th century. One after another, leading admirals and naval theorists, looking for battle advantage, started to abandon the old sense of regularity as the underlying principle of the well-conducted battle. Roughness, imbalance, asymmetry, concentration on one part of the enemy, the breaking open of accepted norms: this, increasingly, became the intellectual pattern of British naval battle in the last part of the 18th century. Classical forms had started to take on Romantic intonations.

By 1780 a system of tactics had been developed in which the idea of crushing part of the enemy had replaced the earlier intention of coming alongside, fleet to fleet, and hoping for the best. A swift and vigorous attack had replaced the slow and watchful defensive. Above all, naval tacticians had come to realise that concentrating as much of the attacking force as possible on the rear of the enemy meant that a devastating victory could be achieved. The leading ships in the enemy's van could do nothing to help their beleaguered rear, at least not quickly, and that period of advantage for the attacker would bring victory before any help arrived. Battle had moved over from something that had seemed essentially fair to an action which was founded on the idea of initial and shocking advantage. From a matter of regular beauty, it had become a question of the devastating sublime.

Three leading British admirals, Hawke, Rodney and Howe, were largely responsible for the change. All, despite their age, Hawke born in 1705, Rodney in 1719, Howe in 1726, stood outside the acceptable mid-century courteous norm. Hawke's victory at Quiberon Bay during the Seven Years War in 1759 off the Breton coast, in a thrashingly wild northwesterly November gale, had broken all the rules. Hawke's blockading squadron heard that the French Brest fleet was at sea and it was spotted by one of his scouts when 40 miles west of Belle Isle. They were making for shelter, hoping to avoid an engagement. Hawke made the signal 'for the seven ships nearest to them to chase, and draw into a line of battle ahead of the Royal George [his flagship], and endeavour to stop them until the rest of the squadron should come up, who were also to form as they chased.' Forming as they chase, pursuing a reluctant enemy on to a wild lee shore: there are pre-echoes here of Trafalgar.

Hawke had no reliable charts of the reef-strewn bay into which he pursued the French. He simply assumed the French themselves would avoid the rocks and shoals and followed them. He used the enemy as his pilot, chasing up behind them as the shore and the night both approached. Two French ships surrendered, two sank, two ran ashore and burnt, seven others ran ashore deliberately, of which four broke their backs. Another nine escaped either into the mouth of the Loire or southwards to Rochefort, where they spent the rest of the war, imprisoned behind the British blockade. It was a model of victory achieved through wild and unregulated pursuit.

Hawke gleams as a Nelsonian hero *avant la lettre*, but he had his heirs. Rodney was intemperate, a gambler, falling so deeply in debt that in the 1770s he had to escape to Paris for four years, a man famed for a dashing attack against the Spanish, on a lee shore, at night and in a storm, always quick to seize an opportunity, and far from polished. He had the habit of 'making himself the theme of his own discourse. He talked much and freely upon every subject, concealed nothing in the course of conversation, regardless who were present, and dealt his censure as well as his praises with imprudent liberality. Through his whole life two passions – the love of women and of play – carried him into many excesses.'

For the first time, at the Battle of the Saints off St Lucia in 1782, this wild womanising gambler of an admiral took the shocking and unprecedented step of leading his fleet *through* the enemy to the other side, an action which won him the battle, 'pulverising' the French and turning the world of naval tactics upside down. To go through the enemy was to become British orthodoxy.

Where Rodney was garrulous, Howe was silent, 'a man universally acknowledged to be unfeeling in his nature, ungracious in his manner and, upon all occasions, discovers a wonderful attachment to the dictates of his own perverse impenetrable disposition.' His courage was famous – Horace Walpole described him as 'undaunted as a rock and as silent' – and his appearance forbidding, but 'Black Dick' was loved by both officers and the men of the lower deck. When the mutinies erupted in 1797, it was the aged Howe whom the supervising committee at Spithead chose as the one admiral they trusted and would deal with. These were the precursors, both of them heroes to the common man, on whom the daring, mould-breaking aspect of the Nelsonian method was based.

In Lord Howe's signal book issued in 1790, there is an entirely new signal, applicable when the British fleet was on the attack either from upwind of the enemy or to leeward of them:

> If, when having the weather-gage of the enemy, the admiral means to pass between the ships of their line for engaging them to leeward or, being to leeward, to pass between them for obtaining the weather-gage. N.B. – the different captains and commanders not being able to effect the specified intention in either case are at liberty to act as circumstances require.

Lines broken through and captains at liberty to act as circumstances require: the world of the orderly dance was over. In the next edition of the signal book, the degree of individual freedom for ships was enhanced still further. Howe included a signal which told the ships of the fleet: 'To break through the enemy's line in all parts where practicable, and engage on the other side.' A manuscript note is added in the Admiralty copy of the signal book: 'If a blue pennant is hoisted at the fore topmast-head, to break through the centre; if at the mizzen topmast-head, to break through the rear.' In either case, the van is to be left to sail away ignored. At the Battle of the Saints, Rodney had led his fleet in line ahead through the enemy line. At the Glorious First of June in 1794, Howe instructed his captains to approach the enemy in line abreast, break through wherever they could and 'for each ship to steer for, independently of each other, and engage respectively the ship opposed in situation to them in the enemy's line.'

There is a deep historical and geographical pattern at work here. The essential disposition of British and French fleets over the whole of the 18th century was governed by geography and the prevailing winds. The strategic position of the British was to be out at sea, to windward, holding their blockading station to the west of the European mainland. Their leeward guns faced the French. The French, emerging from port, approached the British from downwind. Their windward guns faced the British. This essential historical structure had a shaping effect on the way in which each side engaged in battle. The British guns, brought down towards the surface of the sea by the heeling of the ships, were habitually aimed at the hulls of the enemy. The French guns, lifted by the heeling of the ships, were usually aimed at the rigging of the ships.

More significantly than that, the French had developed the habit during battle of slipping off to leeward, avoiding the decisive contact, dancing away in front of the British eyes, compelling the British ships to turn towards them and allowing the French to rake their enemy on the approach. The great innovation of the Howe method in particular was to slip through the gaps in the enemy to leeward and then to hold them between the mouths of the British guns and the wind, since a fleet to windward cannot slip away. It is seized in a murderous grasp, the coherence of the fleet broken into fragments over which the French admiral has no control. The Howe method, in other words, *dared* to recreate the mêlée which 150 years previously the invention of the line of battle had been designed to avoid. It is, like so much of what was happening in European consciousness at the time, a return to the primitive, to the essential brutal realities of battle in which deep and violent energies are released by dispensing with the carapace of courtliness which the 18th century had done so much to cultivate. It is, in a phrase, Romantic battle, in which, as tacticians describe it, there is 'the utmost development of fire-surface'. It was the method by which a fleet could develop an overwhelming attack of the most violent kind. And it released the possibilities of heroism. This morning, off Trafalgar, Nelson made a signal to the fleet, expressing an intention which in all likelihood his captains had already assumed: he would break through the enemy line and engage them on their leeward side.

The battle which made Nelson famous, fought off Cape St Vincent in 1797, is an example of this thinking. Commanding the British fleet was Sir John Jervis, who would be created Earl St Vincent as a result of the victory. He surprised a scattered Spanish fleet off Cape St Vincent on the northern edge of the Bay of Cadiz. The by now familiar signal went up; 'The admiral intends to pass through the enemy's line.' But Jervis then made a mistake, asking his fleet to 'tack in succession' meaning that they should follow him in a single line ahead through the enemy, pursuing in other words the Rodney tactic. Only Nelson grasped the mistake, which would have allowed the Spanish the time to get away. On his own initiative, Nelson in the *Captain* converted the order into a version of Howe's method of attack: all turn for the enemy together, in line abreast, not an orderly file but a flock of aggression descending on the Spanish fleet. Followed by Collingwood, Nelson broke through the middle of the Spanish fleet, created the havoc he required, destroyed the Spanish admirals' system of control and captured two ships in the process.

Fascinatingly, there is an account of this battle written by a Spanish observer, Don Domingo Perez de Grandallana, who identified the core of the new English fighting method:

> An Englishman enters a naval action with the firm conviction that his duty is to hurt his enemies and help his friends and allies without looking out for directions in the midst of the fight; and while he thus clears his mind of all subsidiary distractions, he rests in confidence on the certainty that his comrades,

actuated by the same principles as himself, will be bound by the sacred and priceless principle of mutual support.

Accordingly, both he and all his fellows fix their minds on acting with zeal and judgement upon the spur of the moment, and with the certainty that they will not be deserted. Experience shows, on the contrary, that a Frenchman or a Spaniard, working under a system which leans to formality and strict order being maintained in battle, has no feeling for mutual support, and goes into action with hesitation, preoccupied with the anxiety of seeing or hearing the commander-in-chief's signals for such and such manoeuvres . . .

Thus they can never make up their minds to seize any favourable opportunity that may present itself. They are fettered by the strict rule to keep station, which is enforced upon them in both navies, and the usual result is that in one place ten of their ships may be firing on four, while in another four of their comrades may be receiving the fire of ten of the enemy. Worst of all they are denied the confidence inspired by mutual support, which is as surely maintained by the English as it is neglected by us, who will not learn from them.

In three acute paragraphs, de Grandallana, who by the time of Trafalgar had become head of the naval secretariat in Madrid, identified precisely the post-systematic nature of the British advantage. He understood it was a cultural and not a technical advantage; reliant on the notion of the 'band of brothers', of which he would not have heard; and intuitively grasping the power of the individual 'emulation to excel' with which the 18th century had coloured the English heart. This is not a description of Trafalgar; it explains, nevertheless, why Trafalgar was won.

ORDER

JMW Turner's immense vision of the ships-of-the-line taking in stores (*above*) and the dignified richness of the naval officer's working uniform – this (*right*) is the coat, with its gold distinction lace and Flag Officer's buttons, in which Nelson was shot – are both founded on the conservative and Enlightenment virtues of strictness, substance and orderliness, all of them underpinning the workings of the Royal Navy and its success at Trafalgar.

WHAT NELSON WAS NOT

Admiral Sir Cloudisley Shovell (*right*) and Admiral John Byng (*below*) stand for the earlier tradition from which Nelsonian war set itself apart.

Shovell, in armour, as was usual for naval commanders until the early 18th century, and Byng, in acres of satin waistcoat, embody the patrician and gentlemanly ideal of the civilised man at sea. Neither had the great Nelsonian quality: maritime competence combined with unbridled aggression.

Shovell drove his entire fleet on to rocks in the Isles of Scilly in 1707, Byng was shot in 1757 for conducting too gentlemanly a battle with the French off Minorca.

THE GREAT SUSTAINERS

Lord St Vincent (*above*) and Lord Barham (*right*), both First Lords of the Admiralty in the first years of the 19th century, brought different qualities to the task. As William Beechey's magnificent head-on portrait of St Vincent shows, this was a fighting admiral, with a keen appreciation of Nelson's 'animal courage', the will to win by which the 1805 Navy was fuelled. Barham, a longtime naval administrator, was a wheedling, finickety and irritatingly self-congratulatory man who nevertheless ensured that the resources needed at Trafalgar were there and in time. It was this combination of qualities which ensured victory.

CAUTION AND AGGRESSION: A certain weakness hangs about the eyes of Sir Robert Calder (*above*), who failed to bring about a Nelsonian victory in July that year off Cape Finisterre and whose career was ruined as a result.

Thomas Fremantle (*above*) evinces the kind of bullish aggression which endeared him to Nelson and allowed him to write a letter a week after Trafalgar regretting Nelson's death largely because it damaged his own career prospects.

SENSE AND SENSIBILITY: Sir Alexander Ball (*above left*) was Governor of Malta, hero of Samuel Taylor Coleridge, a figure of pure rationality, 'a tideless man'. The young William Beatty (*above right*) Surgeon on the *Victory*, through his sensitive description of Nelson's last hours, did more to shape the inherited idea of Nelson than any other.

ELEGANCE AND BRUTALITY: Henry Blackwood (*above left*) was Nelson's leading frigate Captain and admired by all, including his enemies, for the grace of his bearing. Thomas Hardy (*above*), Nelson's Flag Captain, was one of the harshest disciplinarians in the fleet, who was nevertheless happy to kiss the dying Nelson twice.

VIOLENCE AND HUMANITY: Thomas Troubridge (*above*) relished the doing of violence and the hanging of criminals; Henry Bayntun (*right*), who points to a chart of the battle and wears his victor's sword and medal, did more than any other British Captain to save French and Spanish seamen in the storm that followed.

Beauty in the destruction of beauty, the heights and depths of sublime war: JMW Turner's great image of *The Battle of Trafalgar 21st October 1805* was painted for George IV in 1824. *Victory*'s foremast falls in a cloud of collapsing canvas; in the foreground men die and suffer.

Even in the imagery by which they are recorded, the leading officers of the Combined Fleet do not have the unity and cohesion of their British enemy. The French commander, Pierre Charles de Villeneuve (*top left*) remains the pre-Revolutionary aristocrat. His leading captain, Jean-Jacques Etienne Lucas of the *Redoutable*, (*bottom right*) stands the other side of that revolutionary divide. The Spanish Commander-in-Chief Federico Gravina (*bottom left*) and his leading Captain, Commodore Cosme de Churruca (*top right*) seem to come from an earlier world altogether.

THE MULTIPLE MAN

In life, as in his portraits, Nelson flickered from one image to the next. Lemuel Francis Abbott's 1800 portrait (*above*) is the ultimate in glamour, the Prince of the Opera, the bejewelled and bemedalled hero.

The portraits by John Hoppner, (*above left*) done in about 1800, by William Beechey, 1801 (*above*) and by Matthew Keymer in the same year (*above right*) show a range of delicacy, sensuousness and even exhaustion which are quite absent from Abbott's more famous, starry vision.

Hero-making in action. Guy Head's meticulous and unheroic painting done in 1798-1799 (*left*) can be set alongside William Beechey's famous 1800 painting (*above right*), now on show in the National Portrait Gallery, London. It is quite obvious that Beechey has added an extra layer of more romantic and wayward hair to the tightly controlled effect in the Guy Head portrait. If an age required a hero, he needed hair and weather to match.

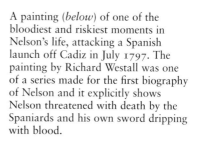

A painting (*below*) of one of the bloodiest and riskiest moments in Nelson's life, attacking a Spanish launch off Cadiz in July 1797. The painting by Richard Westall was one of a series made for the first biography of Nelson and it explicitly shows Nelson threatened with death by the Spaniards and his own sword dripping with blood.

The Battle of Trafalgar, 21 October 1805: End of the Action painted by Nicholas Pocock in 1808. This glamour-free portrayal of the last phase of the battle was a favourite among naval men for its exactness and reality. This is battle as dismantling yard, not the sublime vision of a Turner, but a place of hideous mutilation and overwhelming destruction.

Two competing visions of the *Death of Nelson*, one painted in 1806 by Benjamin West (*above*) and the other by Arthur William Devis (*right*) a year later. Both draw on imagery associated with the death of Christ but one is ridiculous, the other deeply moving. West portrays a public and national event, out on the quarterdeck; Devis a hidden tragedy within the dark confines (although painted too tall) of the *Victory*'s orlop deck. West's painting gets it wrong not only actually (French musket fire would within minutes have killed everyone in his crowded canvas) but psychologically. The power of Nelson's death, as Devis recognized, was not its public glory but its simple humanity.

THIS SHALLOP,
Which brought the Body of the ever to be lamented
LORD NELSON

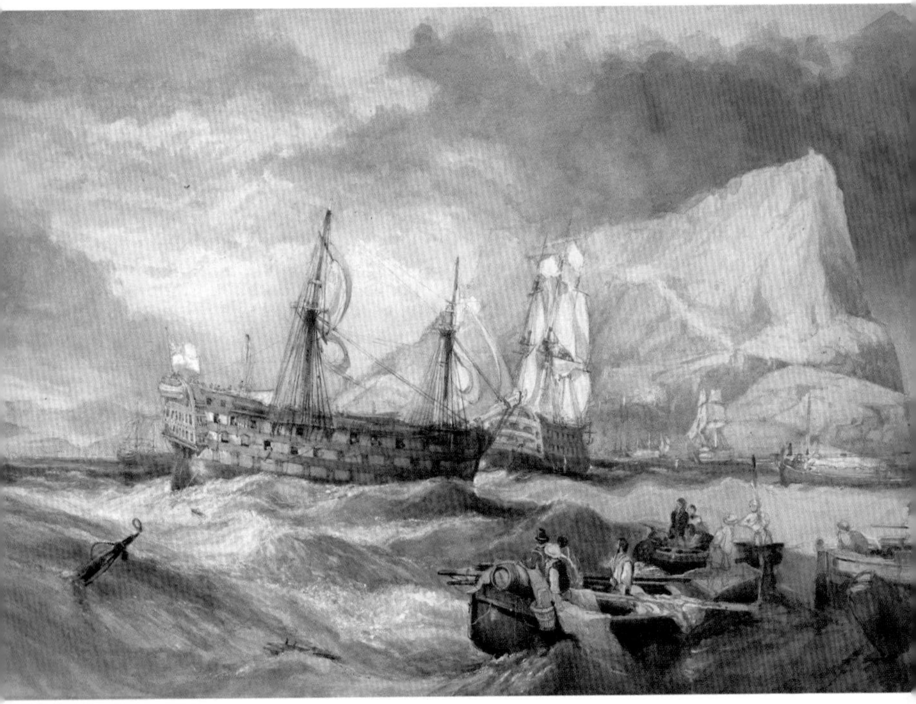

Two memorials to Nelson. In January 1806, he is absorbed (*top*) into the world of the British Establishment, a royal barge taking his body to a funeral in St Paul's from which those he loved most were excluded. By the 1850s, when Clarkson Stanfield painted the *Victory* being towed into Gibraltar after the storm (*bottom*), another meaning had taken over. The jury-rigged *Victory* holds the secret within her decks, the body of the admiral preserved in a barrel of spirits, lashed tight and stood over by a Marine, essentially tragic and like all tragedies, essentially private.

Up to the eve of Trafalgar, and beyond, there were officers in the Royal Navy who had not grasped the essence of the new idea. The fleet engagement that had occurred most recently before Trafalgar was a text-book case of what the new thirst for uncompromising victory no longer thought adequate. Sir Robert Calder, the admiral commanding a British squadron off Cape Finisterre, the northwestern tip of Spain, had enjoyed by any account a glitteringly successful career, winning prizes, making his fortune, acting as Sir John Jervis's flag captain at the Battle of Cape St Vincent, promoted to vice-admiral in 1804, both a knight and a baronet.

In the summer of 1805, Calder's responsibility was one of the most essential nodes in the British defence network, cruising off the deep-water port of Ferrol, both to blockade the Spanish ships arming and victualling in there and to catch Villeneuve's fleet as it returned from the Caribbean. The British force, reinforced by Barham in early July, consisted of fifteen ships-of-the-line, stretched out in a curtain to the west of Cape Finisterre. On 22 July, in a thick fog, they fell in with Villeneuve's superior fleet, twenty to his fifteen. Calder found himself downwind of the French, but he managed to engage them and capture two Spaniards before night intervened. The poor man was honourable, personable and charming but not cast in the Nelsonian mode. He thought he had achieved a victory and sent a modestly heroic dispatch to London. The following day, he was anxious to secure his prizes, to attend to the battered condition of one or two of his own fleet and to avoid being caught by the huge fleet, consisting of Villeneuve's 18 plus the 15 that would come out of Ferrol to join him, which now threatened him. Imagining that discretion was still the better part of valour, he did not seek to re-engage.

The newspapers in England were full of contempt for Calder's lack of fighting spirit, for his ridiculous interest in preserving his little Spanish prizes and his failure to destroy the enemy. Lord Howe's explanatory notes to the Fighting Instructions issued in 1799 had been unequivocal:

> If there should be found a captain so lost to all sense of honour and the great duty he owes his country, as not to exert himself to the utmost to get into action with the enemy, or to take or destroy them when engaged, the commander of the squadron . . . is to suspend him from his command, and is to appoint some other officer to command the ship.

If the admiral himself behaved in such a pusillanimous way, public ignominy was the only possible outcome. The tradition of Hawke, Rodney, Howe and now Nelson had created an environment in which Calders could not survive.

When the news of the state of public opinion reached the fleet, Calder requested a court martial at which he might defend himself, feeling, as officers usually did in this predicament, that without a hearing his silence would be interpreted as accepting the calumnies against him. At the same time, an acutely political Admiralty required him to return home to England, realising equally powerfully that the London populace would never accept as good enough such an inconclusive form of fighting the French. The delays in communication between the fleet at sea and the Admiralty meant that Calder's personal crisis persisted for the rest of the year. By the time the decision was made to send Calder home, it was mid-September. Nelson had by then returned to the fleet off Cadiz, where Calder was flying his flag in the 98-gun *Prince of Wales*. Such a ship would be an immensely important asset in any coming battle with the Combined Fleet. On instructions from the Admiralty, Nelson decided, at first, to remove the admiral from his flagship and send him home in the *Dreadnought*, still a ship-of-the-line, but the fleet's worst and slowest sailer.

He wrote to Calder to say so and Calder, in a highly emotional state, replied:

> Prince of Wales, at Sea
>
> I am this instant honoured with your Lordship's letter: I own I was not prepared for its contents. Believe me, they have cut me to the soul, and, if I am to be turned out of my Ship, after all that has passed, I have only to request I may be allowed to take my Captain, and such Officers as I find necessary for their justification of my conduct as an Officer, and to be put into such ship with them . . . as your Lordship shall deem proper for my passage to England, and that I may be permitted to go without a moment's further loss of time. My heart is broken! and I can only say I have the honour to be, my Lord, with all due respect, your Lordship's obliged and faithful humble servant, ROB. CALDER

Nelson relented, allowed Calder to remain in the *Prince of Wales* and on 30 September wrote to Barham:

> I may be thought wrong, as an Officer, to disobey the orders of the Admiralty, by not insisting on Sir Robert Calder's quitting the Prince of Wales for the Dreadnought, and for parting with a 90-gun Ship before the force arrives which their Lordships have judged necessary; but I trust I shall be considered to have done right as a man, and to a Brother Officer in affliction – my heart could not stand it, and so the thing must rest.

Calder was popular among the other captains, capable of giving life-enhancing dinner parties for twenty of his captains at a time on board the *Prince of Wales*, the object of far more affection, for example, than stiff, solitary, wooden Collingwood, 'another stay-on-board Admiral, who never communicates with anybody but upon service,' as Captain Codrington of the *Orion* described him. It is possible, in this light, to see Nelson's leniency as an act of war: its respect for an officer's honour would have bound the captains of the fleet to him with a gesture only they would have understood. Such trust would win a battle in a way that the mere presence of the *Prince of Wales* might not.

Nevertheless, Nelson was worried about Calder, anxious about the outcome of the court martial, not sure that Calder quite understood the severity of his predicament, and was acting 'too wise', as Nelson wrote to Collingwood. The court martial was held on 25 December 1805, but even by then Calder had not understood. Defending himself against the charge that he did not renew the action the following day, he said:

> I deprecate the idea that an engagement must be continued by a commanding officer as long as he can continue it, even though he should put at a hazard the advantage he has before gained. I maintain, that to encourage such an idea, would one day prove fatal to the officer, and dangerous to the country. The necessity of continuing an engagement must always depend on its own circumstances, and the discretion of the officer who commands, subject to that responsibility which attaches to the situation in which he is placed.

Not to have done what he did, he said, would have been 'rash and imprudent'. He congratulated himself on having exercised 'a sound discretion'. He did not like the idea, as he wrote to Barham, of the 'danger I must have exposed my squadron to, as also the country, if I had madly and rashly done what John Bull seems to have wished me to have done.' Pompous, wordy and non-Nelsonian, everything Calder disparaged was precisely what, in the light of Trafalgar, he should have done: rashness, imprudence, exposure to danger, madness, what John Bull wished for – all this was central to Nelson's grasp of the heroic.

At his trial, Trafalgar had come and gone and Calder had missed it:

> By being placed under the necessity of demanding this inquiry, I have been prevented from sharing in the glories of that day; and, believe me, that has been no small part of my sufferings (*the gallant admiral turned round, and wiped a tear from his eye*). The judgment of this Court will, I hope, reinstate me in society, and restore to me unsullied that fair fame and reputation which have been so cruelly attacked.

He had no such luck; he made the appallingly thick-skinned error of claiming that, although he had been absent from Trafalgar, he was nevertheless due his share of the £300,000 prize money voted by parliament after the battle; and the judgement of the court must have driven a stake into the poor man's tender, 18th-century heart.

> The Court is of the opinion, that the charge of not having done his utmost to renew the said engagement, and to take or destroy every ship of the enemy, has been proved against the said Vice-Admiral Calder; that it appears that his conduct has not been actuated either by cowardice or disaffection, but has arisen solely from error in judgment, and is highly censurable, and doth adjudge him to be severely reprimanded, and the said Vice-Admiral Sir Robert Calder is hereby severely reprimanded accordingly.

The world had moved on past him and Calder was never asked to serve at sea again.

* * *

Nelson had an instinct for devastation and the people of England detected it in him. He knew in his bones that the public demand was for convincing and destructive violence, not a harmless strategic victory. It was what he had gone for at Cape St Vincent and delivered at the Nile and again in Copenhagen. He had tried and failed to deliver the same in the Canaries and in a catastrophic raid on Napoleon's invasion fleet in Boulogne. In the media-rich environment of early 19th-century London, this was, if nothing else, a canny stance. He was, consciously or not, the hero-thief. In August 1805, for the fortnight he was back in London, he was mobbed in the streets like a star. His old friend, Lord Minto, chanced on him one morning:

> I met Nelson in a mob in Piccadilly, and got hold of his arm, so that I was mobbed too. It is really quite affecting to see the wonder and admiration, and love and respect of the whole world; and the genuine expression of all these sentiments at once, from gentle and simple, the moment he is seen. It is beyond anything represented in a play or in a poem of fame.

Those last words are acute: the Nelson story was rising up into the realms of fiction and theatre. Later he was seen in the Strand:

> The crowd which waited outside of Somerset House till the noble Viscount came out, was very great. He was then very ill, and neither in look nor dress betokened the naval hero, having on a pair of drab-green breeches, and high black gaiters, a yellow waistcoat, and a plain blue coat, with a cocked hat, quite square, a large green shade over the eye, and a gold headed stick in his hand, yet the crowd ran before him and said, as he looked down, that he was then thinking of burning a fleet, &c.

His appearance was irrelevant. These were inner qualities, only apparent to the adoring crowd, seeing in his slightest gesture, as they see in all heroes, the workings of a wild and catastrophic heroism. He was summoned for interviews by ministers and officials. The country looked to him for its prodigies of conflict and its miracles of victory. On 24 August he wrote to Captain Keats, one of his Mediterranean band of brothers, from the house at Merton, to the west of London, which he shared with Emma Hamilton: 'I am now set up for a Conjuror, and God knows they will very soon find out I am far from being one.' The country expected magic; Nelson, who had been careful throughout his career to promote this mould-breaking, magic-delivering idea of himself, now found the wave he had set in motion taking on a life of its own.

The fantasy of sudden and violent victory at sea was something deeply shared in England. It reached what, at this distance, seems like the most unlikely of corners and was far more widely spread than merely among the jingoistic, navy-admiring French-haters. William Wordsworth, for example, who in the 1790s had been agonisingly alert to the savagery and psychic destruction of war, nevertheless nurtured a half-guilty, voyeuristic vision of himself as a fighting sailor.

> I cannot at this moment read a tale
> Of two brave Vessels matched in deadly fight
> And fighting to the death, but I am pleased
> More than a wise man ought to be; I wish,
> I burn, I struggle, and in soul am there.

It is, for Wordsworth, a moment of visionary apocalyptics, a shuddering, vicarious delight at the tales of battle and the need for courage, resolution and skill which they impose. The received ideals of courteous politeness no longer satisfy. Those, perhaps are what a wise man should delight in, but they are not enough. Deadly fighting and fighting to the death reaches deeper into the modern heart than politesse and the observance of rank and order. Wordsworth's guilty confession acknowledges a new world bubbling up under the skin of the old. And to the general populace Nelson, more than any other man in the country, looked as if he had the secret of that new world in his hand. For Wordsworth, Nelson's genius consisted, more than anything else, in 'turbulence'.

Fascinatingly, in the terms they use to describe what they do, Nelson's approach to battle mimics Wordsworth's idea of what poetry needed to be. This is not to claim that battle is guided by aesthetic concerns, merely that Nelson's form of battle, so clearly drawing on the Hawke-Rodney-Howe inheritance, but given heightened intensity in the psychically dynamic and inventive years around Trafalgar, takes as its essential merits precisely those qualities which Wordsworth requires for the new poetry: immediacy; a dignity given to the common man; dispensing with the fripperies; a sense that the moment of crisis is engaged with the ultimate metaphysical realities; interested more in the essence of what is to be done than the niceties of form; quite unaffected in manner, 'scrambling into action'; inspiring in a way those around both Wordsworth and Nelson cannot quite explain; richly, deeply and humanly sympathetic; ruthless in its pursuit of the ideal; prepared to engage with the broken, the anarchic and the chaotic in pursuit of the goal either of victory, which is a form of revelation, or revelation, which is also a form of victory.

In both of them there is a deep distrust of the affected world of 18th-century society. From the beginning, Wordsworth proudly declared his crudeness, his lack of courtesy, his plain truth.

> 'Those who have been accustomed to the gaudiness and inane phraseology of many modern writers,' he declared in the 1802 manifesto-preface to the *Lyrical Ballads*, 'if they persist in reading this book to its conclusion, will, no doubt, frequently have to struggle with feelings of strangeness and awkwardness: they will look around for poetry and be induced to inquire by what species of courtesy these attempts can be permitted to assume that title.'

This is battle without decorum, without the pretty and elegant evolutions on which poetry had previously relied. Like Nelson, never loath to repeat his essential point, Wordsworth's language, he says again and again, is 'the real language of men in a state of vivid sensation', 'the very language of men' addressing 'the essential passions of the heart' in 'a plainer and more emphatic language.' 'What is a Poet?' he asked, as Nelson might have asked what a fighting man might be. 'He is a man speaking to men. He is the rock of defence of human nature; an upholder and preserver, carrying everywhere with him relationship and love.' In this light, it becomes clear that Wordsworth's basic conception of the human condition is battle.

This is no more than core Rousseauism, a rejection of 'social vanity', but given a new fighting ferocity. It is as if Wordsworth, in his programme for a new kind of poetry and a new kind of society, is drawing up a plan of attack, whose forms and emphases mimic Nelson's in the months and years before Trafalgar. 'All good poetry is the spontaneous overflow of powerful feelings,' Wordsworth famously wrote, just as Nelson insisted, again and again, that the purpose of battle was to annihilate the enemy by a release of essential fighting energies. A fusion of slow understanding, the application of the will and an unbending enmity towards the hypocritical, the weak, the affected and the wrong drives them both. 'I have at all times endeavoured to look steadily at my subject,' Wordsworth wrote. 'The style is manly,' and whatever beauty, he wrote modestly, may be found in his poetry, it resides 'in the sense of difficulty overcome.' Poetry is victory. In such a martial conception of art and life, beauty and victory become the same thing. Poetry is no longer bound up in books and metrical forms. Poetry, as Hazlitt would describe it, was to be found 'wherever there is a sense of beauty, or power or harmony.'

Direct, fierce, daringly bereft of ornament or complexity, focusing on the central task, impatient with frippery, allowing the plain and open approach its vigour and clarity, Wordsworth, at precisely the same historical and cultural moment, had become to poetry what Nelson was to battle. Both were driven by a desire for the primitive and the passionate, that dreamed-of, unequivocally manly moment in the history of the world when daring coloured the acts of men:

> The earliest Poets of all nations generally wrote from passion excited by real events; they wrote naturally, and as men: feeling powerfully as they did, their language was daring and figurative.

Action would erase the effeminate hypocrisies to which both poet and admiral considered themselves opposed. 'The ready way to make a mind grow awry is to lace it too tight,' Coleridge had written in his notebook in November 1801. Here were his passionate contemporaries, both of them his heroes, looking for resolution in violence.

Nelson had been dwelling on how to bring the French and Spanish fleet to a conclusive and final victory at least since October 1803. The long and grinding months on blockade off Toulon, the chase across the Atlantic and back again, the couple of weeks and the hectic discussions in England in August 1805 had all provided him with the opportunity to develop a plan. He was clear from the start. There was to be no shilly-shallying. 'The business of an English Commander-in-Chief,' he wrote in a memorandum probably written off Toulon in 1803, was to lay 'his ships close on board the Enemy, as expeditiously as possible; and secondly to continue them there, without separating, until the business is decided.' There was to be none of this long-distance elegance. It was to be close, bloody, attritional, naked and decisive. At this stage, he was thinking only of a relatively small fleet action, involving perhaps eight or nine ships on each side. Nelson's initial plan was quite conventional: to bring his full force to bear on a part of the enemy fleet, push through them to leeward, *à la* Howe, accept that some damage would be done to the British ships during the attack, but confident that straight dealing would overwhelm the enemy in detail.

Two years of dwelling on the question developed it. Nelson, predicting he would have more ships with him than turned out on the day, initially decided to attack in three divisions. One, made up of the fastest ships, would be held in reserve, to windward, to descend on any part of the battle where it looked as if they were needed. With the other two, as he told Sir Richard Keats, strolling on one of those August mornings in the garden at Merton,

> 'I shall go at them at once if I can, about one third of their line from the leading ship.' He then said, 'What do you think of it?' Such a question I felt required consideration. I paused. Seeing it he said, 'But I will tell you what *I* think of it. I think it will surprise and confound the Enemy. They won't know what I am about. It will bring forward a pell-mell Battle, and that is what I want.'

This, as the great naval historian Sir Julian Corbett described it, was 'a return to primitive methods: the three squadrons, the headlong charge and the mêlée. He seems to insist not so much upon defeating the enemy by concentration as by throwing him into confusion, upsetting his mental equilibrium in accordance with the primitive idea.' A scribbled note, recently discovered among a file of letters from Nelson to his elder brother, seems to have, on its reverse side, a rough sketch by Nelson of exactly such a plan in action, clearly describing his method of attack when in London in August 1805.

After Nelson joined the fleet, he described the plan to his captains on 29 September in the great cabin of the *Victory*:

> When I came to explain to them the 'Nelson touch' it was like an electric shock. Some shed tears, all approved – 'It was new – it was singular – it was simple!' and from Admirals downwards it was repeated – 'It must succeed, if ever they will allow us to get at them!'

The 'Nelson touch' was a phrase Nelson had often used in letters to Emma. Between them, it carried slight erotic overtones: 'Touch and take' was another variant he often used, implying closeness, that electricity, an intimate violence. Its meaning is nowhere spelled out, but it certainly cannot mean overwhelming the rear of the enemy fleet, nor of driving through them to the leeward side, as both of those tactics had been well known in the navy for 20 years. What it is much more likely to mean is the *style* of the attack: giving Collingwood complete command of the lee division; trusting his captains to their own initiative once the battle had begun; creating an atmosphere among them in which it felt impossible not to win; and as Collingwood wrote to Admiral Sir Thomas Pasley after the battle, 'to substitute for exact order an impetuous attack in two distinct bodies.' Those are the electrifying atmospherics which lie behind the victory at Trafalgar, the introduction of chaos as a tool of battle.

The written memorandum Nelson issued to his captains on 9 October is highly detailed: three divisions, two to attack, one as reinforcement; Collingwood's line to attack 12 from the rear of the enemy fleet; Nelson attacking in the centre; the enemy van to be left to its own devices. The plan, as described in the memorandum, does *not* describe a hell-for-leather chase all morning across the ocean to get to the enemy. The British fleet are to arrange themselves in their divisions just out of gunshot of the French, in close order, sailing parallel to them. Only then would the signal be given to attack, Collingwood's division first, in line abreast, followed by Nelson's, also in line abreast, the third division hanging off, waiting to see where its force could be brought with greatest effect.

This is so unlike what happened at Trafalgar that it left most of the captains confused. There was no reserve squadron and the ships designated for the reserve squadron were mostly attached in a slightly muddled way to Collingwood's line. The two columns did not gather themselves into coherent aggressive bodies just out of gunshot but each ship of each column plunged into battle one by one. The distance between the head and tail of each of the British columns was about 7 miles. As they approached, Collingwood gave the signal for each ship to make for the enemy ship nearest to him in the rear of the Combined Fleet, each pushing through, according to one of Howe's signals. Nelson apparently feinted towards the enemy van, keeping Villeneuve in a state of uncertainty, and then pulled back towards the centre and drove into the enemy in line ahead, pretty much on the Rodney model.

To a critical mind the whole approach was not only chaotic but intensely dangerous. There is one document in particular, anonymous but almost certainly written by an officer on board the *Conqueror*, Lieutenant Humphrey Senhouse, and almost certainly written soon after the event, which, a little tentatively, dared to criticise the haste and confusion with which Nelson jumped his fleet into the attack. 'Of the advantages and disadvantages of the mode of attack adopted by the British fleet,' Senhouse ventures, 'it may be considered presumptuous to speak, as the event was so completely successful.' The pall of perfection was already beginning to fall on Nelson's great battle. Senhouse then described what should have happened:

> If the regulated plan of attack had been adhered to, the English fleet should have borne up together, and have sailed in a line abreast in their respective divisions until they arrived up with the enemy. Thus the plan which consideration had matured would have been executed, than which perhaps nothing could have been better; the victory would have been more speedily decided, and the brunt of the action would have been more equally felt.

Senhouse was no bewigged stick-in-the-mud; he had volunteered for the terrifying role of sailing fireships into the Combined Fleet still at anchor in Cadiz. Nevertheless, this is the non-Nelsonian voice of order, consideration and regulation. It is the 18th century addressing the spontaneity and near-anarchy of Nelson's method. By the original plan, all except the lumpen sailers, the *Britannia*, *Dreadnought* and *Prince*, would have come into action at the same moment and the rear and centre of the Combined Fleet would have been crushed and eventually annihilated by the impact.

But that wasn't how Nelson did it on the day. Without forming into mutually supportive bodies of ships, the British fleet, raggedly arranged in its two columns, were even now being thrown into action like confetti at a wall, the difference being that this confetti was explosive and the wall far from strong. The reason for the British success at Trafalgar was not tactical. The tactics were immensely weak. The success depended on the independent ferocity and fighting aggression of each British ship and on the example of leadership given by Nelson to his captains. As Lieutenant Senhouse put it:

> The mode of attack, adopted with such success in the Trafalgar action, appears to me to have succeeded from the enthusiasm inspired throughout the British fleet from their being commanded by their beloved Nelson; from the gallant conduct of the leaders of the two divisions; from the individual exertions of each ship after the attack commenced, and the superior practice of the guns in the English fleet.

In others words, love, honour, zeal and skill won the day. Without those qualities, this officer maintained, or even with them when faced with a resolved and skilful enemy, it is perfectly possible that Trafalgar would have been a catastrophe.

Senhouse, after the event, allowed himself the luxury of imagining disaster. The two columns of the British fleet, in their slowness, are drifting down in the light airs towards the enemy. The day is calm and clear. The swell pushes through. All is alert. The bands are still playing. The British ships seem to hang, almost immobile, in front of the enemy cannon arrayed so thickly before them.

> The disadvantages of this mode of attack appear to consist in bringing forward the attacking force in a manner so leisurely and alternately, that an enemy of equal spirit and equal ability in seamanship and gunnery would have annihilated the ships one after another in detail, carried slowly on as they were by a heavy swell and light airs.

He is expert enough to know what a British fleet would have done if they were defending against such an attack.

> At a distance of one mile, five ships, at half a cable's length apart [100 yards] might direct their broadsides effectively against the head of the division for seven minutes, supposing the rate of sailing to have been four miles an hour; and within the distance of a half a mile three ships would do the same for seven minutes more, before the attacking ship could fire a gun in her defence.

Assuming a firing rate of a broadside about every 90 seconds, and each broadside firing an average of 37 guns, the leading ship would in the space of about quarter of an hour be sailing through a block of air filled with about 1,000 roundshot, each one aimed at its hull and rigging. If the wind fell, or a sudden calm came on, the leading ships would, in Senhouse's words 'be sacrificed before the rear could possibly come to their assistance.'

These are not the armchair thoughts of an amateur strategist reflecting much later on Trafalgar after all is over. This, among officers of the British fleet, is the quality of apprehension on the morning of Trafalgar itself. What is Nelson doing? Why does he not allow us to come up? What mad daring is this? How can he hope to survive? And among the French and Spanish, those questions must have been equally insistent. Nelson, for friend and enemy alike, was imposing exactly what he had told Keats a couple of months before: 'I think it will surprise and confound the Enemy. They won't know what I am about. It will bring forward a pell-mell Battle, and that is what I want.'

Confusion and its attendant chaos was, for all his planning, Nelson's chosen method of battle. He knew he would win like that, even if at some terrible cost to the British fleet. As the great 19th-century French naval historian Julien de la Gravière wrote, '*Le génie de Nelson c'est d'avoir compris notre faiblesse.*' The genius of Nelson was to have understood our weakness. Or, as Miles Padfield has written more recently, the chaotic, piecemeal mode of attack adopted by Nelson at Trafalgar was 'the tactics of disdain'.

Everything was visible as they approached: the broadsides of the enemy, with their iron teeth turned towards them, now and then trying the range of a shot to gauge the distance, so that they might, 'the moment we came within point blank (about six hundred yards) open their fire upon our van ships.' The *Santísima Trinidad*, with four distinct lines of red painted the length of her hull between the gunports, was clearly seen about eleven ships back from the van of the Combined line. Nelson was driving his column towards her. On the *Neptune*, just behind him, one of Fremantle's midshipmen, 16-year-old William Badcock, was gazing at the Spanish flagship,

> her head splendidly ornamented with a colossal group of figures, painted white, representing the Holy Trinity, from which she took her name. This magnificent ship was destined to be our opponent. She was lying to under topsails, top-gallant sails, royals, jib and spanker; her courses were hauled up; and her lofty towering sails looked beautiful, peering through the smoke, as she awaited the onset. The flags of France and Spain, both handsome, chequered the line, waving defiance to that of Britain.

Everything on every ship was now in order. The galley fires had been extinguished, flashproof screens made of thick woollen cloth known as 'fearnought' had been fitted around the hatchways through which powder from the magazines, where it was stowed in copper-hooped barrels which would make no sparks, would be passed; the shot racks in which the 18lb, 24lb and 32lb balls were stored had been drawn out from under their usual coverings; the guns, usually triced up tight to prevent movement at sea, had been cast loose. Crowbars – handspikes – used to lift and point the guns were lying at hand beside them on the decks. Goats and pigs had been sent down to the cable tier, the deepest and most protected level on the ships; the captain's ducks and geese were more often left in the coops to take their chance; Collingwood didn't move his pigs from their sty and they were killed during the battle. In the near lightless depths of the cockpit on the orlop deck, sails were spread out on chests, the surgeon's saws, knives, probes, bandages and tourniquets all put in order. The surgeon's task, as the Admiralty described it, was 'to be prepared for the reception of wounded men, and himself and his mates and assistants are to be ready and have everything at hand for stopping their blood and dressing their wounds.' The carpenter and his crew were ready down below with shot boards and plugs of wood with which to repair underwater damage from enemy fire.

Silence prevailed as the men and boys stood to their guns. Men tightened their handkerchiefs around their heads. On the leading ships, shot fell short alongside and then went over. Then, in *Victory*, a shot went clean through the main topgallant sail. Then seven or eight ships opened fire on her, 'a heavy and unremitting cannonade' and within a minute or two, as Dr Scott, Nelson's secretary, was speaking to Captain Hardy on the quarterdeck, a roundshot killed him. That is casually said, but what exactly happened when a cannonball hit a body?

It could cut a man in two; it could remove his head or any one of his limbs, not neatly but leaving a ragged tear where the limb had been. The man died either through sheer destruction of life-critical tissue – the hammocks in their netting were spattered with it – or through the rapid loss of very large quantities of blood. For a few moments, the heart might respond to the trauma by increasing the pulse-rate, but that response would only have the effect of killing the victim faster. Scott's blood would have pumped out all over the quarter-deck, his flesh would have begun to turn pale, his mashed remains would have been thrown over the side, and the only memory of this sophisticated, multi-lingual, doggedly loyal man, who wrote letters to Emma on Nelson's behalf, would have been a pool of blood on *Victory*'s pale deck timbers of Prussian deal.

'Is that poor Scott who has gone?' Nelson asked, suddenly looking round, a question that reveals how death could appear so casually here; a man Nelson knew as well as any other, walking on his quarterdeck, speaking to his captain, and then, in the next instant gone, not lying there as an elegant corpse, but his identity erased, his body not butchered or hurt but mangled and distorted, a muddle of blood and bone and half-human features where a man had been.

When *Victory* was 500 yards from the enemy line, her mizzen topmast was shot away. Another shot struck and destroyed the wheel. Within another two minutes, a double-headed shot – a heavy, stubby bar of metal which spun through the air – sliced through a line of eight marines, killing every one of them. Yet another smashed into a launch, hit the deck of the *Victory* and a splinter flew towards where Hardy and Nelson were walking on the quarterdeck. It tore off the buckle from Hardy's left shoe.

> They both instantly stopped, and were observed by the Officers on deck to survey each other with inquiring looks, each supposing the other to be wounded. His Lordship then smiled and said, 'This is too warm work, Hardy, to last long.'

For young Lieutenant Nicolas on the *Belleisle*, newly challenged to the display of phlegm, war became suddenly horrifying:

> The shot began to pass over us and gave us an intimation of what we should in a few minutes undergo. A shriek soon followed – a cry of agony was produced by the next shot – and the loss of the head of a poor recruit was the effect of the succeeding, and as we advanced, destruction rapidly increased. A severe contusion on the breast now prostrated our Captain, but he soon resumed his station. Those only who have been in a similar situation to the one I am attempting to describe can have a correct idea of such a scene. My eyes were horrorstruck at the bloody corpses around me, and my ears rang with the shrieks of the wounded and the moans of the dying.

On the decks of the *Belleisle* a dozen men lay dead. Ten more were wounded and in the hands of the surgeon far below. Between the decks, at least protected by the thickness of the oak, there was nevertheless tangible fear: no noise, no laughter, no show of hilarity; perhaps some jokes but nothing more. Men stood there listening, or peering out through the gunports to judge the distance. 'I felt a difficulty in swallowing,' one sailor, Charles Pemberton, remembered of just such an attack a few years later.

> Now if we had gone at it at once, without this chilling prelude, why I dare say I should have known very little about that thing which we call fear. 'Stand to your guns!' at last came in a peal through the stillness from the captain's speaking trumpet; it swept fore and aft with such clear force, as though it had been spoken within a foot of the ear, and seemed to dash down into the holds, and penetrate to the very keel.

> Take good aim! Ready the first platoon. Ready? Aye, every one was ready; stern, fixed, rigid, in soul – pliant, elastic in body

When at sea, the drummer beat the men to quarters every night. The entire ship knew what its fighting quarters were, eight men and a boy to the lightest guns, fifteen of them to the heavy 32-pounders, and they habitually sang to the drummed rhythm.

Not now though. All is perfect death-like silence. The guns have been shotted and the slow-matches lit and placed in their tubs, a stand-by system in case the flintlocks misfired. The lieutenants have been through the decks, reminding the marines and those seamen who are designated as boarders, what to do if they were ordered to board the enemy. Pikes, cutlasses, and pistols have been issued and stowed. Buckets of good sweet drinking water and tubs of cinders or sand, for when the deck becomes wet or slippery, have been placed between each pair of guns. Behind them the grape and canister, the roundshot, the waddings, the powder cartridges and the powder horn are all laid out according to designated patterns. Pistols are kept ready in case a gun should fail to discharge when the flintlock is released. If a gun 'hangs fire' like that, a 'pistol with half a cartridge of powder fired slantway down the touch hole of the gun will always discharge the gun.' As it does so, a burst of blame drives up from that touch hole and scorches the deck beams above. The captains have toured all parts and urged the men 'to courage and duty'.

On the *Neptune*, Thomas Fremantle speaks to his men at their different quarters. They were to think of their country, and all that was dear to them. The fate of England, as Able Seaman James Martin remembered Fremantle's words

> Hung upon a Ballance and their Happyness Depended upon us and their Safty also Happy the Man who Boldly Venture his Life in such a Cause if he shold Survive the Battle how Sweet will be the Recolection and if he fall he fall Covred with Glory and Honnor and Morned By a Greatfull Country the Brave Live Gloryous and Lemented Die

That's why Nelson loved Fremantle: because Fremantle loved England and everything in it and understood what might be called the 'Achilles Deal' which Nelsonian battle required. What Martin may not have realised is that Fremantle was remembering the inspirational words he had read in Pope's translation of the *Iliad*, Book V, in which Diomed addresses the Greek warriors:

> Ye Greeks, be men! the charge of battle bear;
> Your brave associates and yourselves revere!
> Let glorious acts more glorious acts inspire,
> And catch from breast to breast the noble fire!
> On valour's side the odds of combat lie,
> The brave live glorious, or lamented die;

Men were stationed in the tops – narrow platforms on each mast which gave an overview of neighbouring ships – their duty both to trim the sails and, in some ships, to fire down with muskets on the enemy poop and quarterdeck if it came to close action. Others on the forecastle and poop had as their task the handling of the sails during the battle: to back the topsails if the ship needed to lose way, to haul on the braces of the great yards if the ship was to tack or wear. Every man was at his quarters. The moment of intimacy was upon them.

Part II

BATTLE

October 21st 1805
12.30 pm to 5 pm

6

VIOLENCE

October 21st, 1805
12.30 pm to 2.15 pm

War: the exercise of violence under sovereign command against withstanders
SAMUEL JOHNSON, *A Dictionary of the English Language*, 1755

Every man stood in the quiet of terror and discipline waiting for the first noise of battle. When it came, it sounded, it was said, 'like the tearing of sails, just over our heads.' But nothing except the air was being torn: this was simply 'the wind of the enemy's shot', a passage of metal at speed through air. If it passed close enough to you, it could, without touching, kill, merely with the shock of the pressure wave that a travelling projectile creates. Unblemished men would fall dead on the deck as the roundshot passed. Others, extraordinarily, found their clothes on fire. The level of noise grew to a pitch nothing else in life could match. Each ship trembled, deep into its frames and keel, with the reverberation of its own guns firing. The ship was a place of yelling, the guns roaring, the blocks and tackles with which they were hauled out through the gunports and manoeuvred to bear on the enemy, screaming and squealing like pigs on the point of slaughter. The noise of ingoing and outgoing fire could scarcely be distinguished. From within the lower decks of the ships, enemy shot could be heard striking on the hull and bouncing away, but all part of a maniacal frenzy of noise, 'like some awfully tremendous thunder-storm, whose deafening roar is attended by incessant streaks of lightning, carrying death in every flash and strewing the ground with the victims of its wrath: only, in our case, the scene was rendered more horrible than that, by the presence of torrents of blood which dyed our decks.'

No account survives of the experience in detail of the gunfight at Trafalgar, but in its place can be put the words of a thirteen-year-old powder-monkey called Samuel Leech, who experienced a brutal frigate action in the 1812 war against the United States. Leech was a political radical, deeply distrustful of the violent methods of navy discipline and of the inadequacy of the officer class. Something of that political and social rage undoubtedly colours his account but does not entirely devalue it. About a third of the crew of his frigate was either killed or wounded in the action against a large American, armed with more and heavier guns. Here, in Leech's words, almost uniquely is the atmosphere between decks in the days of sailing battle. It is a scene of unequivocal horror. The firing has already begun:

> I was busily supplying my gun with powder, when I saw blood suddenly fly from the arm of a man stationed at our gun. I saw nothing strike him; the effect alone was visible; in an instant, the third lieutenant tied his handkerchief round the wounded arm, and sent the groaning wretch below to the surgeon.

In this, as in most battles, cause and effect seem scarcely to relate. The damage seems to emerge from the air itself.

> The cries of the wounded now rang through all parts of the ship. These were carried to the cockpit as fast as they fell, while those more fortunate men, who

were killed outright, were immediately thrown overboard. As I was stationed but a short distance from the main hatchway, I could catch a glance at all who were carried below. A glance was all I could indulge in, for the boys belonging to the guns next to mine were wounded in the early part of the action, and I had to spring with all my might to keep three or four guns supplied with cartridges. I saw two of these lads fall nearly together. One of them was struck in the leg by a large shot; he had to suffer amputation above the wound. The other had a grape or canister shot sent through his ankle. A stout Yorkshireman lifted him in his arms and hurried him to the cockpit. He had his foot cut off, and was thus made lame for life. Two of the boys stationed on the quarter deck were killed. They were both Portuguese. A man, who saw one of them killed, afterwards told me that his powder caught fire and burnt the flesh almost off his face. In this pitiable situation, the agonized boy lifted up both hands, as if imploring relief, when a passing shot instantly cut him in two.

I was an eye-witness to a sight equally revolting. A man named Aldrich had his hands cut off by a shot, and almost at the same moment he received another shot, which tore open his bowels in a terrible manner. As he fell, two or three men caught him in their arms, and, as he could not live, threw him overboard.

The sheer shambolic squalor of these battles is not to be underestimated. The ships were smeared with blood. The blood rolling to and fro across the deck painted patterns on the clean-scrubbed deal. Afterwards, large parts of the ships had to be repainted and each ship carried in its stores the paint necessary to efface the gore.

Nor were these single crises. The cannonading, or the 'smart salute' of the broadside, as 19th-century commentators on naval warfare often liked to call it, went on often for an hour or even more at a time. There was no quick solution to the destruction of men for the most part hidden within the walls of their floating wooden blockhouse. Down on the maindeck, manfully bringing his powder to the guns from the magazine, Leech saw death and wounding around him again and again.

> One of the officers in my division also fell in my sight. He was a noble-hearted fellow, named Nan Kivell. A grape or canister shot struck him near the heart: exclaiming, 'Oh! my God!' he fell, and was carried below, where he shortly after died.

Grape and canister shot poured through the port-holes 'like leaden rain'. The sound of the large shot striking the ship's side was 'like iron hail'. The whole body of the ship was shaken by their impact, a deep, groaning thudding. Even worse, when these 24lb or 32lb balls penetrated the hull, giant splinters, several feet long, would go spinning through the confined space of the gundecks, killing and maiming any bodies trying to inhabit what had become knife-filled air. A shot that came through the gunports was called 'a slaughtering one' and it usually killed or wounded the entire gun crew. The dead were then shoved out into the sea by the hole through which their death had come.

Men, in these circumstances, do not react, as one might imagine, with shrinking terror. There is a mindlessness to a battle of this intensity. What is repeated again and again, in all accounts of Trafalgar and other battles, is the cheering, 'the deep roar of the outpoured and constantly reiterated 'Hurra! Hurra! Hurra!' They cheer each other on, filling with the noise of their own voices the space which terror might inhabit. Leech addresses the strangeness of that behaviour:

The battle went on. Our men kept cheering with all their might. I cheered with them, though I confess I scarcely knew for what. Certainly there was nothing very inspiriting in the aspect of things where I was stationed. So terrible had been the work of destruction round us, it was termed the slaughter-house. Not only had we had several boys and men killed or wounded, but several of the guns were disabled. The one I belonged to had a piece of the muzzle knocked out; and when the ship rolled, it struck a beam of the upper deck with such force as to become jammed and fixed in that position. A twenty-four-pound shot had also passed through the screen of the magazine, immediately over the orifice through which we passed our powder. The schoolmaster received a death wound. The brave boatswain, who came from the sick bay to the din of battle, was fastening a stopper on a back-stay which had been shot away, when his head was smashed to pieces by a cannon-ball; another man, going to complete the unfinished task, was also struck down. Another of our midshipmen also received a severe wound. A fellow named John, who, for some petty offence, had been sent on board as a punishment, was carried past me, wounded. I distinctly heard the large blood-drops fall pat, pat, pat, on the deck; his wounds were mortal. Even a poor goat, kept by the officers for her milk, did not escape the general carnage; her hind legs were shot off, and poor Nan was thrown overboard.

I have often been asked what were my feelings during this fight. I felt pretty much as I suppose every one does at such a time. That men are without thought when they stand amid the dying and the dead is too absurd an idea to be entertained a moment. We all appeared cheerful, but I know that many a serious thought ran through my mind: still,

> what could we do but keep up a semblance, at least, of animation? To run from our quarters would have been certain death from the hands of our own officers; to give way to gloom, or to show fear, would do no good, and might brand us with the name of cowards, and ensure certain defeat. Our only true philosophy, therefore, was to make the best of our situation by fighting bravely and cheerfully.

Although there is no direct evidence of coercion by British officers at Trafalgar, Leech distinctly heard one of the reasons that the men kept at their work on his frigate. 'A few of the junior midshipmen were stationed below, on the berth deck, with orders, given in our hearing, to shoot any man who attempted to run from his quarters.' It was a violent and unhappy ship but there were equally violent and disciplinarian captains at Trafalgar. The prospect of instantaneous execution by one's own officers might well have persuaded the reluctant to fight longer and harder than they otherwise would. There is certainly evidence from Trafalgar of intense loathing between the lower and the quarterdecks. The seaman known as Jack Nastyface, on the *Revenge*, later told a grisly story:

> We had a midshipman on board our ship of a wickedly mischievous disposition [a more serious accusation in early 19th-century English than nowadays], whose sole delight was to insult the feelings of the seamen, and furnish pretexts to get them punished. His conduct made every man's life miserable that happened to be under his orders. He was a youth not more than twelve or thirteen years of age; but I have often seen him get on the carriage of a gun, call a man to him and kick him about the thighs and body, and with his fist would beat him about the head; and these, although prime seamen, at the same time dared not murmur. It was ordained however, by

> Providence, that his reign of terror and severity should not last; for during the engagement, he was killed on the quarter-deck by a grape shot, his body greatly mutilated, his entrails being driven and scattered against the larboard side; nor were there any lamentations for his fate! – No! for when it was known that he was killed, the general exclamation was, '*Thank God, we are rid of the young tyrant.*'

Here, then, is the amalgam of the British ship-of-the-line going into battle: on the quarter-deck and among the officers of the marines, an overwhelming sense of what needs to be done, of the 'parts that became them' in the drama of violence. Zeal, order, honour, love and daring were all aspects of duty, as was the steady doing of violence to the enemy. That is what Nelson's signal to the men of England had meant. The officers are beautifully dressed, wearing silk stockings and shoes, not the seaboots most of them wore at sea, maintaining the upright stance of men indifferent to terror. Heroism for them was violence phlegmatically done. Collingwood, on the *Royal Sovereign*, as the shot flew around them, as his men were dying, carefully and elaborately folded up a studding sail, which was hanging over the starboard bulwarks, saying to his first lieutenant that they could not know when they might need it next. Watched by the Spaniards, they stored it away in one of the *Royal Sovereign*'s boats. On the *Belleisle*, as her great guns and those on the *Fougueux* dealt out to each other mutual and dreadful slaughter, Captain Harwood, walking on the quarterdeck, came across John Owen, who was his captain of marines, and offered to share with him a bunch of grapes. The two of them stood on the quarter-deck, watching the battle in which the *Fougueux* lost her mainmast and mizzenmast and the *Belleisle* lost all three, eating grapes, discussing the future.

Around them, on the decks below them and in the

rigging above, the men, the people, were acting to different urges. For every £1,000 of prize money which a captain might expect to receive from a captured enemy vessel, the average seaman might receive £2 or £3. That is a measure not of a continuum between the two classes but a chasm, the two sorts of people occupying different mental worlds. The band of brothers did not include the men below. They were below physically, socially and conceptually and their reaction to this air thick with violence was the opposite of the stoical refined silence which honour imposed on the officers. The crews did not contain the tension but released it by pure aggression and bellowing, some of them even in mid-battle unable to resist poking their 'heads through an idle port [to see the smoke] bursting forth from the many black iron mouths, and whirling rapidly in thick rings, till it swells into hills and mountains, through which the sharp red tongue of death darts flash after flash. The smoke slowly rolls upwards like a curtain, in awful beauty, and exhibits the glistening water and the hulls of the combatants beneath.' That seaman, Charles Pemberton, later became a playwright. His memories, recollected in tranquillity, are coloured by a retrospective literariness in a way that Leech's are not, but still his account of battle seems to describe an engagement with brutalism which is only rarely recorded from warfare but explains much of what happens during it. For Pemberton, quite explicitly battle is a moment of extreme and passionate violence:

> Often we could not see for the smoke, whether we were firing at a foe or friend, and as to hearing, the noise of the guns had so completely made us deaf, that we were obliged to look only to the motions that were made. Sulphur and fire, agony, death and horror, are riding and revelling on the bosom of the sea; yet how gently, brightly playful is its face! To see

> and hear this! What a maddening of the brain it causes! Yet it is a delirium of joy, a very fury of delight!

There, in a rare moment of excess, some kind of truth is uttered. For those in the horror of battle, it is not horror but delight, a form of the sublime, a moment in which the collapse and disintegration around them, the excess of energy, finds sudden and explosive release in 'a very fury of delight.'

Nelson wanted a conflict that was indescribable, not in the sense of moral revulsion, but as a plain narrative fact. The pell-mell battle, the anarchy in which the individual fighting energies of individual ships and men were released, could not submit to narrative convention. The fleets become their ships, the ships their men, the men their instincts. Decision-making moves from admirals to captains, to gun captains, to the powder-monkeys, the surgeons and their assistants buried in the bloody dark of their cockpits. Life – and death – in Nelsonian battle is atomised, broken into its constituent parts, made to rely not on the large scale manoeuvring of destructive force, but the will to kill and to live. Already, in the first moment of engagement, as *Royal Sovereign* entered the killing zone, that atomisation had begun. Every ship in all fleets considered that they fought Trafalgar almost entirely on their own. The literal fog of battle threw them in on themselves, a half-blind and in most places nearly fearless frenzy from which the British emerged victors and the French and Spanish destroyed. It was the chaos which Nelson required and which his daring approach had imposed on the enemy.

Trafalgar, nevertheless, can be seen to have three distinct phases: the first battle between Collingwood's division and the rear of the Combined Fleet; the long-drawn-out mutual battering between Nelson's division and the centre of the

Combined Fleet; and finally, the battle between the van of the Combined Fleet, which had sailed away from the battle to start with, and a series of individual British ships which, very late in the battle, it had turned to attack. The two conflicting principles of war and of human organisation are apparent in all three phases: fragmentary British aggression, as if the British fleet were an explosive charge, breaking and scattering into tens of equally explosive pieces, coming up against the defensive wall of the Combined Fleet. That wall was inadequate because it was broken from the start, and the detonating elements of British aggression – the individual ships – found their way between the blocks of which it was made, so that their violence did not break like a wave against a seawall, but entered the body of the enemy's defences and destroyed them from within.

The leading ships, of all three navies, knew that this was to be a tight, close-range affair. Spanish and French ships had prepared for the battle with grappling irons and extensive training in boarding the enemy which those irons held alongside. Grenades were prepared to be thrown down the enemy hatches from the tops of all three masts. The British had loaded their guns with two or even three shots each: ineffective at long range but delivering multiple killing and splinter-creating blows at short range. Every British ship, and several of the Combined Fleet, were armed with short range, large calibre, deck-mounted guns known as carronades, which were mounted not on a conventional gun carriage but on a pivot and swivel which would allow them to sweep the decks of enemy ships alongside. British crews were also provided with lengths of line, which once they had got deep among the mass of the enemy, they could use to lash the French and Spanish ships to their own, holding them there, not hundreds of yards away, not even a few feet away, but bound to each other, their hulls touching at water level, their yards and bowsprits tangled up high above, so that the enemy could not withdraw from the murderous onslaught of the broadsides which one after another were fired through them and into them. Close to, guns were loaded with reduced powder, to slow down the shot and ensure it remained within the hull of the enemy alongside and didn't burst through to damage a friendly ship beyond it. Guns on high decks were aimed below the horizontal so that the shot would smash their way downwards through deck after deck. The big guns on the lowest tier were aimed upwards, so that in the enemy ship their shot would erupt through the decks beneath men's feet, destroying men's bodies from below. It is as if a boxer, with one hand, was holding the head of his opponent which, with his other, he then bludgeons into submission.

The intimacy of this battle meant that in some ships the muzzles of the French and English guns touched each other. An average British ship, like the *Polyphemus*, eighth behind the *Royal Sovereign,* expended 1,000 24lb shots and 900 18lb shots in the course of the battle, a weight equivalent to 18 tons of cast iron fired at a muzzle velocity capable of killing men and destroying masts at the range of a mile, but here fired into the faces of people six or eight feet away. In many ships, more than 7,000 lbs of gunpowder was used during the engagement. What is extraordinary is not that people died or that ship structures were savaged but that anyone or anything survived.

That story repeats itself again and again at Trafalgar, beginning at the moment that the *Royal Sovereign* broke into the Combined line. Collingwood had aimed just astern of the *Santa Ana*, who had backed her mizzen top-sail to take the way off her. The British ship fired not a shot, apart from one or two to create a curtain of smoke around her, until her guns bore on the Spanish flagship. Collingwood had ordered his guns double-shotted and as they passed under the windows of the stern galleries, the huge, glazed glories of a ship-of-the-line, set in dazzlingly carved and gilded woodwork, the most theatrical, most honourable and in retrospect most absurd aspect of a ship-of-the-line, behind which admirals and captains had their cabins, and providing by far the weakest point in the entire structure, the *Royal Sovereign* gunners fired one by one, as their guns came to bear.

Any shot that entered through those galleries would travel the length of the ship on all three of its decks. No bulkheads or transverse timbers would interrupt their flight. They would slaughter without difficulty every creature, human and animal in their path. To achieve this longitudinal devastation of a ship – called since the mid-17th century a 'raking' – from a position in which no enemy broadside could be brought to bear, was the aim and the ideal of all late-18th-century ship tactics and the moment of the *Royal Sovereign*'s passing of the *Santa Ana*, achieved through Nelson's daring perpendicular approach, was the apotheosis of the killing craft.

The *Santa Ana* carried a crew of some 800 officers, marines and men; 240 of them were killed or wounded in the first raking broadside from the *Royal Sovereign*. If Collingwood's flagship was travelling at about 2 knots, gliding forward at a rate of about 3 feet a second – in the very light airs, both studding sails and the main- and fore-courses were shaken out; they wanted every bit of speed out of her they could – she would have taken almost exactly a minute to pass under the stern of the *Santa Ana*. That first minute of Trafalgar devastated the Spaniards, half of them recently swept up from the gutters of Cadiz. One Spaniard after the battle was found still to be in the Harlequin clothes he had been wearing when taken from the theatre where he had been entertaining the people of Cadiz. During this minute on the *Santa Ana* they were killed and wounded at a rate of nearly 4 men a second, a

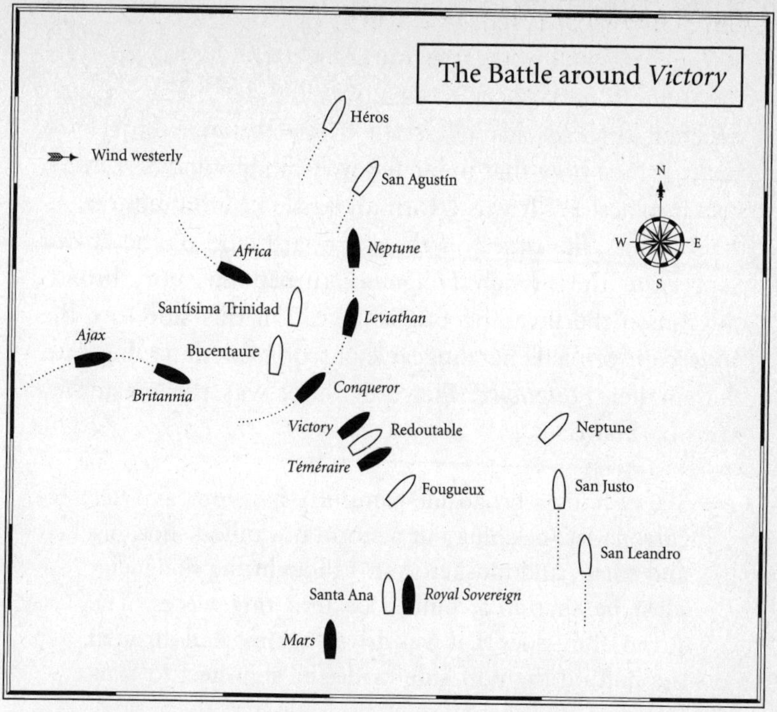

screaming, frenzied, terrifying minute, from which there would have been no escape, and in which the scenes between decks must have been beyond description.

On the long approach of the *Royal Sovereign*, they had scarcely managed to land a single shot on target. The cold silence of the approaching English guns, and the knowledge that this enemy, with such a ruthless reputation, was planning to pass under their desperately vulnerable stern – that can hardly have helped Spanish resolve. Now the *Sovereign*'s weight of metal plunged through her crew, totally disabling 14 of the *Santa Ana*'s guns, the full broadside of 50 guns fired once, half of them able to fire again. This was shock and awe. As Collingwood stood on the quarter-deck of his calmly advancing ship, he called out to his captain: 'Rotherham, what would Nelson give to be here?' There was delight in battle if battle was like this, in the supremely effective imposition of overwhelmingly damaging force. Two miles away to the northwest, Nelson watched through his telescope from the quarter-deck of *Victory*: 'See how that noble fellow Collingwood carries his ship into action'. It was a form of battle he admired too.

At the same time, on the starboard side of the *Royal Sovereign*, the French *Fougueux* turned her port broadside on to the invading Englishman. On this side too, the *Sovereign* replied, her huge weight of iron slamming into the smaller *Fougueux*. Pierre Servaux was the master-at-arms on board:

> She gave us a broadside from fifty-five guns and her carronades, belching out a storm of cannon shot, big and small, and musket-shot. I thought the Fougueux must be shattered, pulverised into tiny pieces. The storm of missiles that was driven against and through the hull on the port side made the ship heel to starboard. The larger part of the sails and the rigging was cut to pieces, while the upper deck was swept clear of most of the seamen who were working there and of the marksmen. On the gundecks below, there was less damage. There, not more than thirty men were put out of action. This preliminary greeting, rough and brutal as it was, did not dishearten our men. A well-maintained fire showed the Englishmen that we too had guns and could use them.

Servaux's cool-headed account of that first blast of the iron wind from a British ship-of-the-line is revealing on several counts. There is, to begin with, the sheer volume of aggressive metal which the big three-decker can deliver. Initial shock, conveyed by hugely powerful ships at the head of the two columns, was central to Nelson's scheme. It established a devastating advantage from which recovery was nearly impossible. But Servaux also makes clear two crucial facts about this form of attack. First, the effect of raking fire and the effect of a broadside received broadside-on is the difference between a battle and a slaughter. Raking fire, poured through the stern or bow of a ship, encountered no obstacle on its way. It met the vulnerable bodies of men and guns as violently as it had left the muzzles from which it had been fired. But gunfire which had to punch its way through the oak walls of the enemy ship could have no such effect. Its killing power was blunted by the density of the wooden defences. Even a broadside that drove the receiving ship over with the impact, as if caught in a vicious squall, did not disable a ship in the way that the *Santa Ana* was smashed by the raking fire on the *Sovereign*'s other broadside. Sailing skill, sheer deftness of manoeuvre and the alacrity with which crews would jump to instructions, either turning the ship into a position where it could rake its enemy, or turn itself away from raking fire, were the factors on which life or death depended.

Further than that, in Servaux's words, the difference could not be clearer between the horror of exposure on the upper decks – the forecastle, the quarterdeck and the poop – and the relative safety of the oak-bulwarked gun-decks below. Those upper decks were where the leading figures of the ship needed to be during the battle. Captains, first lieutenants, and masters were all to be found on the quarterdeck, boatswains, other petty officers and prime seamen on the forecastle, marine officers on the poop. These places were where the killing and wounding was done and so among these ranks, in ship after ship, the proportion of casualties often rose to well over a third or even a half. The more significant the man at Trafalgar, the more vulnerable he was.

These conditions were common to all sides, given the current technology. Why, one might ask, did the commanders not have constructed for themselves a quarterdeck shelter, in which they might be as protected from shot and musket-fire as those on the decks below them? Was self-exposure so central a part of the code of honour that a sailing ship-of-the-line, governed as these were, would not in fact have been operable in battle without it? It may be, at some subliminal level, that this self-sacrificial style of command also fed into the fighting capacity of ships. If his officers were prepared to expose themselves to so much danger, then what could a man do but follow their lead? It is precisely the opposite of generals commanding later battles from many tens of miles behind the front. Here the commanders placed themselves on the point of the spear.

It was not a complicated method, it was inherently bloody and it meant that officers needed to wait in the danger zone for long periods while the great guns did their work. That long period of exposure was an inescapable part of the theatre of battle. They had no protection, beyond the hammocks in their netting containers on either side of the quarterdeck, and the horizontal nets drawn taut above their heads to save them from falling debris. Neither was any use against roundshot, langridge or musket-fire. And the theatrical role played by honour, combined with the style of personal leadership Nelson had developed, meant that neither he nor any other officer could hide. Exposure of the person was more than an inherent hazard; it was an essential part of the task.

But there is one further and governing point which emerges from Pierre Servaux's words: a deep, inbuilt sense of inferiority. They were not 'disheartened' by the brutal aggression. They could show the Englishmen that they had guns too. That is the language of defeat, of keeping one's end up, of showing the better man that you are a man too. In that innermost, erosive doubt much of the outcome of Trafalgar is decided.

Collingwood was many minutes ahead of the next ship behind him, the *Belleisle*. Gathering to the aid of the *Santa Ana*, French and Spanish ships clustered like wasps around the intruder: the *Fougueux* raked the *Royal Sovereign* from astern; the *San Leandro* from ahead; the *San Justo* was cannonading her from 300 yards off her starboard bow; the *Indomptable* from off her starboard quarter. Shots were perfectly visible as they came towards the men on board, at least from the upper decks, and in these few minutes, so many were being fired at the *Royal Sovereign* that the crew frequently saw shots from different ships collide, or glance off each other, as if in a game of demonic aerial billiards. But the *Royal Sovereign* stuck to her guns. Once past the stern of the *Santa Ana*, Collingwood turned hard to port and ranged his ship right alongside the Spanish flagship.

Muzzle to muzzle for about two hours they fired man-killing shots into each other's bellies. The British fired perhaps eighty broadsides in that time, the Spanish perhaps twenty-five or thirty. The aim was not to sink the other ship but to kill the other crew, or at least enough of them for their officers to consider any continuation hopeless, and those mathematics are the facts on which victory was founded. By about 2.15, the officers of the *Santa Ana* decided to surrender. Her starboard side, next to the *Sovereign*'s guns, had been 'very nearly beaten in' by the shot fired into it. Nearly all her officers were dead or wounded and they surrendered, as was the convention, by hauling down her flag. At almost the same moment, the mizzenmast on the *Royal Sovereign* collapsed, shot through by the fire of the five ships which had surrounded her. A few minutes later, the mainmast followed, leaving only the foremast standing, and that, as the expression of the time had it, 'tottering and wounded'. Records and figures of dead and wounded on French and Spanish ships are sketchy, but on the British ships exact. There were 47 men dead on the *Sovereign* and 95 wounded, half of them severely, out of a ship's company of about 600. The Spanish had inflicted casualties at a rate of about 25%; the British had probably killed or wounded about 50% of the enemy. That is the winning difference.

The *Belleisle* strode in after the *Royal Sovereign*, through the same gap Collingwood had entered, and the *Belleisle* again savaged the *Santa Ana* from astern, another double-shotted load with a canister of grape shot on top of them. These methods of warfare do not aim at individual destruction; they make environments murderous. The air between decks in a well-raked ship was as unsurvivable as any No-Man's-Land over which machine guns played.

On all ships engaged in this form of brutal action, winning or losing, the damage was horrifying. 'I now went below,' Samuel Leech wrote of his encounter with a heavily armed American frigate in 1812, after his own outgunned ship had surrendered,

> to see how matters appeared there. The first object I met was a man bearing a limb, which had just been detached from some suffering wretch. Pursuing my way to the ward-room, I necessarily passed through the steerage, which was strewed with the wounded: it was a sad spectacle, made more appalling by the groans and cries which rent the air. Some were groaning, others were swearing most bitterly, a few were praying, while those last arrived were begging most piteously to have their wounds dressed next. The surgeon and his mate were smeared with blood from head to foot: they looked more like butchers than doctors.

Here the sea was full of the bodies of scorched, butchered and mangled people. On board the defeated ships, the scene confronting the British officers was one of cinematic horror. A British midshipman went on board the *Santísima Trinidad*:

> She had between 3 and 400 killed and wounded, her Beams where coverd with Blood, Brains, and pieces of Flesh, and the after part of her Decks with wounded, some without Legs and some without an Arm; what calamities War brings on, and what a number of Lives where put an end to on the 21st.

The companionway steps, leading down from deck to deck, were in the most brutalised ships so covered in blood that you could hardly walk on them without slipping. Nor is the sense of revulsion a modern reaction. 'Such was the horror that filled' the mind of the chaplain on board the *Victory*, the Rev. Dr Scott,

> that it haunted him like a shocking dream for years afterwards. He never talked of it. Indeed the only record of a remark on the subject was one extorted from him by the inquiries of a friend, soon after his return home. The expression that escaped him at the moment was, 'it was like a butcher's shambles.'

Lieutenant William Ram of the *Victory* was brought down into the cockpit where the surgeons were working on the wounded. Ram was not aware as he was carried down below quite how desperate his condition was. The surgeon looked at him and the young man was told the seriousness of his wound.

> On discovering it, he tore off with his own hand the ligatures that were being applied, and bled to death. Almost frenzied by the sight of this, Scott hurried wildly to the deck for relief, perfectly regardless of his own safety. He rushed up the companion-ladder, now slippery with gore, to the scene above [where] all was noise, confusion, and smoke.

On board the *Leviathan*,

> a shot took off the arm of Thomas Main, when at his gun on the forecastle; his messmates kindly offered to assist him in going to the Surgeon; but he bluntly said, 'I thank you stay where you are; you will do more good there:' he then went down by himself to the cockpit. The Surgeon (who respected him) would willingly have attended him, in preference to others whose wounds were less alarming; but Main would not admit of it, saying 'Avast, not until it come to my turn if you please.' The Surgeon soon after amputated the shattered part of the arm, near the shoulder; during which, with great composure, smiling, and with a clear steady voice, he sang the whole of 'Rule Britannia'.

A note survives on Thomas Main, written by his captain, Henry Bayntun, dated December 1st 1805, Plymouth:

> I am sorry to inform you, that the above-mentioned fine fellow died since writing the above, At Gibraltar Hospital, of a fever he caught, when the stump of his arm was nearly well. H.B.

* * *

In an area of sea about one and a half miles long and half a mile wide, a series of individual ship-actions developed in which the brutal facts were laid out: if one ship in the encounter could kill more of the people on the other, the victory went to them. The ships of each fleet manoeuvred into contact with their enemy. Each attempted to find those positions ahead or astern from which they could inflict ultimate damage and have none or little done to them in return. It was like a wrestling match, close to and sweaty, in which each was looking to turn the other.

Astern of Collingwood, the *Belleisle* found herself

embroiled with crowds of French and Spanish ships coming on to her as the rear of the Combined Fleet sailed up into the battle. The *San Juan Nepomuceno*, the *Fougueux*, the French *Achille*, the *Aigle*, the *San Justo* and the *San Leandro* and the French *Neptune* all attacked her one after another. Her masts fell in a vast tangle of rigging, sails and spars which blocked her gunports and prevented her from either manoeuvring or firing in her own defence. Only when ships in Collingwood's column crowded into the same mêlée, was she saved from utter destruction. Of all the British ships, she was the most horrifically damaged. All three masts and bowsprit had been shot away. Her hull was 'knocked almost to pieces'. The only place they could raise an ensign on board was on the end of pike held aloft. Without her rig above her, the body of the mauled *Belleisle* rolled like a hog in the swell. But here is a strange and significant fact. No ship in the British fleet should have been more murderously treated and yet, at the end of the battle, out of her crew of 750, only thirty-one of her men were dead and 93 wounded. Here too is one of the governing facts of Trafalgar. The captains and gunners of the Combined Fleet failed in the one essential: killing large numbers of the enemy.

The *Polyphemus* came to the *Belleisle*'s rescue, then the *Defiance*, the *Tonnant* and the *Swiftsure*. The crews of each ship cheered as the others came past and drove into the fighting. The *Mars*, miscalculating a manoeuvre, suddenly found herself stern on to the *Monarca* and the *Algésiras* and then bow-on to the *Pluton*. Captain Duff had allowed his ship to become caught in the most dangerous geometry which sailing battle could offer. It was then that a ball from the *Pluton* struck him on the chest, drove upwards, removed his head and left his trunk lying dead on the gangway just forward of the quarter-deck. The same shot scything through flesh, killed two seamen behind him.

The men of the *Mars* gathered the trunk of their dead captain, held it up and gave three cheers 'to show they were not discouraged by it, and they returned to their guns'. Duff's first lieutenant, William Hennah, appalled at the death of a man he loved, instantly took over command. The ship then drifted out of the battle, all three of her masts still there but with not a single foot of standing rigging having survived the high-aimed and slashingly destructive fire that had been poured into her and killed and wounded 98 of her crew. If a single sail had been raised, the masts would have collapsed. In the ship's log, her master Thomas Cook wrote, in words thicker with emotion than most logs allow for, 'Poop and Quarter Deck almost destitute the carnage was so great.' Even so, none of the ships of the Combined Fleet attempted to take either the *Mars* or the *Belleisle*, one of the failures which measures the gap in morale between the two fleets.

How do men sustain this behaviour? Certainly, the culture of violence had by 1805 entered very deeply into the thinking of the British naval officer. It is true that in his famous prayer on the morning of Trafalgar, Nelson had prayed for the greatest 'humanity' after the action, but humanity could only follow on from annihilation. Goodness depended on the riding and revelling. It is the paradox at the heart of moral war.

Sir Thomas Troubridge was not at Trafalgar but more strikingly than any other of Nelson's captains he personifies qualities in the British naval officer of the early 19th century which were so excitedly engaged with violence that they seem to border on the unhinged. Apart from a fit of jealousy and a falling-out towards the end of Nelson's life, Troubridge was always intimately close to Nelson. Nelson loved him as he loved others like him and did his best to promote him and reward him. They had been boys together on the *Seahorse* and as Nelson, favoured with better connections in the high echelons of naval command, outstripped him in his career, he ensured that Troubridge kept step. St Vincent singled Troubridge out, as he did Nelson, for the aggressive fighting qualities he recognised in both. Both Nelson and St Vincent admired Troubridge for his extraordinary courage in the 1794 mutiny at Spithead when he had seized ten of the mutineers himself. Nelson made sure that Troubridge, who through sheer bad luck drove his ship aground before the Battle of the Nile, nevertheless received a gold medal as the other captains had. He procured him a baronetcy and persuaded Ferdinand King of Sicily to give him jewels, a pension and boxes of gold coins. For Nelson, Troubridge was 'My honoured acquaintance of twenty-five years, and the very best sea-officer in His Majesty's service.'

In 1799, he was sent by Nelson to blockade the French in the city of Naples and to take the islands in the bay – Procida, Ischia and Capri – from the enemy. His task was 'to extirpate the rebels' who had risen against the authority of the Sicilian Majesties, with whom Nelson was then obsessed. On Ischia, Troubridge found priests preaching revolt against the Sicilian kings. Sir Thomas summoned a judge and then wrote to Nelson. The judge

> talks of it being necessary to have a bishop to degrade the priests, before he can execute them. I told him to hang them first, and if he did not think the degradation of hanging sufficient I would piss on the d–d jacobins carcass, and recommended him to punish the principal traitors the moment he passed sentence, no mass, no confession, but immediate death, hell was the proper place for them.

In a separate letter he added, 'If we could muster a few thousand good soldiers, what a glorious massacre we should have . . .' and then apologised that he was unable to send on to Nelson the head of a Jacobin which he had been sent by a Sicilian loyalist but which Troubridge feared he could not forward to Nelson as the weather was too hot and the head would rot on passage.

Nelson went about the task of executing rebels with equal relish. As he wrote to Captain Edward Foote of the frigate *Seahorse* 'the hanging of thirteen Jacobins gave us great pleasure: and the three priests [who had been sent to be degraded in Palermo] I hope return in the *Aurora*, to dangle on the tree best adapted to their weight of sins.' Perhaps they were brutalising conditions, but the brutality found ready candidates in these men. Perhaps it was of a piece with the necessarily aggressive constitution of a successful military man. Nelson knew this about himself and knew the man he was. He was not smooth. This was, for him, quite explicitly, a war on terror. As he told Sir John Acton, the Neapolitan prime minister, republicanism 'is the system of *terror*, by which terror the French hold all Italy.' In those circumstances, 'A fleet of British ships of war are the best negotiators in Europe; they always speak to be understood and generally gain their point.' His aggression was part of the new 'unpoliteness' – a word used by Nelson in thanking the Lords of the Admiralty for sending 'gentlemen to sea instead of dancing with nice white gloves.' It is a phrase that marks him out as part of the great revolution against politeness which swept Europe at the end of the 18th century. When a certain Mr Hill attempted to blackmail him in 1803, by threatening to publish a true account of what had gone wrong during a desperately unsuccessful raid led by Nelson on the French flotilla outside Boulogne, Nelson responded with almost Shakespearean grandeur: 'I have not been brought up in the school of fear,' he wrote, 'and therefore care not what you do. I defy you and your malice.'

St Vincent had said that 'predatory war' was Nelson's *métier* and he was certainly capable of the kind of uncomplicated, direct, unelaborated violence in which predators specialise. When commander of the *Boreas*, he had flogged in 18 months 54 of his 122 seamen and 12 of his 20 marines, eight of them for mutinous language. He famously said he would be happy to hang a mutineer on Christmas Day and St Vincent's final verdict on the greatest naval commander Britain has ever known was coldly evaluative: 'the sole merit of Lord Nelson,' the ancient earl wrote in a letter written deep into the 19th century, was 'animal courage'.

This was undoubtedly one of the grounds on which the characters of Nelson and Troubridge met. It was, as so often with Nelson, a friendship charged with high passion. In January 1800 Troubridge had written to him warning him of the immorality of the Sicilian court – 'We have characters, my lord, to lose; these people have none.' – and of the dangers of being seen with Emma Hamilton gambling deep into the night. Nelson loved Emma and revered the Bourbon queen, at whom Troubridge had openly sneered, and wrote back to his junior captain a letter which has not survived but which was clearly smoking with rage and destruction. Troubridge replied:

> It really has so unhinged me, that I am quite unmanned and crying. I would sooner forfeit my life, my everything, than be deemed ungrateful to an officer and friend I feel I owe so much to.

Only a few weeks later, in March that year, Troubridge wrote a letter to Nelson which takes the relish in death and violence to new heights. The British were besieging the French garrison in the port of Valetta on Malta. In attempting to escape, the *Guillaume Tell* had been taken by Henry Blackwood and others and four English deserters had been found on her, savagely wounded. Troubridge wrote to Nelson:

> Two died of their wounds the other two are here one with both legs off & the other has lost his arm, a court martial is ordered, if they will but live Monday, they will be tried and meet their deserts immediately, we *shot & hung* a Maltese for carrying in two fowls & tomorrow I hope will be gala day, for the old lady who I have long been wishing to hang, that carried in the intelligence. She swore she was with child, and possibly she will try some stout fellow: even then it will be good policy to destroy the breed.

What to make of such a series of statements? They are – almost technically in the last phrases – fascistic. They describe the scenes which Goya would paint in the Peninsular War a year or two later. They might be excused as coming from a man too long exposed to the facts of war, but they are words written in the expectation of approval from their recipient, bitter, dehumanising words which still shock at the distance of two centuries.

Perhaps the way to explain this is to see in Nelson the particular form of genius which is able to absorb contradictory qualities and to see no contradiction between them. He was an amalgamator, a bringer-together, a collector of qualities, an animator of spirits, an intuitionist, with a mind in which the rational and spontaneous, the instinctive and the systematic, and perhaps the violent and the loving were not strictly separable or distinct. As Coleridge said, no doubt repeating what he had heard from Sir Alexander Ball,

> [Nelson] with easy hand collected, as it passed by him, whatever could add to his own stores, appropriated what he could assimilate, and levied subsidies of knowledge from all the accidents of social life and familiar intercourse. When the taper of his genius seemed extinguished, it was still surrounded by an inflammable atmosphere of its own, and rekindled

at the first approach of light, and not seldom at a distance which made it seem to flame up self-revived.

That flickering and beautiful description of the workings of Nelson's mind, as if it were partly a butterfly net, partly a chemical or electrical experiment, partly of the Enlightenment, partly of the Romantic world, has never been equalled. Nelson required, in his lieutenants, something of the violence of Troubridge. But he also valued its opposite. Few men in the navy could match the systematic and Olympian calm of Alexander Ball, a 'tideless man' as he was described at the time. 'Courage,' Ball once told Coleridge, 'is the natural product of familiarity with danger.' No *sturm-und-drang* there, just the Virgilian emergence of virtuous behaviour from the virtuous man. In 1797 he had saved Nelson's ship, the *Vanguard* in a storm on a lee shore off the coast of Corsica, without even raising his voice. Ball had taken the *Vanguard* in tow but Nelson had, again according to Coleridge,

> considered the case of his own ship as desperate, and that unless she was immediately left to her own fate, both vessels would inevitably be lost. He, therefore, with the generosity natural to him, repeatedly requested Captain Ball to let him loose; and on Captain Ball's refusal, he became impetuous, and enforced his demand with passionate threats. Captain Ball then himself took the speaking-trumpet, which the fury of the wind and waves rendered necessary, and with great solemnity and without the least disturbance of temper, called out in reply, 'I feel confident that I can bring you in safe.'

But that neoclassical firmness of purpose in Ball (who also enjoyed a fearsome reputation as a disciplinarian) was not enough. It needed the addition of Troubridge's troubled, violent and intemperate spirit. 'Whenever I see a fellow look as if he was thinking,' Troubridge said when asked how to impose discipline on a ship's company, 'I say that's mutiny.' Each man and each quality contradicts the other. They cannot tolerate each other. One looks like liberal civilisation; the other unprincipled barbarity; one is patrician (Ball's father was a large landowner), the other of the street (Troubridge's childhood had been poor); one is controlled, the other anarchic; but in battle neither is adequate without the other. Victory depends on their fusion, a melding of contradictory qualities. It is the contradiction between that grim controlled silence in the long approach to battle and the ruthless killing minute of the double-shotted broadsides pouring into the stern of the *Santa Ana*, tearing apart the flesh and bones of those within. They are twinned, the Apollonian and Dionysian aspects of war. Troubridge and Ball were Nelson's closest fighting allies. Once, according to Coleridge,

> when they were both present, on some allusion made to the loss of his arm, he replied, 'Who shall dare tell me that I want an arm, when I have three right arms – this (putting forward his own) and Ball and Troubridge?'

* * *

If Nelson was, as Byron described him, 'Britannia's God of War', it was due to his intuitive understanding of the intimacy of violence, love, courage, honour, classlessness and victory. That was the amalgam which undoubtedly drew the mass of the ships' companies at Trafalgar into their deep love and admiration of him. He was the conjuror of violence. As commander of the inshore squadron off Cadiz in the summer of 1797, already a vice-admiral, promoted after the battle of Cape St Vincent in February that year, Nelson and the great Thomas Fremantle had plunged off in his ten-oared barge, accompanied by Nelson's boatswain

John Sykes, to take part in the most dreadful, bloody slashing mêlée of his entire career. The British boats fought gunwale to gunwale with three Spanish gunboats which had come out from Cadiz. Boatswain Sykes twice saved Nelson's life, at the cost of some terrible deep cutting wounds to his head, pushing himself between his admiral and his admiral's death. Eighteen Spaniards had been killed out of about 26 and the rest wounded before they surrendered to this whirlwind of violence and aggression. In his dispatch Nelson, without affectation, put the name of Sykes the boatswain alongside those of Captains Miller and Fremantle, two of the gilded élite of the Navy. In Nelson's own words, it was a moment at which 'perhaps my personal courage was more conspicuous than at any other part of my life.' Needless to say, the navy as a result, especially the seamen of the navy on whose level he had put himself, in precisely the way Alexander the Great used to put himself again and again into the bloody crux of battle, came to regard him with still greater awe, admiration and love. That is another way of expressing the amalgam: shared violence is the stimulus for the love on which the violence depends for its success.

This is the world of violence in which, as Wordsworth was writing in *The Prelude* during the summer of 1805, there was 'A grandeur in the beatings of the heart,' where 'danger or desire' made

> The surface of the universal earth
> With triumph, and delight, and hope, and fear,
> Work like a sea . . .

Danger and desire, hope and fear, triumph and delight, violent exposure, removal from the ordinary, on the brink of destruction and self-destruction – this is the heartland of Romanticism, in which the immediate, the spontaneous, the intense and the primitive take over from anything more adult or known. As Coleridge wrote again and again in his notebooks 'Extremes meet – Nothing & intensest absolutest Being'. Crisis is revelatory. In that, intensely contemporary with Trafalgar, are the seeds of the idea that battle is the place of ultimate reality, and the reason that Trafalgar came to occupy such an iconic place in the British imagination.

7

HUMANITY

October 21st 1805
2.15 pm to 4.30 pm

Humanity: great tenderness of heart
EDMUND BURKE, *An Appeal from the new to the old Whigs*, 1791

As the *Victory* approached the allied line, she had already suffered 20 dead and 30 wounded. The dead had gone over the side, if only to prevent their blood making the workspace of battle unusable. The wounded were already clogging the surgeons' tables in the cockpit. According to Nelson's specific instructions, their knives were warmed. The coldness of the steel at the amputation of his arm in the Canaries was something he wanted no one else to suffer. The silence was over; the shrieking came up from below.

Even though, as usual, the crew had duplicated many of the lines in the running rigging, replacing some with chain rather than hempen rope, *Victory*'s top hamper was now in tatters. The studding sail booms on her foremast had all been shot away close to the yard-arms. The mizzen top-mast had been toppled and hung over the poop deck. The foresail itself was hanging in strips. A shot had destroyed the wheel and the ship was now being steered by commands shouted down (perhaps through a speaking tube) to 40 men manning tiller ropes in the gun room below.

This wounding of ship and crew, before a single shot had been fired in response, was an entirely conscious part of Nelson's plan. He knew that the spearpoints of the two British columns would take the most terrible battering from the enemy fleet. He had decided that the strongest ships in the squadron, the three-deckers, should lead those columns and that they should be captained by men he knew and trusted from the long campaigns in the Mediterranean over the previous five years. And he knew, equally well, that both he and Collingwood should be in the lead. That was the essence of the tactics at Trafalgar: a front-loading of fire-power, inspiration, exposure and damage. Thus equipped, the leading ships of the British attacking columns could apply overwhelming force to the centre and rear of the allied line. It was the equivalent of a heavily armoured thrust, strong enough to resist the cannonade with which it would be greeted on the way in, devastating when it arrived.

The battle would be won in its beginnings, which is why Nelson had to be at the front. He conceived Trafalgar, at its heart, not as a corporate action, of the fleet acting as a single disciplined body; but as an action in his image. That was its primitivism. Where he and Collingwood led, others must follow, not by attending to the orders which he would issue – for he would issue none – but by doing what he had shown them to do. It was the most elemental form of command: leadership by example; a throwback to the days of heroism, when warrior kings did not direct, but demonstrated by their own prowess how war was to be conducted. There was honour in exposure, but the honour was not futile. Honour – like zeal, order, daring, love and violence – was an instrument of battle. The heroism, of which those were the constituent elements, was in the service of one thing only: victory.

Sailing warships were in many ways delicate things. If topgallant masts and even topmasts and yards were not 'struck' or lowered in severe weather, they and their rigging would break. A line-of-battle ship was not made and manufactured in the shipyard as a finished object. It was in constant transformation, a continuous process of repair, attended to, battered by the sea and wind, endlessly nurtured by officers and crew. In a storm, fleets could not be held stiffly in position; they had to give before it, running with the wind, before returning to resume their stations after the stress was over. A ship was, in many ways, its habit of care. For Nelson, outstandingly among contemporary naval officers, that habit extended to the wellbeing of the men he commanded. The mountains of lemons ordered for the fleet, the onions at every meal, the standing as godfather to the children of the wounded, the recommending of positions for men he knew and trusted, the courtesy to the slightest, the punctilious delivery of notes and letters: humanity to one's own crew, just like the nurturing of the ships themselves, was what in the end would annihilate the enemy.

That is the context in which to understand the approach of *Victory* to the Combined line. That ship, like those that followed, was one of the most carefully maintained objects in the world. Everything, for month after month, would have told the officers and crew of a ship to attend to its orderliness, to nurture its systems, to be careful.

Now, at this moment, all of that had become an irrelevance. As they approached the line, first aiming astern of the *Santísima Trinidad*, then aiming for a gap just astern of the French flagship, the *Bucentaure*, the French ship behind it, the *Redoutable*, began to close the gap. Hardy looked anxiously ahead and realised that the *Victory* could not pass through the allied line without 'running on board' or colliding with one of their ships. He asked Nelson what he should do:

> His Lordship quickly replied, 'I cannot help it: it does not signify which we run on board of. Go on board which you please: take your choice.'

Hardy is to decide. Damage and devastation were now the currency of victory, just as, a moment before, care and system had been the necessity. Prudence, so essential to the wellbeing of a fleet, was now to be abandoned. Choice did not signify. This was neither bravado nor bloodlust, but the application of a highly attuned mind to the essence of battle. It is a form of negative capability, a trans-rational sense of when interference and attentiveness, the giving and structuring of orders, becomes secondary. It is the point at which the preparedness of a system is so all-encompassing that the system no longer needs to be looked after. If a system is good enough, it must be abandoned to something far more wildly energetic, the thing that creates victory out of the destruction it wreaks.

'Everything seemed,' Collingwood wrote lovingly and loyally after the battle, 'as if by enchantment, to prosper under his direction. But it was the effect of system, and nice combination, not of chance.' That was true, and at least hinted at the whole truth. Collingwood could not stomach the common and received idea, which was everywhere in England, that Nelson was a magician, the conjuror of victory, that he achieved it by a kind of 'spell'. But in the sense that in this battle Nelson relinquished pattern and rationality, there is an element of truth in the word 'enchantment'. Nelson's victory at Trafalgar would not have occurred unless he had allowed and encouraged free rein to the less conscious forces of devastating aggression, the desire to excel, the desire for prizes, the desire to kill and the desire to win. His potency as a commander rests in this very moment as *Victory* comes within a few yards of the stern of the *Bucentaure*. Here his method – you might say his art

– flicks over from careful to careless, from control to anarchy, from commander to conjuror. His method bridged those contradictory qualities, embodying and practising a negative capability which did not need to choose between them.

Almost exactly two years before, in late October 1803, Coleridge in his notebook had asked himself the point of all his thought and work, and answered:

> To support all old & venerable Truths, to support, to kindle, to project, to make the Reason spread Light over our Feelings, to make our Feelings diffuse vital warmth thro' our Reason – these are my Objects – & these my Subjects.

That radical crossing of categories, and the deeply humane nature of the enterprise, pursued through extreme, difficult, self-destructive and often lonely conditions, is the quality that unites Nelson and Coleridge. For both, the method is radical, the purpose deeply conservative, concerned for 'all old & venerable Truths' in a world threatened with change and destruction. It is the zeitgeist speaking through them, joined in this most ardent moment in English consciousness.

As Collingwood wrote of Nelson after Trafalgar:

> There is nothing like him left for gallantry and conduct in battle. It was not a foolish passion for fighting for he was the most gentle of all human creatures and often lamented the cruel necessity of it, but it was a principle of duty which all men owed their country in defence of her laws and liberty.

Those are deeply affectionate and understanding words, embracing the contradictions of the systematic-irrational, humane-violent, intolerant-generous, powerful-suffering hero whom he worshipped. As *Victory*'s bowsprit came across the stern of the *Bucentaure*, Collingwood would have seen nothing of it. He was already deep into the smoke and fire of his own battle a mile to the south. But he would have known what was about to happen.

The wind has dropped, the studding sails have been shot away, the others are like sieves or riddles, and *Victory* slows to the point of encounter. The slight bowing of the allied line, to north and south of her, allows both broadsides to be fired with advantage before she breaks through it. As the guns fire, it is as if the air is sucked out from between decks. Every apocalyptic vision the men have heard or dreamed of starts to become real.

> The one was cloth'd in flames of fire,
> The other cloth'd in iron wire,
> The other cloth'd in tears and sighs
> Dazzling bright before my eyes.

The whole ship, in its massive timbers, shudders with the reverberations of the 100 guns. Then the starboard bow of *Victory* collides with the *Redoutable* and *Victory*'s forecastle is astern of the *Bucentaure*. The French flagship is so close that if there were more of a wind the great French ensign hanging from the peak of her spanker, her aftmost sail, could have been snatched at by men on the deck of *Victory*. As it is, the *Victory* rolls in the swell coming under her and the main yard-arm on the port side just touches the vangs on the Frenchman's gaff – the system of lines holding up the spar to which the spanker is bent. That close, intimate brushing of the enemy – with its strangely erotic undertones of initial, stroking seduction – is what Nelson had in mind. It is the Nelson Touch.

Then the necessary murder: on *Victory*'s forecastle, one on each side, is a pair of huge 68-pounder carronades. They are loaded with a single large calibre roundshot and a canister of 500 musket balls. The portside carronade is fired straight into the stern windows of the *Bucentaure* and its charge travels the length of the gundecks in the French flagship: a single avenging destroyer followed by its cloud of disciples. One by one, as they come to bear, the 50 guns of the *Victory's* port broadside then fire, double-shotted, down the same open alleyway. The metal shot, each 6¼ inches wide, ricochet through the men and guns that lie in their way, a bowling arcade in which the bowls do their work on the nine-pin Frenchmen. Twenty of the great guns on *Bucentaure*, each weighing nearly three tons, are turned over and made useless. The condition of the people can scarcely be imagined. Afterwards, British officers saw the bodies lying on those gundecks, many of them strangely beheaded by the passing shot. What the *Royal Sovereign* had done to the *Santa Ana*, the *Victory* is now doing to her French counterpart. The dust from the *Bucentaure*'s smashed woodwork settles on the shoulders of Nelson and Hardy. Black smoke from the broadside rolls back into the gundecks on *Victory* where each gun has burning beside it a lantern to illuminate the darkness of battle. Hundreds of men on the *Bucentaure* had been killed or wounded in the two minutes *Victory* had taken to sail past her. They listened for the crash made by their shot 'with characteristic avidity'.

In front of them now, and to the right, the French *Neptune*, 80 guns, opened fire on the *Victory*'s bow. Damage everywhere; splinters the size of pick-axe handles flying across the deck; the foremast 'wounded'; the bowsprit hit and the yards carrying the spritsails that were hung from it shot away. The weak structure at the bows of the ship takes a series of roundshot, each one slicing into the smoke-filled spaces between decks. These are the moments in which the *Victory* has more men killed than at any other. Their bodies are thrown over and, as Turner would later quite accurately paint it, the sea becomes coloured with their blood, the Atlantic turned murky with its stain. In other ships, the blood is seen running from the scuppers, down the topsides, streaking the paintwork.

Hardy, meanwhile, ordered *Victory* to starboard, towards the *Redoutable*. Instructions are shouted down to the men at the tiller ropes, and the flagship begins her slow turn around the bow of the *Redoutable*. A broadside was poured into her as *Victory* crossed her bows. The *Redoutable* fired back, took some shots at the British *Téméraire* which had followed *Victory* into battle, and then, to the consternation of the British, closed most of her lower deck gunports, presenting an almost blank, unarmed face to the enemy. Jean-Jacques Lucas, her tiny, fierce captain, had decided to confront the British not with the great guns but with musketry. The ports were closed to prevent the British boarding through them. Within a minute or two, the *Victory* and the *Redoutable* lay alongside each other. The British gunners kept at their work, unable to run the guns out through their ports as the hull of the *Redoutable* walled them in. They fired from within the *Victory*'s own decks, where the black smoke made nothing visible. Where they could, they fired through those of the *Redoutable*'s ports that were open, destroying Frenchmen down the length of a dining-room table. If not for one peculiar bit of luck, the effect of *Victory*'s broadsides might, through sheer Newtonian physics, have driven the two ships apart. By chance, though, *Victory*'s starboard fore topmast studding sail boom iron – the metal fixing holding the boom on to which the fair-weather sail to starboard of *Victory*'s topsail was bent – caught in the side of the *Redoutable*'s fore-topsail. It was enough, in the very light airs, to hold the ships together and, together with the grappling hooks which the Redoutable threw across to *Victory*, that small piece of forged iron created the conditions in which Nelson died.

The killing continued. The carronade on the starboard

side of the *Victory*'s forecastle had not been fired. Now it surveyed, with its terrifying mouth, the open upper deck of the *Redoutable*. The *Victory*'s boatswain, using the carronade, loaded with canisters of musket balls and hugely heavy single shots, swept the gangways clean of living Frenchmen. Life was not sustainable there.

Meanwhile, of course, Captain Lucas of the *Redoutable* had his response. The guns on his maindeck were now being fired into the *Victory*. Muskets were being shot through some of their gunports into the gunports of the enemy, obliterating the Englishmen working at the great guns only a few feet away. But Lucas had also placed men with muskets in the 'tops' – solid wooden platforms on each of the three masts, set some 30 feet above the deck. They were substantial structures: a musket ball fired from below would not penetrate them and so musketmen in the tops could shield themselves from British fire with the timbers on which they stood. In the main and fore tops, small brass mortars called 'cohorns', filled with odds and ends of man-killing metal called 'langridge' – a piece of which had struck Nelson on the forehead during the Battle of the Nile, exposing a section of skull one inch wide and three inches long – were sweeping *Victory*'s forecastle.

It was a killing game, and, because of the nature of the projectiles, bound to be a long one. Explosive shells had been in use in naval warfare since the 17th century; Colonel William Congreve, working at the Royal Arsenal in Woolwich, had developed explosive rockets; and there were explosive mines and explosive grenades. Nevertheless, established naval opinion was for the moment largely against them. The *Redoutable* was equipped with grenades, which men in the tops and the rigging threw down on to the the British decks and through the hatchways. Despite that, the central armament of the fleet was inert metal, in the form of the musket ball, the canister, grape shot or round-shot. None could, in itself and singly, destroy or disable a ship, as an explosive round would have done. Damage could only be cumulative, and victory in pre-explosive battle was achieved either by the imposition of a huge concentration of fire-power in a short time in a confined space; or, between more equally matched opponents, in a simple slugging match. The ships were very nearly unsinkable, unless their magazines caught fire and they exploded. Ships could continue to float and fight even when their hulls and rigging were largely destroyed. A battle was won only if so much damage was inflicted on the enemy's people that they could no longer fire back.

Speed of repeat firing became the key. As in draughts, the more you were winning, the more you were likely to win. It was nearly impossible to claw your way back from a losing position. It was a question, as in business, of trends. A small advantage, slowly opening, would in the end bring you victory. If one set of gun crews could fire faster than the other; or if they could begin, as *Victory* had, with a devastating initial attack, it was difficult for the enemy to catch up. Once behind, the gun crews – the heaviest guns needed 14 men each – would be broken apart by the incoming cannonades. Every time they attempted to reorganise, the next broadside would again destroy them. It was a task for Sisyphus.

British gun-training insisted that every man in each gun crew should be able to perform every task in the elaborate, dangerous heavyweight ballet of loading, firing, cleaning and reloading a gun. That was more rarely the case among the French and Spanish, but at least the defensive thickness of the hulls, and the presence behind them of officers who would shoot them if they deserted their posts, meant that losing crews did not instantly surrender. A certain amount of time was needed before a decision would emerge. That moment – marked by the silence of the guns – was when the beaten ship should strike her flag. This was not maniacal berserker battle: to continue with slaughter when it had become obvious there would be no other outcome, was a mark of inhumanity, not courage. Nearly always there was a precise moment at which the battle was turned from on to off. Until that moment the duty was to reply to their guns with yours. After fighting a Frenchman to a standstill at the Glorious First of June in 1794, and having completely silenced her, the Honourable Thomas Pakenham, younger son of the Earl of Longford, famously hailed her through a speaking trumpet with a string of oaths:

> '–, –, you! Have you surrendered?' Back came a faint reply, 'Non, Monsieur.' Then he thundered, aggrieved to the very soul, 'Why the – don't you go on firing?'

These technological boundaries established the moral terms of battle. You could not dash in and out, to deliver a killer punch and then retire. If you were to win you had, in the word they used, to 'engage'. You had to stay there in close proximity to their killing power for a certain length of time until you had overcome them or they had overcome you. If you wanted to shorten this time, and kill more of them more quickly than your great guns were achieving, you could board an enemy, and kill them in hand-to-hand fighting, which if successful could bring an instant result. That was a tactical variation. The essence remained the same: kill enough of the enemy for them to surrender. You could then take their ship as a prize, which would make you rich.

The effect of this was to create a battle environment in which the humanity of the combatants – their reality as people – was the guiding principle at work. A non-explosive technology which was effective only at short range; and an ideology of honour, which insisted on the exposure of the commander to the greatest danger: that combination made battle intimate, and ensured that the faces of the enemy were visible. And that in turn shaped the way in which the battle was conceived, described and remembered.

This is both the most important and the most unexpected aspect of Trafalgar. Nowhere does this fleet's 18th-century inheritance become more obvious. The preceding hundred years had seen a revolution in the English sense of humanity. The 17th century had understood man essentially in relationship to God. The 19th century would agonise over the fate of his individual self. The 18th century in England saw man's existence neither in those abject metaphysical terms nor in the lonely isolation of the romantic soul but as essentially social, engaged with others, part of a society which gave his life meaning. God himself in this 18th-century vision was social. He had created man to be social and social sympathy was at the heart of humanity. Human togetherness was what made life worth living, and nothing was more conducive to happiness – a key 18th-century word, which had meant nearly nothing to 17th-century puritans, and would be abandoned by the Romantics as inherently suspect. As William Hutton, the free commercial thinker and bookseller in Birmingham, wrote in 1781:

> For the intercourse occasioned by traffic gives a man a view of the world and of himself; removes the narrow limits that confine his judgment; expands the mind; opens his understanding; removes his prejudices; and polishes his manners. Civility and humanity are ever the companions of trade; the man of trade is the man of liberal sentiment; a barbarous and commercial people is a contradiction.

These are, of course, the ideas on which Adam Smith drew. Sociability, never more than when in the service of commerce, was goodness. Virtue was no lonely thing, as it had been for the puritan. It was a full and generous humanity, an acceptance of the human reality of other people and a duty of benevolence among men. Burke thought solitude 'as great a positive pain as can almost be conceived' and that sense of the need for a shared humanity is powerfully in play at Trafalgar. The events that followed the opening of the battle on the quarterdeck of *Victory*, and after that deep below in the dark of her cockpit, as well of course as on other ships, are described with an intense focus on the men involved, on their reality as people. There is, in those descriptions, quite clearly an appetite not only for glory but for sympathy. The way in which people are seen to die at Trafalgar is in fact more pathetic than heroic, more an appeal to the human heart than to an admiration for the achievements of the great. It is one of the paradoxes of heroism that a sense of humanity is one of its essential components. What, in the end, would Nelson be without humanity? As cold and admired as the Duke of Wellington.

Much has always been made of the Christ-like analogies of Nelson's death: the suffering, the sacrifice, the acknowledged fate, the period in the tomb, the rise to glory. That element is undoubtedly there, not least in Nelson's own mind. He knew, and had discussed with the American painter Benjamin West, the great picture West had made in 1770 of General Wolfe dying at Quebec during the Seven Years War. West's masterpiece portrayed Wolfe quite openly in the visual terms which painters had used since the Middle Ages to depict Christ as he was brought down from the Cross: the pale skin, the dead body slumped in the arms of the acolytes around him, the light falling on the central scene, the sense of dark and apocalyptic violence behind, the central grieving, the shock and honour of the moment, the tall Union flag, or King's Colour, half-furled so that in the composition it plays the part of the Cross itself.

When Nelson had gone with the Hamiltons to Fonthill, William Beckford's medievalist fantasy abbey, for Christmas in December 1800, Benjamin West, then President of the Royal Academy, was among the other guests. He and Nelson spoke. The vice-admiral confessed he knew little about art:

> But he said, turning to West, 'there is one picture whose power I do feel. I never pass a print shop where your "Death of Wolfe" is in the window, without being stopped by it.' West of course made his acknowledgements, and Nelson went on to ask why he had painted no more like it. 'Because, my lord, there are no more subjects.' 'Damn it,' said the sailor, 'I didn't think of that,' and asked him to take a glass of champagne. 'But, my lord, I fear your intrepidity will yet furnish me with such another scene; and if it should, I shall certainly avail myself of it.' 'Will you?' replied Nelson, pouring out bumpers, and touching his glass violently against West's – 'will you, Mr West. Then I shall hope that I shall die in the next battle.'

Perhaps the story is not entirely to be trusted. It was only written down late into the 19th century and Nelson, in the bumper-filling exchanges, sounds too much like a joshing, stupid military man for the incident to ring quite true. But in the opening remark you can hear his finer voice, the voice of his letters: 'There is one picture whose power I do feel.' That sounds like Nelson, as does the straightforward admission that he knows it from reproductions in shop windows. Several engravings were made, many of them bearing the rubric: 'The hero is dying at the very moment he has won a continent for the Anglo-Saxon race' – a pre-figuring of Trafalgar of which the imperialist Nelson-Wolfe-Christ was apparently entirely conscious.

There are subtle and important distinctions to be made here. West's *Death of Wolfe* was so greatly admired not because it was a portrait of a hero; nor because it demonstrated triumph; nor, overtly anyway, because it mimicked the moment of Christ's death; but because it made heroism social. Wolfe is shown as a slight and fading figure. He is an anti-Hercules, neither a strong nor a beautiful man. He might have wandered in from administering an estate somewhere in the English Midlands, the sort of figure Gainsborough would have painted, regarding the acres he was so carefully improving, his hand stroking the muzzle of his dog. Wolfe is ordinariness itself and West's picture shows sacrifice, valour, honour, courage and death emerging from that ordinariness, as part of the global-scale enterprise on which the humane and social civilisation of the Anglo-Saxons was embarked. West caught the moment because he had translated heroism into the realm of the humane. That model of the modern death is what shaped both Nelson's enacting and the later telling of his own death at Trafalgar. It was not the death of a god; it was the death of a man.

In all accounts of Trafalgar, even from the beginning, the method of the story now becomes slow and intimate. The scene draws on the great slow deaths: of Jesus, of Arthur, perhaps even of Socrates. In unrelieved close-up, England was invited to watch the dignified, anxious and intensely moving humanity of Nelson in his final hours. That knowledge of the man, naked in his humanity, surrounded by the men he loved and who loved him, deeply embedded in the social reality of an England which he loved, marked him out as a hero. One of the great paradoxes of Trafalgar is that, for all its unbridled violence, it can be seen in the end as a deeply humane event.

A few minutes after 1 o'clock that afternoon, the slight figure of Nelson was walking alongside the huge bulk of Captain Hardy, taller, broader, fatter, taking their 'customary promenade' on the quarterdeck. Almost everything is known about the moment. Their walk to and fro, as the battle raged, was 21 feet each way. At the after end, they turned just in front of the smashed stanchions of the *Victory*'s wheel. At the forward end, they turned by the combings of the cabin ladder-way – the rail around the steps down to the Commander-in-Chief's quarters. There is some doubt whether they were walking on the starboard side of it, nearer the *Redoutable*, as was usual for flag officers on a quarterdeck, or on the port side. Whichever it was, at about 1.15, they were within one pace of the ladder-way combings. Hardy took the extra step, but as he did so, Nelson suddenly spun around to his left. Hardy, now one step away, turned to see him in the act of falling. Nelson fell on his knees, with his left hand, his only hand, just touching the deck, holding him up for a moment. Then the arm gave way, and Nelson fell on to his left side, just at the point where John Scott, his secretary, had been killed. Nelson's clothes, in Surgeon William Beatty's euphemistic phrase, 'were much soiled' with Scott's blood. Translated into a modern idiom, that can only mean Nelson was drenched in it. The stains of Scott's blood can still be seen on the sleeve and the tails of Nelson's coat, now in the National Maritime Museum in Greenwich.

Hardy called out, hoping Nelson was not too badly hurt. 'They have done for me at last,' Nelson said. 'I hope not,' Hardy said again. 'Yes,' Nelson said, 'my backbone is shot through.' A musket ball had entered the top of his left shoulder, burning through the front of the epaulette with such speed and force that some of the gold bullion cords of which it was made were fused to the lead of the ball. They, a piece of the blue serge of the coat, and fragments of gold lace were found attached to the musket ball when it was retrieved from deep in Nelson's body several weeks later. A life-size drawing was done of the strange and potent relic, with its clustering attachments, an engraving was made of it and published, Beatty had a gold setting made for the ball and it was given to the King. It is still at Windsor Castle.

From the geometry of the place of death, it is almost impossible that the French musketeer aimed at Nelson. The *Bucentaure*'s mizzen top was about 40 feet from where Nelson and Hardy walked. That was near the limit of an accurate range for a musket, although musket balls could kill more randomly at far greater distances. Even so, Nelson was almost certainly hidden from anyone in that top by *Victory*'s mainsail, which was brailed up to its yard but still hung beneath it. The musket ball was probably a ricochet, one of the pieces of metal with which the air was filled that afternoon. It broke the edge of his left shoulder blade, drove down through the body, broke two ribs, passed through his left lung and a branch of the pulmonary artery, cut downwards again and then across, breaking several vertebrae and lodged itself in the muscles of the back.

The external wound from a musket is small, but it does massive internal damage. Around the ball, as it penetrates the body, a high-pressure shock wave develops, spreading out from the track which the ball takes. As it carves its way through the organs, a cavity forms behind it. The cavity is only temporary, and as the ball drives onwards, the tissues tend to snap back into their former position. Very rapidly, the cavity pulsates, collapsing and re-expanding a few times before it finally disappears. Wherever the musket ball goes, this sudden, repeated and local expansion has the effect of an explosion within the tissue. It is as if something the size of a fist has been fired through it. By the time the ball comes to rest – and in Nelson, its lead was chipped and dented where it had collided with his bones – the internal organs have been ploughed and scarified by its passage. The body cavity then begins to fill with blood.

As the blood pumps out through the smashed tissues, the heart rate goes up and the veins constrict. The autonomic systems in the body are making their attempt to limit the damage and keep enough blood in circulation for the vital organs to continue to operate. Blood drains from the face and limbs, which soon turn pale and even bluish. But with anything approaching such a massive wound, there is nothing to be done. Blood pressure drops and the wounded man goes into shock. Without blood transfusion, a treatment unknown in 1805, he is now certain to die, within three hours at most. A tourniquet could be applied to an external wound, to staunch the flow of blood and preserve the man. Nothing could be done for widespread internal damage. Even in modern war, most soldiers suffering wounds that result in severe internal haemorrhaging die before they reach field hospital. The 'shedding of blood' is the way in which battle is conventionally and even politely described. The irony is that the shedding of blood – exsanguination – was precisely and dreadfully the mechanism by which battles such as Trafalgar were won and lost.

Nelson knew exactly what had happened to him. He had intense pain in the back where the ball had come to rest. His lower legs were losing sensation. His spinal cord may well have been cut. 'At every instant,' as the ship's surgeon William Beatty reported to the Admiralty in December, which means at every beat of the heart, 'he felt a gush of blood in his breast.' That was his life pumping out of him. He was carried below to the cockpit, with a handkerchief covering his face and lying across the stars on his coat, so as not to dishearten the men of *Victory*. As he was laid in the cockpit among the other wounded, the battle was coming to its climax around him. It is a measure of the raging violence and noise of battle that it was perfectly possible for Nelson to be mortally wounded on the *Victory* and for only a small proportion of the crew even to realise he was missing from the quarterdeck.

A mile to the south, in the fight for the rear of the Combined Fleet, the *Fougueux* and the *Belleisle* had fought each other to a standstill. They drifted apart, mutually wrecked. The *Mars* was already out of the battle, drifting and dismasted, her captain dead, still lying where he had been decapitated, his body now covered in a Union flag. To the south, the *Tonnant*, after compelling one Spanish ship to surrender, went on to engage in a fearsome hand-to-hand fight with the flagship of Admiral Magon, the *Algésiras*. The two ships were clasped to each other in one inseparable mass, the French bowsprit tangled inextricably into the *Tonnant*'s main rigging. Captain Tyler of the *Tonnant* was shot in the leg and carried below. The *Tonnant* lost her main and mizzen topmasts, the *Algésiras* her entire foremast. The pair of them looked like a shipyard in chaos and covered in gore. On neither of their upper decks could men survive and the two ships' companies fired destruction at each other from the great guns down below. The French attempted to board with most of the crew of the *Algésiras* climbing through the rigging. All but one of them were killed in the attempt, shot down by musket and clouds of grape shot fired at them from a few feet away. One Frenchman reached the *Tonnant*'s upper deck, to which an English sailor pinned him through the calf with a pike.

Here, too, is an emblematic moment in the story of Trafalgar. The fighting is absolute, frenzied and horrifying. The scene is probably as intense a combination of the intimate and the bloody as any in the history of warfare. At this moment, a Frenchman lies held to the deck, screaming for his life, while other English sailors are making for him with their own cutlasses and pikes. But at that moment, a British officer intervened: the switch had flicked from violence to humanity, from one aspect of the Atlanticist Anglo-Saxon culture to another, and the Frenchman was saved, to be sent below to the surgeon to have his leg wound tended.

That extraordinary moment, when uncompromising aggression suddenly reverts to care, comes to characterise the later stages of the battle. The ending of violence, its control, is even more mysterious a moment than its beginning. Tension can erupt into aggression; but how does aggression transmute into calm and even generosity? There is evidence from Trafalgar that this capacity for the humane was not simply a product of exhaustion or battle fatigue. More than that, it seems to be evidence of a mature understanding, which had emerged from 18th-century English culture, of the role and limits of violence. The *Algésiras* finally surrendered when her two remaining masts fell, shot through deep within the ship, always the sign of unspeakable devastation between decks. Admiral Magon was found dead on his own quarterdeck, lying in his blood at the foot of the poop ladder.

At the fight between the *Victory* and the *Redoutable*, Hardy remained on deck as the admiral was carried below. It was a desperately anxious time. After the battle, his silver pencil case was found to have the impressions of his teeth deeply embedded in it, where quite unconsciously he had chewed on the silver in the heat of battle. All round him Captain Lucas's musketmen in the tops were having a savage effect on the *Victory*'s upper deck. The French musket fire killed and wounded about fifty men there and those British sailors remaining unhurt left the deck for their own safety.

The *Victory*'s great guns continued to fire below, but from the French there was a curious silence. As the

Victory's upper deck had no one left alive, the musketmen had no further targets to aim at. The *Redoutable* was now not firing at all with her own great guns. Hardy thought for a moment the Frenchman had struck. His own guns had been doing steady and uncompromising destruction below decks. *Victory*'s shot had been driving into the *Redoutable*, through the men and guns, and out again the other side. So close were the *Victory*'s muzzles to the French gunports that the British were afraid that the belch of flame from their own guns, and flaming wads which the detonating gunpowder blew out of the barrels after the shot, would set the *Redoutable* on fire. After each shot, men from the *Victory* threw buckets of water through the holes in the *Redoutable* which their shot had made, to extinguish any fire they might have ignited. A fire aboard the *Redoutable* would also have destroyed the *Victory*. This was a form of battle in which the enemy had to be nurtured if he was to be defeated. The possibility of Mutually Assured Destruction was perfectly available to them and had even been hinted at in Nelson's suggestion that he would willingly have half of his fleet burnt to bring about the destruction of the French. But it was not a tactic which either the men of the lower deck or the lieutenants and midshipmen commanding them, were prepared to countenance. Hardy, having taken the care, now thought he had won this fight and ordered the *Victory*'s starboard battery to cease firing.

A strange moment of silence descended between the two ships at the heart of the battle. Gunfire from other fights echoed around them. The banks of smoke hung like curtains above the slowly stirring sea. Both captains, their officers and crews were waiting for the other to surrender. Both thought they had won and Captain Lucas prepared to board the *Victory*. He ordered his mainsail yard cut down so that it would bridge the gap between the two ships. He prepared his men to rush up from below, armed quite literally to the teeth – a cutlass held between the teeth allowed one arm to hold on to the rigging, another a pistol – but at that very moment Nelson's tactical conception paid off.

This was not, as the old convention had ordained, a battle in which one ship would confront one other and duel with honour. This battle involved the massing of forces against enemy ships in order to bring about their surrender quickly and savagely. Just at the moment that Lucas's boarding party was prepared on the *Redoutable*, 200 men gathered in a mass, the British *Téméraire* materialised on his port side. The *Téméraire* – 98 guns, three-decker, under Captain Eliab Harvey – was as formidable a fighting machine as the *Victory* herself. The *Redoutable*, a two-decker, found herself sandwiched between these two terrifying opponents. As a fierce musketry fight developed between the men of the *Redoutable* and the men of the *Victory*, killing 19 Britons and wounding 22, Harvey coldly ordered his upper tier of guns to fire across the decks of the *Redoutable*. The two hundred men were all killed or wounded. Lucas himself was hit but not killed. In the *Victory*, the lieutenants in charge of the divisions on the lowest decks had their guns treble-shotted, with a reduced charge of powder, and ordered their muzzles to be lowered so that as the roundshot from each broadside hammered through the *Redoutable*, they wouldn't drive on into the *Téméraire* beyond her.

This was the savage centre of Trafalgar. On one side the *Victory* was still firing with her port guns into the *Bucentaure*, with her starboard guns into the *Redoutable*. The *Redoutable* herself was suffering massacre from the *Victory* on one side and from the *Téméraire* on the other. Men in the *Redoutable*'s tops, and even on her yard-arms, were throwing incendiary grenades down into both the *Victory* and the *Téméraire*. At the same moment, the *Téméraire*, on her far side, was getting ready to receive a

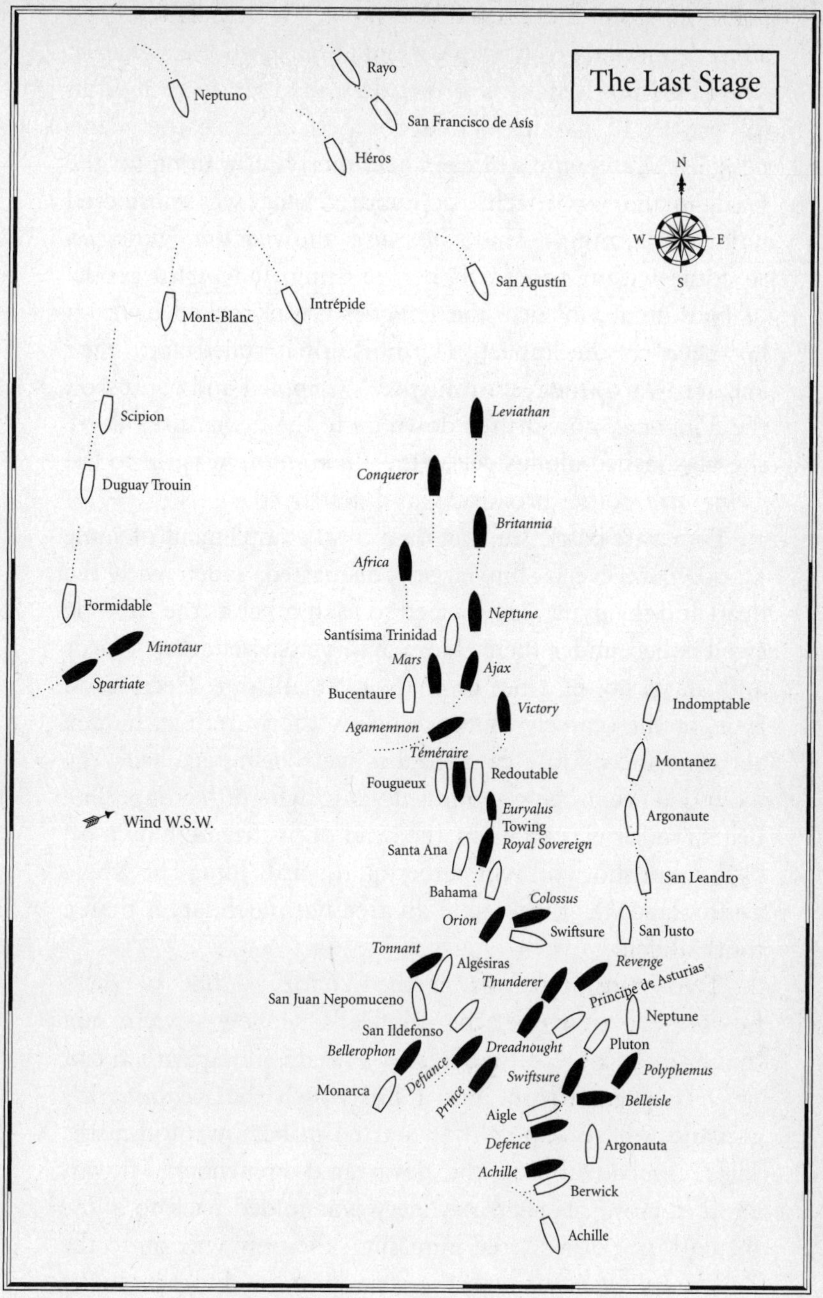

The Last Stage
N
W
E
S
Neptuno
Rayo
San Francisco de Asís
Héros
San Agustín
Intrépide
Mont-Blanc
Scipion
Duguay Trouin
Formidable
Minotaur
Spartiate
Leviathan
Conqueror
Britannia
Africa
Neptune
Santísima Trinidad
Mars
Ajax
Bucentaure
Victory
Agamemnon
Téméraire
Fougueux
Redoutable
Euryalus
Towing
Royal Sovereign
Santa Ana
Bahama
Indomptable
Montanez
Argonaute
San Leandro
San Justo
Wind W.S.W.
Colossus
Orion
Swiftsure
Tonnant
Algésiras
Revenge
Thunderer
Principe de Asturias
San Juan Nepomuceno
Neptune
San Ildefonso
Bellerophon
Dreadnought
Pluton
Defiance
Swiftsure
Polyphemus
Monarca
Prince
Belleisle
Aigle
Defence
Argonauta
Achille
Berwick
Achille

collision from the French *Fougueux*, which had moved away from her earlier bloody encounter with the *Belleisle*. The *Téméraire*'s starboard broadside had yet to be fired in the battle. It was in its state of perfect pre-battle readiness. The *Téméraire*'s officers held their fire, waiting for the Frenchman to approach; 200 hundred yards was considered point-blank range. The *Téméraire* allowed the *Fougueux* to come within 100 yards before firing. It was the model of Nelsonian violence: the *Fougueux* was rocked back on her heels by the impact. The noise of it rolled across the ocean towards the rest of the fleet. 'Crippled and confused', the *Fougueux* now drifted down on to the *Téméraire*, where she was lashed alongside, as the *Redoutable* was on to the *Téméraire*'s other broadside, and destroyed.

Four vast battle ships, with a total complement of some 3,000 men, every ship largely dismasted, laden with the dead and the dying, lay clasped to each other as the Atlantic swell rolled under them. None had yet surrendered. Yards and masts lay in a net of chaos over all four. Deep in all four, in the scarcely lit decks below the waterline, hidden sorrows and private catastrophes were being enacted. The wounded were being wounded again where they lay. One British sailor was killed by the head of his friend, blown off by a roundshot and sent careering towards him. The whole assemblage was gathered in an area not much larger than a football field.

Two midshipmen from the *Victory* – one of them Edward Collingwood, the admiral's nephew – were sent by Hardy in one of the flagship's boats, along with six or seven seamen, to put out a fire which the *Redoutable*'s grenades or 'stink-pots' had started in her own forecastle. They climbed aboard the devastated Frenchman. It was another moment where savagery was folded back to allow the entrance of a shared humanity: the only way on to the *Redoutable* was through the stern ports and as the young

British officers climbed in, they were greeted warmly and politely by the French sailors inside. Beyond those proffered hands they encountered, even on a day of such horror, a scene of which they were unable to leave a description.

The *Redoutable*'s mainmast and mizzenmast had both gone by the board. Her bowsprit was shot through and her fore topmast gone. She lay rolling in the water, bedraggled and broken. Her rudder was destroyed and her massive oak hull was in pieces. Several guns had burst, killing everyone around them. The human damage was unconscionable. Of her complement of 643 men, 522 were dead, dying or unable to stand. Two hundred and twenty two of them were lying waiting to be operated on by the surgeons. Three hundred dead lay on the decks. Only those who had managed to spend the battle below the waterline were still in one piece. Everyone who had been on any one of the gundecks was dead or wounded. Neither the French nor the Spanish heaved the dead overboard, as the English practice was, and the sight on the *Redoutable* was of a blood-drenched chaos, the bewildered and bruised faces of young men, an unheroic scattering of limbs and bodies.

No British image, drawn or painted, addressed the squalor of Trafalgar, in the way that Turner would paint the field of Waterloo on the evening of the battle, the ground surface itself merging with and even indistinguishable from the rippling, billowing landscape of the dead, a downland of corpses, lit by the flames of distant fires. But the accounts of those who saw these sights are, if anything, strangely ashamed, bemused, almost as if there were an embarrassment to battle, an awkwardness at the lowering of the cultural guard. In battle, in the sight that greeted these young midshipmen as they walked across the *Redoutable*, a level of human life had been exposed where humanity, in its dignified and socialised form, the most precious thing their civilisation possessed, had been for a while horribly suspended.

It is not perhaps surprising that their urge to humanity was turned to so quickly and so warmly. The horrors of battle, not during it, when the adrenaline was running, but as it ended, created a need for that warmth, for a repairing of the rupture. By about 2.15, four of the six pumps on the *Redoutable* had been destroyed by shot and the water was now fast rising in the hold. The *Téméraire* was then in possession of her prize, as she was of the *Fougueux* on the other side of her. Together, they represented perhaps £100,000 of prize money, a good £5–6 million today, the equivalent of £20,000 for each of the lives taken in the winning of her.

Victory was slipping away to the north, having pushed herself off from the *Redoutable* with giant booms. Over an hour had passed since Nelson had been carried below. The musket ball that had entered his shoulder was only part of a storm of metal then engulfing the *Victory*'s quarter-deck. Between forty and fifty men were carried down to the *Victory*'s orlop deck at the same time as the admiral. Several had died in the arms of the seamen on their way down, but still the cockpit to which the wounded were carried was crowded. As Nelson was brought in, the wounded seamen around him called to the surgeon, William Beatty, 'Mr Beatty, Lord Nelson is here: Mr Beatty, the admiral is wounded.' He was taken to a midshipman's berth, and the men carrying him very nearly dropped him as they tripped in the crowded dark. Nelson was laid on a bed, stripped of his clothes and covered with a sheet. His coat was rolled up and used as a pillow for a midshipman with a head wound beside him. The young man's head was leaking so much blood that after the battle the coat had to be cut from his hair. Wounds to the lower back almost inevitably destroy any control of the bowel or bladder. In the sanctified atmosphere of Nelson's last hours, this is never mentioned, but among the other horrors of that place, Nelson and those around him would certainly have been lying in his own urine and faeces.

The received image of Nelson's deathbed is of a place of quiet and privacy, surrounded by his chosen companions, as if in a shrine. It cannot have been like that. The thumping and shuddering battle was still shaking *Victory* to her bones. Just above his head the 32-pounder battery was still bellowing and roaring at the enemy. 'Oh *Victory*, *Victory*,' Nelson said, murmuring to himself as the recoil from another broadside shocked the air inside the battleship, 'how you distract my poor brain.' The cockpit was full of the *Victory*'s eighty wounded men. The shouts of those above reached down into the flickering dark. Nelson, even from the beginning, was able only to whisper, knowing he was dying, full of anxiety, repeating himself, returning to the great secret of his life. He told Beatty he was 'gone' and then whispered to him, 'Remember me to Lady Hamilton. Remember me to Horatia. Remember me to all my friends. Doctor, remember me to Mr Rose; tell him I have left a will and left Lady Hamilton and Horatia to my country.'

As one by one the French and Spanish ships around *Victory* struck their flags, the men cheered and at each new shout Nelson asked what the noise meant. On one of these occasions, the flag lieutenant John Pasco, who was also lying wounded in the cockpit, said it was the surrender of a Frenchman. Nelson must have known that but it betrays his frame of mind, something that has also been forgotten in our knowledge of the British victory. Nelson was intensely anxious about the battle's outcome. 'He evinced great solicitude for the event of the battle.' Doctor Alexander Scott and the purser, Walter Burke, a cousin of the great Edmund Burke, tried to calm him. The two of them supported his back so that he lay in a semi-recumbent position, which was how he felt least discomfort. The huge internal loss of body fluids made him thirsty. He asked again and again for 'drink, drink' and 'fan, fan' and they gave him sips of lemonade, as was given to the other wounded, as well as water and wine. They fanned him with a paper. He became desperate for cool air. Their reassuring words irritated him. Burke told him he would carry the news of the great victory to England. 'It is nonsense, Mr Burke,' Nelson said, 'to suppose I can live.' Dr Scott, the ship's chaplain, told him he should trust to Providence to restore him to his friends and to his country. 'Ah Doctor!' Nelson said, 'it is all over; it is all over.'

These are the words people say on their deathbeds. They murmur and repeat. Sharpness turns hazy, and present reality gives way to drift and uncertainty. The dying man is with the people who surround him and then profoundly alone. He thinks urgently of present needs and then just as suddenly moves into a much longer perspective, scarcely tethered to this life. Sudden moments of the old self appear, as if floating up in the mist. A young midshipman brought a message down from Hardy, desperately busy on the quarterdeck. Nelson asked who the boy was. It was Hardy's aide-de-camp, a young midshipman called Richard Bulkeley. 'It is his voice,' Nelson said, his eyes clearly closed, and then: 'Remember me to your father.' Lieutenant Richard Bulkeley had been an army officer with Nelson in a desperate campaign in Nicaragua twenty years before, and had remained his friend ever since. It was to Lieutenant Bulkeley that he had told the story of his teenage vision, in which the radiant orb of heroism and glory had come to him on board the *Dolphin*.

Nelson wanted Hardy and called for him again and again, thinking his absence must mean that the captain had also been killed. They were undoubtedly friends. Hardy loved and revered his admiral and Nelson loved being loved by him. Their friendship contained within it their difference in rank, but when Hardy came down to see him, over an hour after Nelson had been wounded, what they said was the conversation between friends. Its every nuance was recorded, as though this friendship and this evidence of friendship was somehow what this battle was for.

As he was told Hardy was coming to see him, Nelson clearly summoned strength from within him, opened his eyes and sat up. They shook hands and Nelson said, 'Well, Hardy, how goes the battle? How goes the day with us?' That is the bright public man speaking, not the haunted, wounded figure, muttering half to himself of Emma and Horatia and the need for drink. 'Very well, my Lord,' Hardy said. 'We have got twelve or fourteen of the enemy's ships in our possession.' 'I hope,' Nelson said, 'none of *our* ships have struck, Hardy?' – surely a smile attached to that? 'No, my Lord,' Hardy said, 'there is no fear of that.' Then Nelson has him come nearer, the public moment quite suddenly giving way to the private. 'I am a dead man Hardy. I am going fast: it will be all over with me soon. Come nearer to me. Pray let my dear Lady Hamilton have my hair, and all other things belonging to me.' Just as much as the public commander, the unexampled imposer of British violence on British enemies, this quiet and tender Nelson is the figure who stands in granite eighteen feet tall on his column in Trafalgar Square. He is the hero humanised.

Nelson comes and goes. He wants to die. He knows he is dying, but he regrets his death. He imagines Emma Hamilton there with him and feels distressed at the distress she must feel. He compares his situation to other sailors he had known who had been wounded in the spine. He talks to Beatty and tells Beatty that he is dying. 'I know it,' he said. 'I feel something rising in my breast which tells me I am gone.' It was, in all likelihood, the tide of his own blood. Beatty tells him that nothing can be done for him and, with the emotion released by expressing the words, the surgeon is then forced to turn away to hide the tears in his own eyes. Again and again, reflecting on his life, Nelson dwells on its two poles, his private and public selves. Between the sips of lemonade and watered wine, he says, almost alternately, 'God be praised, I have done my duty' and to the Rev. Dr Scott, 'Doctor, I have *not* been a *great* sinner,' the smile in that quite audible now, two hundred years later.

Overhead, the battle continued. In front of *Victory*, the *Bucentaure* had been raked in turn by the *Téméraire*, *Neptune*, *Leviathan* and *Conqueror*. The ship scarcely existed any longer. Almost every ally around her either sailed onwards, deserting their flagship, or fell away to leeward where they could play no part in defending her. The British savagery descended on the *Bucentaure*. Her captain was wounded in the mouth; her first lieutenant lost a leg. The senior unwounded officer was the second lieutenant and the surgeons could not cope. In all, some 450 men were killed or wounded out of a ship's complement of about 800. Men bled to death in the dark. No seamen were left on the upper deck; there was no rigging left for them to handle and none of the upper deck guns were serviceable. Villeneuve sent the few remaining men below to save their lives.

The admiral alone, aware of the catastrophe happening to his ship and fleet, stayed above, walking to and fro on his quarterdeck. But no piece of flying metal saved him from ignominy. By about 1.40, half an hour after Nelson had been shot, all three of the *Bucentaure*'s masts went over the side. All the boats had been destroyed by gunfire. There was nothing Villeneuve could do but surrender. The imperial eagle was thrown into the Atlantic and the French admiral struck his flag. Within the remains of his ship, the dead were no longer recognisable but lay along the middle of each deck in rough piles of blood and guts through which the roundshot and the splinters had ploughed again and again. The British officers who went aboard to take command of the ships picked their way past these sights which left them with memories of little but disgust.

The fire of the huge 136-gun *Santísima Trinidad*, the only four-decker in the world, with a crew of 1,115 men, just ahead of the *Bucentaure*, was doing terrible damage to those around her, shots removing the stomachs and arms of the British gunners. One shot, striking one of the great guns, split into jagged pieces, each one of which killed or wounded its man. But for all that, it was only a question of time before the *Santísima Trinidad*, surrounded by five or six British ships, surrendered. First, as an officer on the *Conqueror* described it, the vast vessel 'gave a deep roll with the swell to leeward, then back to windward, and in her return every mast went by the board, leaving an unmanageable hulk on the water.' Every sail in the *Santísima Trinidad* was deployed to its fullest extent, as she had been trying in the lightest of airs to make her way out of the encircling pack of British ships: 'her immense topsails had every reef out, her royals were sheeted home but lowered, and the falling mass of the squaresails and rigging, plunging into the water at the very muzzles of our guns, was one of the most magnificent sights I ever beheld.' It is something of the effect, but tripled and quadrupled, which Turner painted in his depiction for George IV of *Victory* losing her foremast: beauty in the destruction of beauty, the summit and depths of the sublime.

Then, a moment of honour. The smallest battleship in the British fleet, the 65-gun *Africa*, captained by Henry Digby, decided to add the *Santísima Trinidad* to his tally of prizes. Her masts and colours had gone; she had ceased firing. He sent his first lieutenant, John Smith, with a party of men, to take command. He climbed up into the wreck of the Spanish flagship. The quarterdeck was mere devastation. None of the leading figures of the Spanish fleet was there to greet Smith. Admiral de Cisneros had been wounded. His commodore, Don Francisco de Uriarte and the captain of the ship, Don Ignacio de Olaeta, were with him also down below, wounded by the British gunfire. There was a Spanish officer on the quarter-deck and he greeted Smith with great courtesy. Smith asked for the surrender of the *Santísima Trinidad*. The officer told him, politely, that he was mistaken. The *Santísima Trinidad* had not surrendered. She had merely paused to provide the guns with more powder, and although she had lost all three of her masts, and she was roiling like a dead whale in the swell, she would soon resume the battle. Lieutenant Smith apologised for his ridiculous and insulting mistake, gathered his men about him, and was escorted back to the ladder, down the side of the flagship to his waiting boat and back to the *Africa*. This was honourable but mere bravado: the *Santísima Trinidad* did not fight again and the British ships left her to be taken in tow later, with her cargo of dead and her freight of wounded pride.

At about 3.30, Hardy came down below again to Nelson and again their conversation makes its turns between the inner and the outer man. The flag captain suggests that Collingwood should take over command of the fleet. Nelson, with sudden energy, attempts to lift himself off his deathbed to deny that position to anyone but himself or at least to Hardy as his deputy. There is no calm going into death here, no Keatsian acceptance of its rest. The level of tension rises in him till the last. But then Nelson falls back into the arms of Scott and Burke. 'In a few minutes I shall be no more,' he says. And then, even more quietly, a sudden need for intimacy, perhaps for love. 'Don't throw me overboard, Hardy.' Hardy says he won't, of course he won't. They have already discussed where he is to be buried: not in the cold enveloping muds beneath Westminster Abbey, where the old memories of the marshes hold a terror for Nelson of dissolution and softness. No, he is to be buried in St Paul's, high and dry on the hill around which the City of London was first made. 'Take care of my dear Lady Hamilton,' Nelson then says, 'take care of poor Lady Hamilton. Kiss me, Hardy.' It is Nelson's cheek that Hardy kneels down to kiss, their faces close, the love acknowledged and the barriers down. 'Now I am satisfied,' Nelson said. There, in that calm sentence, is a kind of private millennium, an arrival, a sense that the race is done. Then again he said 'Thank God, I have done my duty.' Hardy stood for a few minutes looking down at the man he loved and admired. Nelson's eyes were now closed, his mind no more than half aware. Hardy knelt again and kissed him on the forehead. 'Who is that?' Nelson said quickly, coming up to consciousness from the depths of his reverie. 'It is Hardy,' the captain said. Nelson slumped back and replied, 'God bless you Hardy.' With that the flag captain left the cockpit for the quarterdeck. He had been with him about eight minutes and he knew he would never see him alive again.

This minute-by-minute account of Nelson's death is due almost entirely to the *Authentic Narrative* published in 1807 by William Beatty, the surgeon. It is, in one sense, Nelson's great memorial, the depiction of the man by which he is most known. All Nelson is there: affectionate, anxious, commanding, impatient, trusting, pious, romantic, heroic, mortal. This is the figure which the 19th century inherited. Beatty's Nelson has an air of completeness and resolution. His duty is done and in the light of that his failings are irrelevant. He worries but his worries are set to rest. Battle has become for him, as it would be for the century that followed, a kind of absolution. Deep in the company of the men who loved him, he is somehow blessed by battle and by his death within it. It is not quite a sanctification, because his sinfulness is not absent. He turns to his own guilt again and again; he thinks again and again of Emma and Horatia, both evidence, in the increasingly austere moral atmosphere of early-19th-century England, of a sin against marriage and its vows. Nelson had treated his wife abominably. In letters to Emma, he had referred to Frances Nelson simply as 'the impediment'; he had cruelly spurned her own attempts to restore their marriage. He had explicitly longed for both her and Sir William Hamilton to die so that he and Emma might be happy together. But the sinfulness is set within the broader frame of the duty having been done, that duty consisting in the animal courage, the imposition of order, faith in his own daring, the love of his fellow officers and men, the acting out here in this bloody cockpit of the humanity of the victor. In short, as Nelson reviews his life, he recognises that, despite its sinfulness, it has been a life of honour.

This is almost a recreation of West's *Death of Wolfe*, but there are differences. Nelson, like Wolfe, expires at the moment of victory, but Nelson's death has moved away from Wolfe's very public setting; this moment has gone downwards and inwards towards privacy. It is an individual, not a public moment. It is a private tragedy not a public loss. West painted a version of the death of Nelson which imitated his *Death of Wolfe*, but the Nelson painting is a failure. It is historically false, as the Wolfe picture is historically false, but the Nelson picture is false in another sense: it rings untrue in the way that its great predecessor did not. West showed Nelson expiring on deck, with half his crew around him. It looks factually ridiculous – one blast from the *Redoutable* would have blown them away – but more than that it looks psychically ridiculous. The setting of the scene, the mise-en-scène, contradicts the meaning of what it hopes to portray. Other, slightly ludicrous paintings were made soon after Trafalgar of Nelson's spirit being wafted up to heaven in the arms of Britannia, the apotheosis of his spirit, but they too are little more than historical curios. Drawing on a visual rhetoric which had meant more in the age of Rubens than of Lawrence or Goya, they were public formalities which missed the point. Only one painting of the death of Nelson registered with the spirit of the time and became, in endlessly recycled engravings and prints, the image of the moment which the 19th century preserved. It was not immensely popular at the time and engravings of it were outsold by prints of West's painting. Nor is it, in itself, a particularly painterly work. There is a slight gaucheness, a lack of authority to the figures and its author, Arthur William Devis, is remembered for nearly nothing else. His father, Arthur Devis, had painted delicate and charming conversation pieces of mid-18th-century squires and their families, scenes from which all rhetorical grandeur had been stripped away. The father's people look more like dolls than humans and the son's paintings, translated forward 50 years, share some of that unreality.

Nevertheless, there is an essence there. Devis's *Death of Nelson* shows the scene in the cockpit. The space between the decks is painted too tall, and there is far too much light, most of it apparently emanating from the body of Nelson himself, but otherwise the scene is accurate, both physically and emotionally. The cockpit of the *Victory* is like a re-creation of the tomb in which Christ's body is laid. There is no publicity, no reference to larger aspects of the battle, let alone to imperial ambitions. The officers are in their uniforms but no Union flag disrupts the humanity of the scene. Benjamin West had sneered at it. It was, the President of the Royal Academy said, 'A mere matter of fact [that] will never . . . excite awe and veneration.' But that is why, for all its unearthly light, and its references to the death of Christ, the English people took it to heart as the image of a hero. A man is wounded; a man is loved; and a man dies. The absence of anything more is a reflection of his greatness. Devis's imagery, curiously, is reminiscent of Christ's birth in the stable.

About a quarter of an hour after Hardy left him, Nelson became speechless. His pulse could scarcely be felt and his limbs and forehead were cold. The blood was draining from his veins. Nelson's steward, Henry Chevalier, called the surgeon who came to him from the other wounded. Nelson suddenly opened his eyes, gazed up at the deck above him and then closed them again. No words passed but the Reverend Scott continued to rub his chest. Beatty left again and within five minutes the spirit left Nelson's body. The steward fetched Beatty again and the surgeon confirmed it. Nelson had died at about 4.30 in the afternoon, two and three quarter hours after he had been wounded.

The battle was won and Nelson knew of his victory. Twenty-five of the French and Spanish ships had been engaged by the British attack. Sixteen of them had by now surrendered. Victory was assured and Nelson had been martyred in its service.

8

NOBILITY

October 21st to October 28th 1805

Nobility: Dignity; grandeur; greatness
SAMUEL JOHNSON, *A Dictionary of the English Language*, 1755

As Nelson lay dying, one English officer was failing him. In the aftermath of Trafalgar, it was easy enough to imagine that everyone had played their part as the dictates of honour required. Certainly, Collingwood was reluctant to criticise any of the officers afterwards and only the faintest echoes survive of anything approaching cowardice in the British fleet. There is some evidence, though, that one of the English commanders, third in command after Nelson and Collingwood, Rear-Admiral the Earl of Northesk (he had unexpectedly inherited the title after the death of his elder brother), was reluctant to engage. As his flag-ship, the *Britannia*, approached the battle, Northesk stood on the quarterdeck, arguing with his captain, Charles Bullen. It was said that, with the fight already raging in front of them, Northesk ordered Bullen to reduce sail. After the battle, there was certainly some bitterness in the British fleet at Northesk's reluctance to dive into the brutal and murderous mêlée which their colleagues were subject to. Edward Rotheram, Collingwood's flag captain on the *Royal Sovereign* noted in his commonplace book afterwards that Northesk, 'behaved notoriously ill in the Trafalgar action.'

The earl never commented on the events of the day. But he had no need of victory or glory to advance his standing in British society. He was already possessed of all it might offer him. And Northesk's holding back at Trafalgar did his name no harm. He became a Knight of the Bath, received the thanks of parliament, wore his gold medal, was given the freedom of the City of London, and its sword of honour, treasured his 300-guinea vase from Lloyd's of London – Trafalgar made the life of British marine insurance brokers a great deal easier – and continued to advance smoothly up the lists of the admirals, as if he too had been ferociously and nobly engaged. Of all the commanders in the battle, only Northesk, when he died in 1835, joined Nelson and Collingwood in the crypt of St Paul's, honoured as one of the three great Trafalgar men, simply because he had been an admiral and he was an earl. However apocalyptic an event Trafalgar might have been, certain social realities endured. Unlike nearly everyone else at Trafalgar, Northesk had more to lose – his life and limbs – than to gain. Secure in his position, he was not subject to the mechanics of honour. Dishonourable behaviour was for him a rational choice in a way it never would have been for the captains around and ahead of him, needing to stake all for glory and riches.

At the same moment as Northesk was shortening sail, an equivalent scene was unfolding in the van of the French fleet. Early that morning, Villeneuve's battle plan had fallen apart when Admiral Gravina's Squadron of Observation had become muddled up with the rear of the Combined Fleet. Villeneuve had been left without a tactical reserve and the Franco-Spanish ships had as a result been exposed, one by one, to the overwhelming superiority of British gunnery and aggression. But Villeneuve had another option. The van of the Combined Fleet might itself have played the part of a tactical reserve. Nelson's attack, just astern of the *Bucentaure*, had left the Combined van, under the command of Admiral Pierre le Pelley Dumanoir, untouched. As the battle developed, Dumanoir continued sailing blithely north. For nearly two hours, with the eight valuable ships of the van around him, in perfect, pre-battle condition, he did not turn. He was abandoning his admiral, his fellow captains and their cause. The logs of the British ships – heavily engaged and buried in gunsmoke – do not comment on Dumanoir's departure. He is simply an absence.

No one has ever resolved whether the reason for Dumanoir's failure to come to the aid of the rest of the fleet was carelessness, cowardice or defeatism. Earlier in the year, he had been in command of the fleet when in Toulon and Villeneuve had been appointed over his head. Like Churruca, he too may have felt that Villeneuve was unsatisfactory as a commander and that to preserve the ships of the vanguard was in itself a practical if inglorious course.

In Dumanoir's column, sailing away from the realm of honour, was a captain for whom such behaviour was unthinkable. On the *Intrépide*, Captain Louis Antoine Cyprian Infernet's eyes remained fixed on the masts of Dumanoir's flagship, the *Formidable*, desperately searching for the signal which he wanted Dumanoir to make: to go about and take part in the Battle of Trafalgar. Infernet was a big man, thought to be as vastly tall as a drum-major (he was 5' 10") and 'as fat as an abbot', rough, uneducated and ferocious, born near Toulon, who bellowed at his crew in the broadest Provençal. He was in other words, a brigand fighter, precisely the sort of man the Revolution had brought to the fore, for whom the idealistic honour of the fight was its own form of nobility.

Villeneuve, in the midst of the chaos and mayhem around the *Bucentaure*, had in fact made the signal for Dumanoir to return but, perhaps because of the gunsmoke,

Dumanoir did not see it and continued northwards. Infernet could tolerate it no longer, and at about 2 o'clock wore ship without Dumanoir's instructions, using one of his ship's boats to bring the *Intrépide* around, as the winds had become so light that the ship would not respond to her helm. Soon afterwards, Dumanoir signalled the whole of the vanguard to reverse direction, and they too needed their ship's boats to haul them round. The manoeuvre took an hour in the light airs. Five of them set off to leeward of the battle. Others including Dumanoir himself in the *Formidable* kept to windward.

Why he should have turned when he did is as much of a conundrum as why he did not turn earlier. Perhaps one can see in it the slow influence of honour, which is not an on-off switch, but a moral force gradually applied. For an hour or so, fear, self-preservation and disdain for Villeneuve may have kept Dumanoir sailing north. But the slow application of honour, as a moral imperative, may by then have had its effect, and forced Dumanoir to turn.

The *Intrépide* was already en route for the enemy. Infernet, when asked for instructions from the master, bellowed to the helmsman: '*Lou capo sur lou Bucentauro!*' – Lay the head on the flagship! With the density of gun-smoke, and the light winds doing little to disperse it, Infernet could not have seen the situation Villeneuve was in. But the pure geometry and mathematics of the day could have told him that the centre of the Combined Fleet, with the brutal firepower of British three-deckers now in among them, was in dire need of help.

A young French aristocrat, Auguste Gicquel des Touches, was a sub-lieutenant stationed on the forecastle of the *Intrépide*. He left a graphic account of Infernet's plunge into the midst of battle, driving down through the wreckage and violence in order to rescue Villeneuve. When they finally reached the flagship, both she and the *Redoutable* lay mashed by the guns of the British fleet. Fremantle in the *Neptune* and Bayntun in *Leviathan* had both slapped into both French ships. The masts were down in both of them, their fire almost silenced, just an occasional gun crew maintaining sporadic shots at the enemy around them. It was not a place, with any reason, that a French ship should go but the drive motivating Infernet was not subject to reason. He wished, Gicquel des Touches wrote,

> to rescue the Admiral, to take him on board, and to rally around us the vessels which were still in a fit state to fight. The plan was insane, and he himself did not believe in it; it was an excuse that he was giving himself in order to continue the fight, and so that no one could say that the *Intrépide* had left the battle while she still had a single gun and a single sail. It was a noble madness, which cost us dearly, but which we did with joy and alacrity: and which others should have imitated.

That is a note which is not found among the British accounts of Trafalgar. For all the hazards associated with Nelson's perpendicular drive at the iron teeth of the Combined Fleet's broadside; for all the questioning among the officers of the Royal Navy of that tactical idea; there is never a suggestion that this way of conducting battle was 'noble madness'. It was calculated risk, thriving on the sense that victory could only emerge from damage, and that annihilation of the enemy required an entry into the zone of acute danger. The difference between these mentalities, in other words, was the difference between death and destruction as a means to an end and as an end in itself. Self-sacrifice might have been accepted by Nelson and others in the British fleet as a possible cost; it was not the purpose of battle, as it had by now become for Infernet.

Collingwood had formed something of a line to resist

the ships of the French van now coming south towards him. Infernet drove past that line. The 64-gun *Africa* fired at him, but the *Intrépide*'s guns bellowed back and *Africa* was silenced. Gicquel des Touches found a young midshipman on the forecastle beside him. His face was calm and his bearing upright, maintaining, with his body, the language of honour. Gicquel offered him a glass of wine, which the boy took, but as he brought it up to his lips he could control himself no longer. His hand shook so much that the wine spilled all over the deck. Perhaps as any man would, Gicquel then grasped the boy's hand and told him that he admired him, and that courage lay not in the absence of fear but in mastering it.

British ships clustered around the *Intrépide*: Bayntun in the *Leviathan*, with rigging and rudder shot away after a bruisingly murderous encounter with the *San Agustín*, but still firing; Sir Edward Berry in the *Agamemnon*; Codrington in the *Orion*; even Northesk's *Britannia* which had by now lumbered into battle. Is it possible to conceive the degree of terror which such a sight would instil in any man, particularly those exposed on the deck of the *Intrépide*, as this ring of death closed around them? These moments on *Intrépide* represent one of the most desperate situations in the battle, entirely brought about by Infernet's drive for self-sacrificial honour.

Gicquel des Touches, frantically applying his men on the forecastle to repairing and reknotting the standing rigging by which the foremast was held up, was also keen – 'my ardent desire' – to use them to board a British ship. Codrington in the *Orion*, fighting the coolest-headed battle of all, saw that his friend Henry Bayntun was in trouble, with the beautiful *Leviathan*'s rig largely shot away, and manoeuvred to take on the *Intrépide* in his place. Bayntun hailed Codrington as he passed 'and said he hoped, laughing, that I should make a better fist of it.'

If there is something of the cricket match in that careless, gentlemanly, amused remark, a moment in which the ideal of the British naval officer seems to be fulfilled, as though a scene in a penny print entitled 'The Gentleman Gives Way' or perhaps 'After You Sir', nothing could be further from the atmosphere of extreme anguish on the *Intrépide*. Gicquel des Touches saw

> the English vessel *Orion* pass in front of us in order to fire a series of broadsides at us. I arranged my men ready to board, and pointing out to a midshipman the manoeuvres of the *Orion*, I sent him to the captain to beg him to steer so as to board.

Savagery was being poured in the *Intrépide*. Two thirds of her men were now killed or wounded. The sea was hosing in below where shot had punctured the hull. The shrieking of the wounded was drowned by the bellowing of guns. The concentration of British firepower in the centre of the battle was focused on her.

In the forecastle, Gicquel des Touches waited for the change of course which would drive her bow into the *Orion* amidships. But no change of course occurred. Codrington's men fired broadside after broadside into the bow of the *Intrépide* as they passed. Alongside, half a pistol shot away, the *Britannia* slammed at her with her upper batteries. This was annihilation in action, precisely the devastation which Nelson had required. The *Orion* slipped beyond reach and Gicquel des Touches went back towards the quarterdeck to find out why his recommendation had not been followed.

On his way there – and this may be the most poignant failure of courage in Trafalgar, a scene for a matching penny print, this one entitled the 'The Midshipman's Dread' – Gicquel des Touches found the boy he had sent back a few minutes earlier, lying down behind the bulwarks of the *Intrépide*, flat on his stomach, terrified by the sight of the

Britannia alongside, unable to move, let alone stand up and walk as far as the quarterdeck to deliver his message. In all the accounts of Trafalgar as they have been preserved, this is the rarest of experiences: paralysing terror. Gicquel des Touches kicked him in the backside and then went on to find Infernet. The captain was breathing fire, slicing off the carved wooden balls on the rail with his sabre and threatening anyone who talked of surrender – undoubtedly the right course of action – with death.

Dumanoir's squadron, coming south, had divided in two, half of it passing to windward of the battle, half to leeward, neither having much effect on the outcome. One ship after another fired at them as they came past: the *Mars*, the *Royal Sovereign*, the *Téméraire*, the *Bellerophon* and the *Victory*. It was these guns firing at Dumanoir's passing ships which Nelson in his last moments heard deep within the bowels of the flagship, shaken by their roaring, to which he muttered, as Beatty so carefully recorded, 'Oh *Victory*, *Victory*, how you distract my poor brain.' Dumanoir kept well to windward. 'It is too late to push in now,' he told his flag captain. 'To join in the battle now would be only an act of despair. It would only add to our losses.' The *Victory*'s log says they 'fired our larboard guns at those they would reach.' But even such long-distance fire was made to tell. The *Formidable* had 65 men killed and wounded on board and the hull was damaged enough for the water to be rising in her hold at the rate of four feet an hour. Her mainyard was broken, her sails shot through, her bowsprit and the mizzenmast shattered. This was damage enough for Dumanoir to claim he had played his part at Trafalgar. It didn't impress Napoleon who after the news of the battle reached France expressed the desire to see Dumanoir either shot or ruined. He eventually escaped either fate and became a distinguished sailor after the restoration of the Bourbons to the French throne.

Dumanoir fired at those British ships that confronted him, and even at the French and Spanish prizes around them. It was a perfectly deliberate act. The *Formidable* was seen to back her topsails so that she would slow down while firing into the prizes, simply to give herself longer on the target. His gunfire killed and wounded several on board, French, Spanish and English, and scandalised the officers. This was not part of the manners of war. Perhaps it adds another possible reason for Dumanoir's strange behaviour this day: panic. He soon made off to the south with his four sail-of-the-line. Eleven ships to leeward joined Admiral Gravina, who was gathering what remained of the fleet, to conduct them in to Cadiz. Several British ships began to chase them but were recalled by Collingwood.

Battered in the midst of the battle, the *Intrépide* was now a mass of wreckage. She had been firing with both broadsides at once and even with her stern-chasers. No living Frenchman remained on her decks. All her masts had been shot away and had gone by the board. The guns were 'clogged with the dead'. The ship itself was a corpse, leaking, all the lids of the gunports torn off. Most of the guns were disabled, eight feet of water was in the hold and rising, despite the efforts of the men at the pumps, 306 officers and men were killed and wounded, 45% of those on board. Even then, Infernet could not bring himself to surrender and his surviving officers had to hold him down while the colours were lowered.

'Ah what will the Emperor say,' he groaned as he watched, 'after I told him that I could fight my way through ten battles and I have failed at the first?' Napoleon, in fact, would honour him. But the crew of the *Intrépide* felt they had done enough. As Gicquel des Touches wrote in his memoir of the battle: 'At least our honour was saved, the task accomplished, duty fulfilled to the uttermost.' It was a demonstration of courage which impressed the British officers. On the *Conqueror*, Lieutenant Humphrey Senhouse said in a letter home that the defence of the *Intrépide* 'deserves to be recorded in the memory of those who admire true heroism.'

At this distance, it is worth interrogating this scene a little more. What was in control here? What drove Infernet to his suicidal mission, to risk all, not for any hope of a positive outcome, because it was surely clear by the time he arrived in the heart of Trafalgar that he could make no difference at all, but simply for the symbolism of martyrdom?

The recent history of France had put a particular spin on the idea of heroism, idealism and self-sacrifice. In some ways, the French Revolution had been profoundly conservative. The modernising trends which had been in play in France throughout the 18th century were cut short in the new revolutionary ideology. In the third quarter of the 18th century, France had been making aggressive strides in the direction of an Anglo-style, commercial, Atlantic entrepreneurial culture. The French nobility, conventionally portrayed as affected, self-indulgent and out of touch, were in fact closely involved in finance, business and industry, especially in the booming Atlantic sugar and slave economy of the West Indies. Nor were they crusty old families, descended from the knights of the Middle Ages. Fully a quarter of all French aristocratic families, 6,000 of them, had been ennobled in the 18th century, bourgeois families who had joined the élite. In their hands, France's foreign trade had increased tenfold in the 60 years before the Revolution.

That entrepreneurial drive had been interrupted and destroyed at the Revolution and replaced with a far more static and Roman ideal of nobility. If the late-18th-century shift in England had been from the Virgilian to the Homeric ideals of manhood, as the dominant ideology of England turned towards market success, in France it went the other way. Paradoxically enough, revolutionary and Napoleonic France was dominated by Roman and even aristocratic ideals.

Livy, Plutarch, the fierce demands and emotional appeal of Roman oratory, Cicero as '*père de la Patrie*' – these were the models to which the revolutionaries appealed. In them they saw the nobility of republicanism, fiercely dividing itself off from the luxury and corruption of the materialist world around them. Civic morality, a Rousseauesque rigour, an enthusiasm for liberty, stoic self-possession and an austere masculinity were all the ingredients of a Roman, republican integrity. The Corinthian enrichments of mid-18th–century Europe gave way to Doric rigour. Even hairstyles, led by the example of actors on the Paris stage, showed the world the sort of man you were. Unlike the elaborated curls of the aristocrats (in which Villeneuve appears, interestingly, in his portraits), straight, unpowdered hair, cropped short and brushed forward – modelled, it was said, on the hair of English roundheads – showed you were a true republican. An article appeared in *Patriote français* in October 1790:

> This coiffure is the only one that is suited to republicans: being simple, economical and requiring little time, it is trouble-free and so assures the independence of a person; it bears witness to a mind given to reflection, courageous enough to defy fashion.

This was, in other words, Infernet hair. It was evidence not of particular actions, but of the condition of your soul, of being in a state of republican grace. The outcome of any action mattered less than your moral wholesomeness when you engaged in them.

Of course there are many echoes in France of changes in

England. The Rousseauist ideas which form such a potent backdrop to Trafalgar – that the good man is not the affected dandy posing at court and lying his way into luxuries of a hypocritical world, but standing foursquare in his honest simplicity, sobriety, stoicism and directness – that is a common European inheritance. But in France, it fed straight into the dazzlingly powerful exporting of the Revolution to the rest of Europe, seen in France not as an act of imperialism but of revolutionary idealism. France was like a citadel of freedom besieged on all sides. Her rampage through Europe had been a break-out from that citadel, releasing a tidal wave of liberty to the benighted: Belgium and Savoy in 1792, the Rhineland and the Netherlands in 1794, northern Italy and Venice in 1797, Switzerland in 1798, followed by Rome, Malta, Naples and Egypt. The people of Europe, and even of the world, were being shown the light.

That is not, of course, how it was seen in England nor by her allies on the continent of Europe, but it is central to the fighting idealism of Infernet's drive into the blood and destruction of Trafalgar. In November 1792, the French National Convention had declared 'in the name of the French nation that she will bring help and brotherhood to all people who want to recover their freedom.' Goethe, witnessing the arrival of the French armies in Germany, thought 'they seemed to be bringing only friendship, and really they did bring it. All of them were in a state of heightened exhilaration, with great enthusiasm they planted trees of freedom, to everyone they promised self-government and the rule of law. In front of our eyes, hope was floating in the air of the future and drew our gaze towards new ways, newly open . . .'

For all the often-remembered horrors and brutalisations of revolutionary and Napoleonic France, there is this underlayer of heroic republican idealism, a sense that the perfect vision of humanity had been glimpsed, before sinking under the blood, shock and terror of a pan-European war. The death and wounding of so many on the *Intrépide* was in the service of that ideal, whose goal was not victory but a state of mind, an honourable freedom, complete in itself, beyond any thought of survival or gain. That was not an English idea. The English wanted victory, but, in that sense, Auguste Gicquel des Touches's words were a precise description of the French: their honour had been saved.

The battle was nearly over and devastation lay afloat on the Atlantic. The mastless hulks, no longer with any sails aloft to act as a stabilising vane, rolled in the swell. On the *Santísima Trinidad*, a Spanish officer surveyed his surroundings.

> The English shot had torn our sails to tatters. It was as if huge invisible talons had been dragging at them. Fragments of spars, splinters of wood, thick hempen cables cut up, as corn is cut by the sickle, fallen blocks, shreds of canvas, bits of iron, and hundreds of other things that had been wrenched away by the enemy's fire, were piled about the deck, where it was scarcely possible to move. Blood ran in streams about the deck, and in spite of the sand, the rolling of the hull carried it hither and thither until it made strange patterns on the planks. The enemy's shot, fired as they were from very short range, caused horrible mutilations. The ship creaked and groaned as she rolled, and through a thousand holes and crevices in her hull the sea spurted and began to flood the hold.

At 6.30, the English took possession of her and began to heave the dead overboard, 254 killed, and others dying among the 173 wounded. In the Combined Fleet as a whole, the number of dead has never been established. It might well have been in the region of 4,000 men. Perhaps twice that number had been wounded and just over 11,000 had been taken prisoner. Between two and three thousand more would be drowned or die of their wounds in the coming days: a total perhaps of 6,500 dead. The number of British casualties is strikingly low and exact: 449 dead, 1,214 wounded, several hundred of whom would also die in the coming weeks, perhaps a total of 650 dead. That was the winning ratio: ten to one.

In one French ship, with only her foresail set, the captain stood on the poop, holding the lower corner of a small French flag, while he pinned the upper corner with his sword to the stump of the mizzenmast. She fired two or three guns, probably to provoke some return fire, and to spare the crew the shame of a tame surrender. The *Conqueror* was alongside her and the British broadside was ready to destroy the Frenchman. Then the *Conqueror*'s Captain Israel Pellew shouted, 'Don't hurt the brave fellow; fire a single shot across his bow.' Her captain immediately lowered his sword, thus dropping the colours, and, taking off his hat, bowed his surrender.

Courtesy and humanity eased into the spaces which battle had opened up. Far down at the southern end of the battle zone, the *Prince,* one of the heavy slow sailers at the rear of Collingwood's division – she was said to have approached the battle like a haystack and her captain, Richard Grindall, was another who was said to have behaved 'notoriously ill' – had come up with the French *Achille*, which had already received the attentions of three British ships. A fire had already broken out in the chest containing arms and cartridges in the top on the foremast. The *Achille*'s fire pumps had already been smashed in the battle and the fire blazed up into the sails above it. Then the *Prince* fired a high broadside into the vessel and cut the foremast in two. The topmast fell with its fire into the waist of the ship, setting fire to the boats and spars that were stored there.

The whole ship was soon ablaze and the *Prince* ceased firing when her captain saw men on the *Achille* jumping overboard. Deep within her, below the waterline, there was a woman on board, Jeannette Caunant, stationed in the passage of the fore-magazine, working to assist in handing up the powder to the men in the batteries. When the firing ceased, she tried to make her way up to the lower deck and then to the main deck, looking for her husband. But passage was impossible. All the ladders joining the decks had either been removed or shot away. It was a desperate situation. Surrounded by the mangled, the wounded, the dead, the body parts, she could see the fire burning down through the decks to reach her. As the flames weakened each deck, the guns themselves burst down through the burning planks on to the decks below, each gun three tons of red-hot metal smashing down like depth charges around her. She climbed out through a gunport and then hung above the water, at the stern of the wreck, awaiting her fate. The little British schooner, the *Pickle* and a cutter, the *Entreprenante*, along with boats from the *Prince* and the *Belleisle* ran in as close as they could to the wreck, 'to save the people which were floating on different spars belonging to the ship', even though the already-shotted guns, as the fire reached them, were blowing off uncontrollably and unpredictably. In all, in a fore-echo of the rescues of the days to come, between two and three hundred Frenchmen were rescued by the British from the *Achille*. Jeannette Caunant was also pulled from the sea, naked, and taken to the *Pickle*, where she was dressed and her wounds tended.

Then the ship blew up. A British officer on the *Defence* watched it:

> It was a sight the most awful and grand that can be conceived. In a moment the hull burst into a cloud of smoke and fire. A column of vivid flame shot up to an enormous height in the atmosphere and terminated by expanding into an immense globe, representing for a few seconds, a prodigious tree in flames, speckled with many dark spots, which the pieces of timber and bodies of men occasioned while they were suspended in the clouds.

It was a vision of explosive war, of the victims of war tossed like the black leaves of a tree radiant with fire and light, fulfilling all the expectations of apocalypse. As the fragments fell back into the Atlantic, and the shattered remains of the *Achille* sank, a black pig was seen swimming strongly through the swell. The men on the *Euryalus* caught, killed, butchered, roasted and ate it that evening.

The battle was nearly at its end. The fervour of the morning had given way not to triumph nor to any sense of glory, but to desperation among the defeated, and to both exhaustion and dejection among those who had won. Very few people knew what had happened to Nelson and it was not his death which governed the final reactions to battle; it was the nature of the battle itself, an experience of bruising mutual destruction from which those involved emerged deadened.

Thomas Hardy, Nelson's flag captain on the *Victory*, when he later returned to England with all 'the Ships Flags and Pendants half Mast on the melancholly occasion' and his admiral's body preserved in the biggest water butt they could find, a leaguer, lashed in the heart of the ship, and stood over night and day by an armed marine, had one thing to tell his navy friends. 'You have often talked of attacking a French line-of-battle ship with two frigates,' he said to Captain Parker of the *Amazon* who came aboard at Spithead. 'Now, after what I have seen at Trafalgar,

I am satisfied it would be mere folly, and ought never to succeed.'

'Mere folly' is a phrase which in early-19th-century English still means 'total and utter folly': and Hardy's remark is in the voice of sobriety and battle-shock, a measure of what had occurred at Trafalgar, of the cold sluice of horror delivered to his appetite for battle. The enemy had responded with a ferocity and obstinacy which neither he nor his friends had been prepared for. The last two major fleet actions had been at the Nile in 1798, when the French had been surprised at anchor, half the crews were ashore and the unprepared gundecks were cluttered with stores and baggage; and at Copenhagen in 1801, when the Danes, also at anchor, had never considered themselves a match for the British fleet. The resistance they had met at Trafalgar had come as some shock.

Hardy's remarks are also astonishingly modern in their tone, full of a sense of battle reality which, we assume too easily, was scarcely known before the twentieth century. But it was known, and the condition that became known as shell shock or battle fatigue could be found in Georgian England. In a fragment written in 1798 and later included in the *Prelude*, the young Wordsworth described how he had met a discharged soldier on the road and walked alongside him:

> While thus we travelled on I did not fail
> To question him of what he had endured
> From war and battle and the pestilence.
> He all the while was in demeanour calm,
> Concise in answer: solemn and sublime
> He might have seemed, but that in all he said
> There was a strange half-absence and a tone
> Of weakness and indifference, as of one
> Remembering the importance of his theme,
> But feeling it no longer.

This half-absence, this dejected disconnection, which Wordsworth later described as 'the ghastly mildness in his look', is the result of horror undergone. The last phase of Trafalgar, and the storm which followed it, both contributed as much to that experience as anything that had gone before.

Lieutenant Philibert on the *Tonnant* surveyed the appalling scene. In the quiet of the early evening, all order had gone. All the beauty of the morning had been shot away. The wounded sobbed as they were moved and shrieked as they had their clothes stripped from them. For all that, a kind of silence had descended.

> The smoke which had enveloped us up to then having cleared, our first glances searched for our fleet; there no longer existed any line on either side; we could see nothing more than groups of vessels in the most dreadful condition, in the place more or less where we thought our battle fleet ought to be. We counted 17 ships from the two navies totally dismasted – their masts gone right down to the deck, and many others partially dismasted.

On the *Conqueror*, Lieutenant Senhouse saw it all as 'a melancholy instance of the instability of human greatness.' Those beautiful fleets which only a few hours previously had been 'towering in all their pride on their destined element' were now these shattered hulks, 'lying like logs on the water, the surface of which was strewed with wreck.' On the *Belleisle* Lieutenant Nicolas thought 'Nothing could be more horrible than the scene of blood and mangled remains with which every part was covered, and which, from the quantity of splinters, resembled a shipwright's yard covered in gore.' Nicolas's comparison was exact: battle was a dismantling yard, a place in which the elaborate assembling of ten thousand separate particulars was disassembled, in which order was converted into disorder and an act of civility turned into pandaemonium, a version of hell drenched in blood, like a gravy. No beauty in this violence, just dis-orientating and re-orientating damage.

Admiral Gravina, that morning, had called the *Argonauta* 'the most beautiful flower in my garden'. Now officers from the *Belleisle* made their way across to her in a pinnace to take the Spaniards' surrender. They could hardly find a living person aboard. It was another wrecking yard of dismantled bodies and disintegrated gear. What remained of the crew was hiding below. The captain was wounded. The men from the *Belleisle* took the second captain, Pedro Albarracin, back to their ship, where they brought him to the cabin of their own captain, Edward Hargood. There Hargood accepted Albarracin's sword and in return offered him what hospitality he could. He gave him a cup of tea. As he and other officers from the *Belleisle* were drinking the tea, exhausted, melancholic, dwelling on the day of chaos and destruction, the death of friends, the shrieks of pain still coming from the wounded far below them in the ship, a lieutenant from the *Naiad* came into the captain's cabin. He had news: Nelson was dead.

On the *Royal Sovereign*, Collingwood was seen in tears. One of his sailors wrote home: 'Our dear Admiral Nelson is killed! So we have paid pretty sharply for licking em. I never set eyes on him, for which I am both sorry and glad; for to be sure, I should like to have seen him – but then, all the men in our ships who have seen him are such soft toads, they have done nothing but blast their eyes and cry ever since he was killed.' Those ships that did not receive the news directly looked out in the evening to the *Victory*. She was lightless and no Commander-in-Chief's night-signal burned in her rigging. After the Battle of the Nile, on that very evening, after the terror and anguish of battle, the British captains held a long, loud and celebratory dinner.

Nothing of the kind happened after Trafalgar and the British fleet ended the day sunk in gloom.

From the *Mars*, where her Captain George Duff had been killed by a roundshot which decapitated him, his 13-year-old son Norwich was transferred into the care of Henry Blackwood on the *Euryalus*, along with his schoolmaster William Dalrymple. In a sea of grief, the collection of letters now written to Sophia Duff, expresses the full range of the aftershock. These letters are, in miniature, a model of the British frame of mind in victory, surrounded by death.

First, Norwich sat down to write to his mother at home in 30 Castle St, Edinburgh. His big, open handwriting carefully followed the lines he had ruled on the paper, occasionally striking through a spelling mistake or an unnecessary word. For the battle, his father had sent him off the quarterdeck and down into the lower gundecks, where according to his schoolmaster he and the other boys 'had fought like young Nelsons.' Now this particular boy-man comforted his mother, to whom his father had been in the habit of writing every day, with words of stoic heroism:

> My dear Mama
>
> You cannot possibly imagine how unwilling I am to begin this melancholy letter: however as you must unavoidably hear of the fate of dear papa I write you these few lines to request you to bear it as patiently as you can he died like a hero having gallantly led his Ship into Action and his memory will every be dear to his King his Country & his friends.

But Norwich cannot keep up this Roman face for long. Now on board the *Euryalus*, Blackwood had been 'very polite & kind to me'. The frigate captain wanted to keep the boy with him, as one of his young gentlemen. But Norwich longed for home:

I would much rather wish to see you & to be discharged into the guard Ship at Leith [outside Edinburgh] for two or three months. My Dear Mamma I have again to request you to endeavour to make yourself as happy and as easy as possible. It has been the will of heaven & it is our duty to submit.

Believe me your obedient and affectionate Son
N. Duff.

It is difficult to believe that receiving such a letter would do anything but exacerbate the pain. Norwich survived into the age of photography to become a Victorian Vice-Admiral. There is a photograph of him looking crusty, be-whiskered and bald, in a frock-coat sitting on a pompous chair, taken in 1860, two years before he died, a version of the world for which Trafalgar was fought and his father died.

At the foot of Norwich's words, the schoolmaster Dalrymple added his own note, hand-wringingly aware of the pain of loss but at the same time wavering between anguish and congratulation, the 19th-century cult of the martyr vying for space in these few lines with the 18th-century cult of sensibility, proud of the dead man, gapingly open to the reality of grief.

Mrs Duff, Dear Madam
It is with sincere uneasiness and regret that I have occasion to offer my condolence to you on the late unfortunate but glorious and honourable fate of our worthy generous and brave captain, whose name will ever be revered and whose character will ever be esteemed. Believe me, I am your ever respectful and obedient humble Servant W. Dalrymple

Duff's first lieutenant, William Hennah, who had commanded the *Mars* in the battle with skill and distinction after Duff had been killed, wrote to Sophia on 27 October, when still off Cadiz. His letter can lay claim to being the most dignified and loving document to emerge from Trafalgar. In all its hesitations, and quivering on the brink of pomposity, in its deep sense of hurt and sympathy, its reticence and reluctance to intrude, its own grief and tender care for Sophia's grief, its half-articulateness, relying at its crucial point on the most commonplace phrases and ideas, it is, to use a word that should only rarely be used, replete with nobility:

> Madam,
> I believe that a more unpleasant task, than what is now imposed upon me, can scarcely fall to the lot of a person, whose feelings are not more immediately connected by the nearer ties of kindred, but from a sense of duty, (as first Lieutenant of the Mars,) as being myself the husband of a beloved partner, and the father of children; out of the pure respect and esteem to the memory of our late gallant Captain, I should consider myself guilty of a base neglect, should you only be informed of the melancholy circumstances attending the late glorious, though unfortunate victory to many, by a public gazette. The consequences of such an event, while it may occasion the rejoicings of the nation, will in every instance be attended with the deepest regrets of a few.
>
> Alas! Madam, how unfortunate shall I think myself, should this be the first intimation you may have of the irreparable loss you have met with! what apology can I make for entering on a subject so tender and so fraught with sorrow, but to recommend an humble reliance on this great truth, that the ways of Providence, although sometimes inscrutable, are always for the best.
>
> By this, Madam, you are in all probability acquainted with the purport of my letter. Amongst the number of heroes who fell on that ever-memorable 21st inst. in defence of their King and Country; after

gloriously discharging his duty to both; our meritorious and much respected Commander, Captain George Duff, is honourably classed; his fate was instantaneous; and he resigned his soul into the hands of the Almighty without a moment's pain.

Poor Norwich is very well. Captain Blackwood has taken him on board the Euryalus, with the other young gentlemen that came with him, and their schoolmaster.

The whole of the Captain's papers and effects are sealed up, and will be kept in a place of security until proper persons are appointed to examine them. Meanwhile, Madam, I beg leave to assure you of my readiness to give you any information, or render you any service in my power.

And am, Madam, with the greatest respect,
Your most obedient and most humble servant,

William Hennah.

That tender tone of voice, which does not seek to obscure the dreadful realities of war but understands the value of life beyond and outside them, might also be seen as the quality for which Trafalgar was fought. It is the opposite of a raging, militaristic delight in violence. It is a return to the world of children, home, quiet and settled ease, in which, as Hennah imagines with a painful reality, the events of 21 October had in the Duff household created such a searing wound. The irony of Trafalgar is that such a world could only be reached through a battle as intense and all-absorbing as the one in which George Duff had died. Even here, almost entirely buried below the level of conscious thought, the deep pattern is steadily at work of millenarian peace reached through apocalyptic violence.

* * *

On the evening of the battle, the men could take stock. In the log of the *Swiftsure*, Thomas Cook, the master, wrote that evening:

> British ships taken sunken or destroyed – none
> Of Combined fleet taken sunk burnt or distroyed –
> 22 of the line

Cook had overestimated slightly. The true total was 17 taken, one blown up, but that, by any measure, was a victory. But the damage was horrific and in all ships the men now had to make their vessels workable. On *Victory*, at 5 o'clock that evening, the mizzenmast fell about ten feet above the poop, 'the lower masts, yards & Bowsprit all crippled, rigging and sails very much cut, the Ships around us very much crippled.' The men set up emergency rigging, runners and tackles, to prevent the other masts from falling over. She got under way 'under the remnants of Foresail and maintopsail', the men deep into the night 'employed Knotting the Fore and Main Rigging and Fishing [reinforcing with an extra timber] and Securing the Lower masts.' The carpenters stopped the shot holes. On the *Mars* all the masts were tottering – 'cut half asunder' – and they had 'no sails fit to set'. Every brace and piece of running rigging had been shot away and not a single shroud was left standing. On the *Africa*, hundreds of feet of oak, elm and deal planking were brought up from the stores for repairs. Three copper sheets and 400 feet of sheet lead were nailed over shot holes in the hull. An anchor stock was used as a 'fish', a reinforcing timber, for the shot bowsprit. Booms and spars were used to fish the mizzenmast. In other less damaged ships, such as the late arriving *Britannia*, it was running rigging that needed repair. On her, buoy rope was used to replace a fore topmast stay shot away. Thousands of feet of rope were rove through the blocks to replace halyards and braces shot away during the action.

But in savagely damaged ships, there could be no such return to neatness. In the *Africa*, the whole of the foremast, the whole of the mainmast and the whole of the mizzenmast, each with their associated topmasts and topgallant masts, with the boom irons and the studding sail booms and yards, had all been lost in the battle. As they fell down, they had crushed the materials on deck. The crew managed to jury rig the ship, using a main topgallant mast as a make-do mizzenmast. The ship's pinnace had been stove in during the action and was now repaired with copper sheeting. The glass in the main cabin which had been shot out was replaced. Only twelve days later, on November 3, did the carpenter make this sombre entry in his accounts:

Used in whitewashing the orlop
Glue 8 lbs
Lime 8 lbs
Brushes 4

With the whitewash they were erasing the memory of blood, deep down in the *Africa*, where the wounded had been treated and the dying had died.

Collingwood was faced with a monstrous task. A fleet of over fifty ships was his to control. Half of them were dismasted. The storm, which all predicted, was in the offing and would undoubtedly be on them before many hours were out. It would come in from the southwest and that would put them on a lee shore fringed with murderous shoals. After the battle, it felt like the revenge of the sea itself. Victory meant prizes and prizes meant money. Surveying the wrecks around them, men on all ships reckoned up their winnings. A midshipman might hope to get £100 from the prize money, a chaplain £500, each seaman maybe £30, a captain perhaps £10,000, enough to set him up for life. These were rewards on a spectacular level, more than four times what the fleet had received after the Battle of the Nile. The total value of the ships they had captured was perhaps

£1.5 million – although Collingwood that evening reckoned on £4 million – somewhere between £75 million and £200 million today. The men, in their exhaustion and their grief, were staring at a sea full of riches; but the storm threatened the haul.

For the next dreadful week, a triangle of forces held the British fleet in its grasp. The three controlling elements in play were the weather, the money and, most astonishing of all, a sense of humanity, a concern for the fate of their enemies. The tenderness of a Hennah or a Dalrymple was not confined to the officers nor directed only to a grieving widow in distant Edinburgh. For day after day, British crews risked their lives to save those of the French and Spanish sailors which the storm was threatening. If it had not been for the storm, the British could have taken their prizes easily in tow and made with them for Gibraltar. If not for the prizes, they might, largely unencumbered, have made their own way to safety. And if not for their humanity, they might quite casually have set the prizes adrift, with no care for the men on board. But each of these three demands was equally insistent and it made for a week of chaos and destruction, as horrifying as the day of battle had been.

The storm did not come on at first, and in the light winds and heavy swells, getting and keeping the heavily rolling dismasted ships in tow was an agonisingly difficult task. Tow ropes parted, towing ships misjudged the wind and were run into by the ships they were attempting to tow. The *Royal Sovereign* smashed into the *Euryalus* and carried away sections of her rigging and superstructure. Other ships were drifting inexorably towards the shoals off Cape Trafalgar. Nelson, early on the day of battle, had ordered the fleet to anchor after the action, and had reminded Hardy of that order as he lay dying. But Collingwood, as any seaman might, dreaded the notion of anchoring off a lee shore, and relying merely on the anchor warps to hold the ships away from the shoals. He wanted his valuable, damaged fleet to sail itself out of difficulty.

On 22 October the first of the ferocious winds came in from the southwest. Ship after ship swayed and trembled in front of the storm that was probably blowing Force 10 or even 11, a steady 50 knots of wind, gusting higher than that. In the *Euryalus*, staysails were split and blown away to shreds in heavy squalls at midnight. Men were sounding continuously with the leads for any warning in the dark of a shallowing sea, listening and looking for breakers to leeward. Early in the morning, just before dawn on the 23rd, *Victory*'s main yard, an enormous piece of timber, was suddenly torn away in the gale, splitting two huge pieces of canvas, the mainsail and the maintopsail, which tore themselves into useless rags in the wind. Twenty minutes later the *Royal Sovereign*'s foremast collapsed overboard, taking with it all the sails and rigging of that mast. She hoisted the signal 314, meaning 'Ship is in distress and in want of immediate assistance'. Guns, including the enormously heavy carronades in the poop, were being tossed overboard by the savagely quick motion of the unmasted ship, on which even seasoned sailors were being violently sick. Everywhere in the scattered, desperate fleet, tow ropes gave way, sheets snapped, loose-flapping sails shot themselves to rags. In the smaller ships of the fleet, the cutters and schooners, giant seas were being shipped aboard while men worked desperately at the pumps. Guns, shot, old and useless sails, anything unnecessary for the task of survival was heaved overboard. The *Leviathan* had to cut away the fore and main courses to save her masts. The *Mars* lost one cutter when the painter by which she was towing her gave way. Another cutter and a pinnace which they were towing were swamped and sank with all their gear. Her rudder was almost in two. At ten to six that evening, what remained of the ship's company gathered together to 'Commit the Body of Captn Duff to the Deep.'

On board those ships which had been smashed and ruined in the battle, life was even more precarious. The *Fougueux* broke her tow and drove ashore, smashing herself apart on the rocks and drowning very nearly every one of the men in her who had not been killed in the battle, a total of 546 dead out of a crew of some 650. One of the survivors described it afterwards only as 'a scene of horror', full of shrieking and groaning, tense with the anger of 'insubordinate men who would not help at the pumps, but only thought of themselves.'

In the *Redoutable*, the space between the decks was still heaped up with the battle-dead, the bodies rolling in a soft, rotten mayhem with each violent motion of the ship. The English *Swiftsure* took her in tow and a prize crew was put on board what can only have been a horror ship. All night long, English and French worked alongside each other at the pumps to keep her afloat, deadening, muscle-wrenching work. Some of the young French midshipmen began to hide arms in dark and secret places in the ship, preparing to re-take her, whispering to Lucas, their defeated captain, of their plans. He took it as a sign of the heroism of young Frenchmen. But at midday on the 23rd, her only remaining mast collapsed, broken away by the rolling of the ship, and five hours later, she signalled the *Swiftsure*. The water was gaining on them in the hold and the *Redoutable* would soon sink. The men of the *Swiftsure* got out their six boats, rowed back through the terrifying seas to the prize and transferred the English prize crew and about 100 wounded and 30 unwounded Frenchmen – all that was left of the 645 officers and men who had started the battle on her – to their own ship, gingerly lifting them down from the quarterdeck where the wounded had been brought up from below and laid out. Again and again the *Swiftsure*'s boats returned to her in seas running desperately high. At seven o'clock that evening, the poop of the *Redoutable* was underwater, and by 10.15 she sank, going down by the stern, taking with her the 300 dead and some 90 wounded who they had not been able to rescue. The men of the *Swiftsure* had taken extraordinary risks, at no benefit to themselves. It was an act, as Nelson had requested, of pure humanity. As they rowed away for the last time, it 'was the most dreadful scene that can be imagined as we could distinctly hear the cries of the unhappy people we could no longer assist.'

But fifty of those men managed to escape her and survive the night in the sea. At half-past-three the next morning, the log of the *Swiftsure* records, 'heard the Cries of some people & out Pinnass & part of the Crew of the Redutable on a raft & brought them on board.' At seven that morning: 'Discovered 2 other rafts with People on them that had saved there lives from the Redutable while sinking.' The men of the *Swiftsure* went out to get them in their boats, but when they came alongside, many of the horribly wounded and exhausted Frenchmen were unable to get up the ship's side, never easy in the rolling of the swell. Some of them died in the boats as the English sailors watched from above. Many were naked and the *Swiftsure* 'Served some slops to those who were destitute of cloaths.' The prisoners were then housed as deep as they could be in the ship, below the orlop deck, in the very nastiest part of the hold. 'Heaved overboard on order of captain to make room for Prisoners water casks 60, Butts 30, Puncheons 31.' Almost the only predicament it can have been preferable to was death by drowning.

On the morning of the 23rd, a small squadron made up of five ships-of-the-line and a few frigates, all of which had escaped with Gravina into Cadiz, came out again in an attempt to recapture some of the prizes. Henry Blackwood on the *Euryalus* was, as ever, writing to his wife.

> Last night and this day, my dearest Harriet, has been trying to the whole fleet, but more so to the Admiral who has the charge. It has blown a hurricane, but, strange to say, we have as yet lost but one ship – one of our finest prizes – *La Redoutable*; but which I feel the more, as so many poor souls were lost. The remains of the French and Spanish fleet have rallied, and are at this moment but a few miles from us – their object of course, to recover some captured ships or take some of the disabled English; but they will be disappointed, for I think and hope we shall have another touch at them ere long.

It was a brave attack. The British took it seriously, and Collingwood dispatched the *Neptune*, the *Britannia*, the *Defence*, the *Dreadnought* and the *Leviathan* to meet the threat, the ships clearing for action as soon as the sails were seen emerging from Cadiz. But the prizes and their damaged British accompaniment were nearer Cadiz than the British force which Collingwood sent to defend them and at first it went well for the Franco-Spanish squadron. The *Neptuno*, under a small British prize crew, couldn't hoist enough sail to escape. The Spanish prisoners on board rose against the prize crew, retook the ship and the *Neptuno* was soon taken in tow by the French frigate *Hermione*. The *Thunderer* felt she couldn't defend herself if she had the giant Spanish three-decker, the *Santa Ana*, in tow and she cast her off. The *Santa Ana* was then towed into Cadiz Bay. The *Conqueror* then abandoned the *Bucentaure* for the same reason and she was driven ashore and wrecked. Two prizes had been retaken, one destroyed. Only the cool-headed Edward Codrington on the *Orion* managed to make off with the *Bahama* in tow.

That night, though, conditions worsened. The Spanish *Rayo* lost all her masts, after her crew refused to climb the masts to reef the sails. She was driven ashore. The *Neptuno* and the *San Francisco de Asís* both dragged their anchors and were wrecked. The *Argonaute* and the *Indomptable* ran aground and broke up in the surf. The *Santa Ana* was safe in Cadiz, but overall the little fleet that had come out to strike a small blow back at the British had been destroyed. This was the end of any threat to revise the verdict of Trafalgar.

The storm still had four days to run before it would begin to ease. Monstrous seas were now rolling into the Gulf of Cadiz. The *Belleisle* which had experienced such a bruisingly dreadful battle was now in the most extreme and anxious danger. All three of her masts had gone and the ship was now attempting to sail on short jury masts rigged by the crew out of a few spare yards and booms, tightly lashed or woolded to the old mast-stumps. She had been under tow by the frigate *Naiad* but the tow had parted in the mountainous seas. Repeated attempts had been made to reconnect the frigate with 'the ungovernable hulk' of the *Belleisle* but the two vessels had crashed into each other and the *Naiad*'s stern virtually smashed in. She had withdrawn to preserve herself. Now the *Belleisle* – and is it any surprise that in these conditions men should attribute to their ships a sort of courage of their own? – was attempting to make her way close-hauled out of the Gulf of Cadiz, around Cape Trafalgar and into the safety of the Strait. But under a jury rig, no ship can keep close to the wind, and for every mile southwards they were making, they were making almost a mile to leeward.

Under the thrashing of the sea, two big 24-pounder guns broke loose from their lashings and careered around between the decks, dealing out damage to men and material as only a loose cannon could. With great difficulty they were 'choked up' with the men's hammocks. Roundshot rolled between the bodies of men who were too exhausted from working the pumps to do anything about them. With each roll, seas were breaking over the quarterdeck. The men on board thought they were going to die. At midnight, the captain summoned his officers to tell them that the *Belleisle* would soon take to the ground and they should prepare themselves. Every man knew what was meant: in raging seas over offshore reefs, men do not survive. 'Shipwreck in such a hurricane was certain destruction to all.' All night they waited, expecting death to come upon them. They lay in the dark, thinking of home. Just before dawn, with the help of a scrap of sail hoisted on a jib-boom that had been rigged up as a foremast, they managed to turn their ship away from the land and its murderous breakers. The next morning the *Naiad* found them again and, with all her sails set, spread fair before the westerly wind, with port and starboard topsail studding sails and royal studding sails on both the main and the foremast, looking like a swan of a ship, every stitch of glory up, towed the *Belleisle* into Gibraltar. The garrison had received news of the victory. They had been looking out for the victorious fleet but this was the first sign of it: a sea- and storm-battered frigate towing behind her a single, mastless, battle-ravaged, jury-rigged, patched and hammered ship-of-the-line. But a huge white ensign was flying from a flagstaff on her taff-rail and, as the *Belleisle* was warped slowly into the Gibraltar mole, every man on every ship in Gibraltar manned the yards and cheered her.

It was time for brutal decisions. Codrington in the *Orion* decided that he could not keep both the *Orion* and the Spanish prize he had in tow, the *Bahama*, off the lee shore. He ordered the tow rope cut, abandoning the 548 Spanish prisoners and the 50-odd men in the British prize crew to their deaths. Or so Codrington thought. In fact, by pure luck, the *Bahama* and its men survived, managing to anchor in the surf just off Cadiz beach the next morning, in a desperate condition, the rudder smashed, seven feet of water in the hold, but at least alive. There, for the time being, they would stay.

On other ships, it is difficult to imagine how men could tolerate such a form of existence. An English lieutenant and four English midshipmen, with 50 English sailors, were guarding about 400 Spaniards on board the *Monarca*. Like every other ship she was making several feet of water an hour and the pumps had to be worked continuously. Her mizzen and mainmast had gone, and the crew was desperately heaving overboard guns, anchors, shot – anything to lighten the ship. The British sailors had broken into the Spanish liquor store and were now lying drunk beside the bodies of the dead which no one had yet thrown into the sea. One of the young midshipmen, the 19-year-old Henry Walker, fell into the deepest despair. Battle had been tolerable compared with this. The fear of the Spanish rising on the few remaining Englishmen in the ship who were not drunk; the threat of the violence of the storm, the worst that even seasoned sailors had ever seen; the presence, for many hours at a time, of the threat of death: all this besieged the midshipman.

> When the ship made three feet of water in ten minutes, when our people were almost all lying drunk upon deck, when the Spaniards, completely worn out with fatigue, would no longer work at the only chain pump left serviceable; when I saw the fear of death so strongly depicted on the countenances of all around me, I wrapped myself in a union jack, and lay down upon deck for a short time, quietly awaiting the approach of death.

Young Henry Walker from Manchester, lying in the dark, wrapped in the union jack, thinking of death; you would scarcely believe such a picture on a stage, or even on a recruiting poster, but there is no reason to doubt its truth. And what does that intuitively chosen action describe? Perhaps the deep melancholy of battle and its aftermath; perhaps an overwhelming fear; perhaps a death conceived as honourable. It may be difficult for us now to see authenticity in a patriotic act, but that is simply a measure of the distance between now and 1805. The midshipman wrapping himself in the national shroud: perhaps one should dare to see in that a noble gesture? But death, however nobly and patriotically imagined, didn't come to Henry Walker. The *Monarca* also, for the moment, survived. The Spanish and the British officers together managed to get the ship before the wind and the next day drove her into the shallows off the Cadiz beaches, where she anchored.

By the morning of the 24th, Collingwood, overloaded with the responsibility of command, and appalled by the situation in which he and his broken fleet found itself, decided to cut his losses. Some of the prizes had escaped. Others had been swept up in the Franco-Spanish sortie of the 23rd from Cadiz. Some had sunk and others had broken up on the shore. Collingwood, apart from anything else, clearly needed some relief from the overwhelming anxiety of his command. To wait here on this lee shore much longer would be to risk the loss of a British ship-of-the-line. At 8.30 a.m. he made a general signal to the fleet. 'Prepare to quit and withdraw men from prizes after having destroyed or disabled them if time permits.' It was the standard language of the signal book, but it meant that between the desire for money and the brutal exigencies of the storm, the storm had won.

At ten o'clock, after Henry Bayntun on *Leviathan* had asked by signal for confirmation of the admiral's intention, Collingwood confirmed, in even more brutal phrases: 'Withdraw English, cut masts and anchors away from prizes.' What then evolved over the next four or five days, as one English ship and crew after another rescued the men – English, French and Spanish – who were on board the prizes that were to be destroyed, is one of the most unbrutal and humane actions ever undertaken by the Royal Navy. It is thought that about 2,000 men drowned in the Trafalgar storm, but there is no case of a Spanish or French crew drowning without men of an English prize crew drowning at the same time. In other words, there was no abandoning of the prisoners. Where they could be saved, they were. Uncounted numbers, perhaps amounting to about 8,000, were rescued. When you consider the sheer hazard of what Henry Bayntun called 'the vast rolling sea' bowling into the Gulf of Cadiz from the southwest, and when you consider what the men had gone through in the preceding days, their state of exhaustion, what they managed was a miracle.

That night, the evening of the 24th, the storm reached its height. The little cutter, the 70-foot *Entreprenante*, lost the jolly boat from her stern, tore the after-leach of her mainsail and carried away her topmast. Soon afterwards, the entire mainsail split and went overboard. Under little scraps of sail, her trysail and storm jib, she attempted to weather the worst. Seas were coming into her, the water was rising in the hold and she made repeated signals of distress with her guns. She was crowded with 157 men rescued from the *Achille*, four times the number of her own crew, more than 200 men in a 70-foot cutter. They were desperately short of water. More and more material was heaved overboard 'to lighten her being nearly Water log^{d}. Split the foresail and storm jib at midnight.'

Again and again boats drove into the breaking waves

inshore to rescue men from the *San Agustín*, the *Monarca*, the *Argonauta*, the French *Swiftsure* and the *Bahama*. Boats from the *Leviathan* took all but 150 of the most dreadfully wounded out of the *Monarca* before she was burnt The *Intrépide*, on which everyone was drunk, was very nearly emptied of its crew, the last four taken off in the dark on to the *Orion*. She was then set alight and blew up as she sank. From the *Argonauta*, 387 were laboriously transported to awaiting British ships.

The vast *Santísima Trinidad* had fifteen feet of water in her hold when she was finally abandoned, only after nearly a thousand people, between three and four hundred of them wounded, had been taken out, mostly through the windows of the stern galleries. 'What a sight when we came to remove the wounded,' a British officer remembered. 'We had to tie the poor mangled wretches round their waists, and lower them down into a tumbling boat, some without arms, others no legs, and lacerated all over in the most dreadful manner.'

As the last of the prisoners were being loaded into the boats, a sailor from the *Revenge* witnessed a scene whose story would be told again and again in 19th-century England:

> On quitting the ship [the *Santísima Trinidad*] our boats were so overloaded in endeavouring to save all the lives we could, that it is a miracle they were not upset. A father and his son came down the ship's side to get on board one of our boats; the father had seated himself, but the men in the boat, thinking from the load and the boisterous weather that all their lives would be in peril, could not thinking of taking the boy.
>
> As the boat put off, the lad, as though determined not to quit his father, sprang from the ship into the sea and caught hold of the gunwale of the boat, but his attempt was resisted, as it risked all their lives;

> and some of the men resorted to their cutlasses to cut his fingers off in order to disentangle the boat from his grasp. At the same time the feelings of the father were so worked upon that he was about to leap overboard and perish with his son.
>
> Britons could face an enemy but could not witness such a scene of self-devotion: as it were a simultaneous thought burst forth from the crew, which said, 'Let us save both father and son or die in the attempt!' The Almighty aided their design, they succeeded and brought both father and son safe on board our ship where they remained, until with other prisoners they were exchanged at Gibraltar.

At the last, British carpenters went aboard the *Santísima Trinidad* and cut holes below the waterline through which the Atlantic poured. As the boats left, the shrieks of the terminally wounded men on the lower decks could be heard as they felt the water rising to drown them. Thomas Fremantle saved a pug-dog from the wreck of the great ship, as well as a statue of the Virgin Mary, which the Fremantle family still treasure at home in Buckinghamshire.

For days and nights the dreadful task continued. The *Donegal,* which had joined the British fleet after the battle from Gibraltar, now performed prodigious rescues on ship after ship. She took 626 men out of the *Rayo*. Hundreds drowned attempting to get on to dry land through the surf. The French *Berwick* had all the wounded Frenchmen taken off and then the English prize crew, but the weather worsened, and the *Berwick* was driven ashore with another 300 hundred men still in her. The *Donegal* then got 184 out of the *Bahama*, helped in the rescue by some Spanish fishing boats.

By the 27th, the winds had started to ease and the anarchy of weather and destruction began to abate. Prisoners were exchanged with the Spanish. British officers, led by Henry Blackwood who hadn't slept or washed for days, dressed themselves in their most dignified uniforms to pay courteous visits to the officials in Cadiz. The Spanish admired them for it. No British ship had succumbed either to the battle or the storm. Even the little *Entreprenante* survived. Of the nineteen prizes they managed to save only four. The others were wrecked, sunk or burnt. It was a financial catastrophe, the hoped for £1.5 million reduced to a fifth of that. Parliament recognised the injustice and boosted the prize money by a special grant of £300,000, so that each captain in the end received £3,362, lieutenants £226, midshipmen £37 each and the seamen £6 10 shillings.

On 28 October, the tough-minded, frightening and ambitious Thomas Fremantle on the *Neptune* was writing to his wife Betsey in Swanbourne. The *Neptune* had the battered remnants of *Victory* in tow. Strapped in her middle gundeck, stood over by a marine, the body of Nelson rested in its giant closed barrel, filled with spirits. But Fremantle wasn't dwelling on the drooping melancholy of the scene. The tone of his letter is a reminder that an aggressively self-interested frame of mind had driven the British fleet to victory and had even played its part in the extraordinary seaman-like and humanitarian efforts of the week of the storm. Fremantle was thinking of the future: 'This last Week,' he told his wife,

> has been a scene of Anxiety and fatigue beyond any I have ever experienced but I trust in God that I have gained considerable credit. I am at present towing the Victory and the Admiral [Collingwood] has just made the signal for me to go with her to Gibralter, which is a satisfactory proof to my mind that he is perfectly satisfied with Old Neptune, who behaves as well as I could wish. The loss of Nelson is a death

> blow to my future prospects here, he knew well how to appreciate Abilities and Zeal, and I am well aware that I shall never cease to lament his loss while I live.

No grief expressed for the loss of Nelson, except in terms of what it would mean for Fremantle's career and hopes of promotion. No sense of sublime triumph. No belief in the beauty of battle. The point of war was to win, to get on in the world, to make some money, to garner the prizes. Still at sea on the long roll of the Atlantic, Fremantle was still acting to the dictates of the go-getting, materialist and driven officer-class which the culture of 18th-century England had created.

A few miles away, on the long beach south of Cadiz, an Englishman, anxious for news of the battle, found a landscape drenched in another mood, the essence of what the century to come would take from Trafalgar:

> As far as the eye could reach, the sandy side of the isthmus bordering on the Atlantic was covered with masts and yards, the wrecks of ships, and here and there the bodies of the dead . . . While surrounded by these wrecks, I mounted on the cross-trees of a mast which had been thrown ashore, and casting my eyes over the ocean, beheld, at a great distance, several masts and portions of wreck floating about. As the sea was now almost calm, with a light swell, the effect produced by these objects had in it something of a sublime melancholy, and touched the soul with a remembrance of the sad vicissitudes of human affairs.

This was printed anonymously in the *Naval Chronicle* and, as the writer recognised, what he was describing was the sublime, the strange, poetic and ambivalent pleasure to be taken from the broken, the dreadful and the damaged, particularly when seen on such a scale. It is a painterly and theatrical image, which had already been imagined, painted and described many hundreds of times in the previous century. The near calm, the removal from battle, is of its essence. 'When danger or pain press too nearly,' the young Edmund Burke had written in his essay on the Sublime, 'they are incapable of giving any delight, and are simply terrible; but at certain distances, and with certain modifica-ions, they may be, and they are delightful, as we every day experience.' Somewhere deep in the substance of Trafalgar, in its victory, its damage and its loss, was something profoundly satisfying to the early-19th-century frame of mind.

England grieved for Nelson as they might for a hero of the theatre or the opera. For the hero to die at his moment of triumph, even as a signal that the triumph had been achieved, was once again the aesthetic requirement of the moment. The version of 'King Lear' with which the 18th century had always been happy, in which Cordelia doesn't die, now for the first time since the early 1700s seemed inadequate. To make the play complete, to bring about the heroic sublime, Cordelia had once again to die, to be carried on stage dead. Can it be a coincidence that Nelson's death, at precisely this moment in his drama, also conforms to the pattern of the tragic sublime? Or that Nelson was the first British admiral to have died in action since 1720?

A decade after the battle, Wordsworth, in his *Thanksgiving Odes*, written to celebrate the final victory over Napoleon at Waterloo, would address the God he was thanking for the victory.

> Thy most dreaded instrument,
> In working out a pure intent,
> Is Man – arrayed for mutual slaughter, –
> Yea, Carnage is thy daughter!

The slaughter of these wars was seen by Wordsworth as divine virtue at work. 'Carnage is God's daughter' was a phrase which shocked his more radical contemporaries, but it would find sympathetic echoes in 19th-century England. Thomas de Quincey agreed that 'among God's holiest instruments for the elevation of human nature is "mutual slaughter" amongst men'. De Quincey thought war allowed man to breathe 'a transcendent atmosphere' and to experience 'an idea that else would perish: viz. The idea of mixed crusade and martyrdom, doing and suffering, that finds its realisation in battle.' The disgusting reality of war – the rolling of the corpses in the mastless hulks during the Trafalgar storm, the blood making its patterns on the deal planks of the decks, the quantities of whitewash needed to obscure the bloodstains on the orlop decks of every ship, the spattering of men's faces with the remains of their friends, the actual appearance of the terrible splinter wounds – that becomes obscured under the sublime and theatrical beauties and the exquisite moral drama of distant violence.

Such a conception of war became the Victorian orthodoxy. For Ruskin, war itself was the foundation of beauty. 'There is no great art possible to a nation but that which is based on battle,' he told a London audience in 1865. It was a frame of mind which drew on the theatrics of Trafalgar, a celebration of what Ruskin called 'creative, or foundational war',

> in which the natural restlessness and love of contest among men are disciplined, by consent, into modes of beautiful – though it may be fatal – play . . . To such war as this all men are born; in such war as this any man may happily die; and out of such war as this have arisen throughout the extent of past ages, all the highest sanctities and virtues of humanity.

These disturbing words – and this habit of mind among 19th-century Englishmen – are the context in which the legacy of Trafalgar and the death of Nelson are to be understood. The great and dreadful victory at sea on 21 October

1805 played itself out in the mind of Englishmen as a near-perfect example of violent moral theatre whose sublime beauty relied on its distance and its dreadfulness. It became for them a form of battle-arcadia, a place in which the ordinariness, the disappointments and the compromises of everyday life were somehow absent. The fact that Wordsworth, de Quincey and Ruskin, like the majority of 19th-century Englishmen, had never been near a war was central to their beautiful conception of it. Neither they nor their audiences had any idea what it was like.

This understanding of war lasted, at full strength, until the shock of the trenches. It is the received idea of Trafalgar, of Romantic Battle, which infuses, for example, a letter written by a young British lieutenant, Alexander Gillespie, on the evening before his company went into the attack at Loos on the Western Front in 1915.

> My dear Daddy,
> Before long I think we shall be in the thick of it, for if we do attack, my company will be one of those in front, and I am likely to lead it . . . It will be a great fight, and even when I think of you, I would not wish to be out of this. You remember Wordsworth's 'Happy Warrior':
>
> Who if he be called upon to face
> Some awful moment to which Heaven has joined
> Great issues, good or bad, for human kind,
> Is happy as a lover, and attired
> With sudden brightness like a man inspired.
>
> Well, I could never be all that a happy warrior should be, but it will please you to know that I am very happy, and whatever happens, you will remember that . . .
>
> Always your loving
> Bey.

Poor Gillespie knew only what the tradition of Romantic Battle, with its roots not exactly in Trafalgar but in the received idea of Trafalgar, had taught him. Only with the mass exposure of Englishmen to the humiliating and nauseating realities of battle could such a conception begin to die. Then the vision was replaced by something like this, lines written by Wilfred Owen:

> If you could hear, at every jolt, the blood
> Come gargling from the froth-corrupted lungs,
> Obscene as cancer, bitter as the cud
> Of vile, incurable sores on innocent tongues.

In the hands of Owen, Siegfried Sassoon and Robert Graves, war came to be seen not as a shrine to innocence, but as its destroyer. The shadow, or perhaps the light of Trafalgar, with its halo of courage, beauty and honour, its powerful and Elysian idea of the Happy Warrior, lasted only until the killing fields of industrial war.

The 19th century had chosen to remember only the Happy Warrior; the 20th century only 'the blood come gargling.' Both are essential to any understanding of Trafalgar: the uncompromising violence; the dedicated grip on the need for 'annihilation'; the seeking of victory through exsanguination; combined with a hunger for honour; a belief in the reality of noble ideas; self-possession as a mark of nobility; and behind all that a tender and active humanity. However reluctant people have become to describe battle in this way, these are the ambivalent ingredients of sublime and noble war, of a kind which Homer and Virgil would have recognised, and all of which were undeniably there on 21 October 1805. It was a brutal amalgam and remains an inheritance with a troubling moral ambiguity at its heart.

BIBLIOGRAPHY

MANUSCRIPTS

National Archives, Kew

Admiralty In Letter Book, Mediterranean Station, May–December 1805 ADM/1/411

Captain's Logs:
September-October 1805

Achille ADM 51/1535
Agamemnon ADM 51/1576
Belleisle ADM 51/1515
Bellerophon ADM 51/1522
Britannia ADM 51/1552
Conqueror ADM 51/1529
Entreprenante ADM 51/4443
Leviathan ADM 51/1526
Mars ADM 51/1493 & 4472
Neptune ADM 51/1545
Orion ADM 51/1635
Revenge ADM 51/1535
Royal Sovereign ADM 51/1533
Swiftsure ADM 51/1550
Téméraire ADM 51/1530
Tonnant ADM 51/1547
Victory ADM 51/4514

Master's Logs:
September-October 1805

Achille ADM 52/3561
Agamemnon ADM 52/3563
Belleisle ADM 52/3734
Britannia ADM 52/3572
Conqueror ADM 52/3742
Leviathan ADM 52/3640
Mars ADM 52/3654
Neptune ADM 52/3657
Orion ADM 52/3662
Pickle ADM 52/3669
Revenge ADM 52/4273
Royal Sovereign ADM 52/3678
Spartiate ADM 52/4323 & 3691
Swiftsure ADM 52/3693
Téméraire ADM 52/3706
Tonnant ADM 52/3707
Victory ADM 52/3711

BUCKINGHAMSHIRE COUNTY RECORD OFFICE

Fremantle Papers

Swanbourne inventory D/FR/41/6
Rice contretemps D/FR/31/5
Post-Trafalgar strategic situation 1807 D/FR/32/2/1

BEDFORDSHIRE COUNTY RECORD OFFICE

Bayntun papers

Out Letter book 1799–1800 X170/4/1
Leviathan's Rough Log Book for 1805 X 170/1/2
Leviathan's Muster Book for 1805 X 170/2/2
1804 Letter to Bayntun on *Leviathan* warning of gale in Gulf of Cadiz X 170/7/2

NAVY RECORDS SOCIETY PUBLICATIONS

Bonner Smith, David, (ed.), Letters of Admiral of the Fleet the Earl of St Vincent, Navy Records Society, 1921, 1927
Corbett, Julian S., (ed.), Fighting Instructions 1530–1816, Navy Records Society, 1905
Firth, C.H., (ed.), Naval Songs and Ballads, Navy Records Society, 1907
Hughes, Edward, (ed.), The Private Correspondence of Admiral Lord Collingwood, Navy Records Society, 1907
Laughton, John Knox, (ed.), Letters and Papers of Charles, Lord Barham 1758–1813, Navy Records Society, 1911
Lavery, Brian, (ed.), Shipboard Life and Organisation 1731–1815, Navy Records Society, 1998
Thursfield, H.G., (ed) Five Naval Journals 1789–1817, Navy Records Society, 1951

BOOKS

Abrams, M.H., *The Mirror and the Lamp, Romantic Theory and the Critical Tradition* (Oxford, 1953)

Ackroyd, Peter, *Blake* (London, 1995)

Adkins, Roy, *Trafalgar: The Biography of a Battle* (London, 2004)

Austen, Jane, *Pride and Prejudice (1813)* (London, 1994)

Bainbridge, Simon, *Napoleon and English Romanticism* (Cambridge, 1995)

Bainbridge, Simon, *British Poetry and the Revolutionary and Napoleonic Wars, Visions of Conflict* (Oxford, 2003)

Barker, Hannah and Chalus, Elaine, (eds.), *Gender in Eighteenth-Century England* (London, 1997)

Barker, Juliet, (ed.), *Wordsworth, A Life in Letters* (London, 2002)

Broadley, A.M. and Bartelot, R.G., *Three Dorset Captains at Trafalgar* (London, 1906)

Burke, Edmund, *A Philosophical Enquiry into the Origin of our Ideas of the Sublime and Beautiful (1757)* (Oxford, 1990)

Burke, Edmund, *Reflections on the Revolution in France (1790)* (London, 1968)

Christiansen, Rupert, *Romantic Affinities, Portraits from an Age 1780–1830* (London, 1988)

Clayton, Tim and Craig, Phil, *Trafalgar: The Men, The Battle, The Storm* (London, 2004)

Chandler, David G., *The Campaigns of Napoleon* (London, 1966)

Clark, Kenneth, *The Romantic Rebellion, Romantic versus Classic Art* (London, 1973)

Cobb, Richard, *The People's Armies* (New Haven and London, 1987)

Coleman, Terry, *Nelson, The Man and the Legend* (London, 2001)

Colley, Linda, *Britons, Forging the Nation 1707–1837* (London, 1992)

Committee on Trauma, American College of Surgeons, *Advanced Trauma Life Support Course* (Chicago, 1989)

Cormack, William S., *Revolution and Political Conflict in the French Navy 1789–1794* (Cambridge, 1995)
Crawford, Capt. A., *Reminiscences of a Naval Officer (1851)* (London, 1999)

Desbriére, Edouard, *The Trafalgar Campaign* (London, 1933)
de san Miguél, Brigadier Don Vicente Tofio, *Atlas Maritimo de España* (Madrid, 1789)
Dear, Ian and Kemp, Peter, *An A-Z of Sailing Terms* (Oxford, 1992)
Downer, Martin, *Nelson's Purse* (London, 2004)
Dull, Jonathan, *'Why Did the French Revolutionary Navy Fail?' Proceedings of the Consortium on Revolutionary Europe XVIII* (2) (1989): 121–37

Eagleton, Terry, *Sweet Violence, The Idea of the Tragic* (Oxford, 2003)
Erskine, David, (ed.), *Augustus Hervey's Journal (1953)* (London, 2002)

Fraser, Edward, *The Enemy at Trafalgar (1906) (*London, 2004)
Fraser, Flora, *Beloved Emma* (London, 1986)
Fremantle, Anne, *The Wynne Diaries* (London, 1933–1940)
Fussell, Paul, *The Great War and Modern Memory* (Oxford, 2000)

Gardiner, Robert, *The Line of Battle, The Sailing Warship 1650–1840* (London, 1992)
Girouard, Mark, *The Return to Camelot, Chivalry and the English Gentleman* (New Haven and London, 1981)
Girouard, Mark, *The English Town* (New Haven and London, 1990)
Goodwin, Peter, *Nelson's Ships 1771–1805* (London, 2002)
Goodwin, Peter, *Men o'War, the Illustrated Story of Life in Nelson's Navy* (London, 2003)

Harbron, John, *Trafalgar and the Spanish Navy* (London, 1988)
Harland, John, *Seamanship in the Age of Sail* (London, 1985)
Hayward, Joel, *For God and Glory, Lord Nelson and his Way of War* (Annapolis, 2003)

Hoffman, Capt. Frederick, *A Sailor of King George, The Journals 1793–1814 (1901)* (London, 1999)
Holden Mackenzie, Col. Robert, *The Trafalgar Roll, The Ships and the Officers (1913)* (London, 2004)
Holmes, Richard, *Coleridge, Early Visions* (London, 1989)
Holmes, Richard, *Coleridge, Darker Reflections* (London, 1998)
Holmes, Richard, (ed.), *Southey on Nelson (1813)* (London, 2004)
Holmes, Richard, (ed.), *Defoe on Sheppard & Wild (1724–5)* (London, 2004)
Horne, Alistair, *The Age of Napoleon* (London, 2004)
Howard, Michael, *War in European History* (Oxford, 1976)
Howard, Michael, *The Causes of Wars* (London, 1983)
Howarth, David, *Trafalgar: The Nelson Touch* (1969) (Adlestrop, 2003)
Humphrey, A.R., *The Augustan World* (London, 1954)

Jaeger, Muriel, *Before Victoria, Changing Standards & Behaviour 1787–1837* (London, 1956)
Jennings, Humphrey, *Pandaemonium, The Coming of the Machine as Seen by Contemporary Observers* (London, 1985)

Keegan, John, *The Face of Battle* (London, 1976)
Keegan, John, *The Price of Admiralty* (London, 1988)
Kennedy, Ludovic, *Nelson and his Captains* (London, 1975)
Konstam, Angus, *British Napoleonic Ship-of-the-Line* (Oxford, 2001)

Lambert, Andrew, *Nelson, Britannia's God of War* (London, 2004)
Laurie, Robert and Whittle, James, *Mediterranean Pilot* (London, 1803)
Lavery, Brian, *Nelson's Navy*, *The Ships, Men and Organisation 1793–1815* (London, 1990)
Lavery, Brian, *Nelson's Fleet at Trafalgar* (London, 2004)
Leech, Samuel, *A Voice from the Main Deck (1857)* (London, 1999)
Le Fevre, Peter & Harding, Richard, (eds.), *Precursors of Nelson, British Admirals of the Eighteenth Century* (London, 2000)

Levey, Michael, *Sir Thomas Lawrence* (London, 1979)
Lewis, Michael, *A Social History of the Navy 1793–1815* (London, 1960)
Lynch, Jack, *Samuel Johnson's Dictionary* (Delray Beach, 2004)

Mackay, Ruddock F., *Admiral Hawke* (Oxford, 1965)
Mahan, Capt. A.T., *The Influence of Sea Power Upon History 1660–1783 (1890)* (London, 1987)
Mahan, Capt. A.T., *The Influence of Sea Power upon the French Revolution and Empire 1793–1812* (London, 1892)
McCalman, Iain, (ed.), *An Oxford Companion to the Romantic Age, British Culture 1776–1832* (Oxford, 1999)
McEvedy, Colin and Jones, Richard, *Atlas of World Population History* (Harmondsworth, 1978)
McMaster, Graham, (ed.), *William Wordsworth, A Critical Anthology* (Harmondsworth, 1972)

Nichelson, William, *A Treatise on Practical Navigation and Seamanship (1765)* (Portsmouth, 1792)
Nicolas, Sir Nicholas Harris, *The Dispatches and Letters of Vice Admiral Lord Viscount Nelson, Volumes I-VII, (1846)* (London, 1998)

Padfield, Peter, *Maritime Supremacy and the Opening of the Western Mind* (London, 1999)
Padfield, Peter, *Maritime Power and the Struggle for Freedom 1788–1851* (London, 2003)
Paley, Morton D., *Apocalypse and Millennium in English Romantic Poetry* (Oxford, 1999)
Perry, Seamus, *Coleridge's Notebooks, A Selection* (Oxford, 2002)
Piper, David, *The English Face* (London, 1992)
Pocock, Tom, *Horatio Nelson* (London, 1994)
Porter, Roy, *English Society in the Eighteenth Century* (Harmondsworth, 1990)

Quirk, Ronald J., *Literature as Introspection, Spain Confronts Trafalgar* (New York, 1998)

Reynolds, Graham, *Turner* (London, 1969)
Ribeiro, Aileen, *The Gallery of Fashion* (London, 2000)

Rodger, N.A.M., *The Wooden World, An Anatomy of the Georgian Navy* (London, 1986)
Rodger, N.A.M., *The Safeguard of the Sea: A Naval History of Britain*, 660–1649 (London, 1997)
Rodger, N.A.M., *The Command of the Ocean: A Naval History of Britain, 1649–1815* (London, 2004)
Rule, John, *The Vital Century, England's Developing Economy 1714–1815* (London and New York, 1992)
Rule, John, *Albion's People, English Society 1714–1815* (London and New York, 1992)

Schama, Simon, *Citizens, A Chronicle of the French Revolution* (London, 1989)
Southam, Brian, *Jane Austen and the Navy* (London and New York, 2000)

Terraine, John, *Trafalgar* (London, 1976)
Thompson, E.P., *The Making of the English Working Class* (Harmondsworth, 1980)
Tracy, Nicholas (ed.), *The Naval Chronicle, Consolidated Edition, Volumes I-V* (London, 1999)
Trilling, Lionel, *Sincerity and Authenticity* (London, 1972)
Tunstall, Brian, *Admiral Byng and the Loss of Minorca* (London, 1928)

Uglow, Jenny, *The Lunar Men, The Friends Who Made the Future* (London, 2002)

Villiers, Alan, The *Way of a Ship*, (London, 1954)
Vincent, Edgar, *Nelson, Love & Fame* (New Haven and London, 2003)

Warner, Oliver, *Nelson's Battles* (London, 1965)
Warner, Oliver, (ed.), *Nelson's Last Diary and the Prayer before Trafalgar* (London, 1971)
Watson, J.R., *Romanticism and War, A Study of British Romantic Period Writers and the Napoleonic Wars* (Basingstoke, 2003)
Wheeler, Dennis, *'The Weather of the European Atlantic Seaboard during October 1805', Climatic Change 48, (2–3)*, Feb 2001: 361–385

Winter, Jay, *Sites of Memory, The Great War in European Cultural History* (Cambridge, 1995)
Wordsworth, Jonathan, Abrams, M.H. and Gill, Stephen, (eds.) *William Wordsworth, The Prelude 1799, 1805, 1850* (New York and London 1979)

INDEX

About the author

About the book

Read on

P.S.

Insights, Interviews & More . . .

*

About the author

Meet Adam Nicolson

ADAM NICOLSON lives on a ninety-acre farm near Burwash, in Sussex, England, with his wife, writer and horticulturist Sarah Raven, and their five children. Topping off his pastoral existence are eighty-five sheep, nineteen Sussex cows, two pigs, twelve piglets, two Labrador retrievers, one poodle, and six rabbits. His notion of perfect happiness integrates "new bread, unsalty butter, spring mornings, Pyrenean beechwood, swimming in a stream, sunshine, snow on the mountains, Sarah, the children, the dogs, completeness, cider, and an afternoon sleep." He divides his time between the farm and Sissinghurst Castle, a family estate featuring far-famed gardens that attract thousands of visitors each year.

Jacky Houdret

He was educated at Eton and Magdalene College, Cambridge. Upon leaving university, he spent two years walking around England and two years walking around France; travel writing emerged from both excursions. He has written books on Eastern Europe, the American West, and the evolution of the small English town. "For the last twenty years I have owned some islands" is the pleasingly odd first sentence of his book *Sea Room: An Island Life in the Hebrides.* He inherited these islands from his father, publisher and politician Nigel

Nicolson, who as a young boy hunted butterflies with Virginia Woolf. In 1959 Nigel published the first British edition of *Lolita*—and thereby brought to each of his professions a fair amount of controversy. Nigel's parents—Adam's grandparents—were gender-bending Bloomsberries, about whom Adam remarks: "Harold Nicolson: diplomat, novelist, cultural biographer, politician, blah blah—gay" and "Vita Sackville-West: poet, biographer, novelist, and gardener—gay." He overheard his prospective mother-in-law warning Sarah upon their engagement: "Are you absolutely sure, darling? You do realize his entire family consists of drunks and homosexuals?" And indeed, one grandparental appetite appears to have influenced him irretrievably: "I always knew," he says, "I wanted to be a writer."

He has won both a Somerset Maugham Award and the British Topography Prize, and has been short-listed for Newspaper Feature Writer of the Year. He remains managing director of Toucan Books Ltd, the publishing company he founded in the mid-1980s. His greatest fear is drowning. He wishes he had written Adam Thorpe's *Ulverton.* He turns to the Cambridge University Library and to abebooks.com for inspiration.

"[Adam's grandparents] were gender-bending Bloomsberries."

Writing *Seize the Fire*
A Conversation with Adam Nicolson

The following interview was conducted by Sarah O'Reilly, January 2006.

What prompted you to write this book?

I knew, of course, that the anniversary of Trafalgar was coming up and that there would be a slew of books to commemorate it, just as there had been in 1905. And I knew that I could not hope to compete with the naval scholars who had devoted the bulk of their lives to a study of the eighteenth- and nineteenth-century natives. In that way, I suppose, the anniversary was something of a disincentive for me.

But it was also an opportunity to write about something on which I had been dwelling for a long time: the idea of Romantic Battle. It had occurred to me that battle, in the early nineteenth century, might be subject to the same deep shift in sensibilities, in the idea of beauty and our relationship to wildness, in the conception of manhood, and even of the self, which was apparent in every other dimension of late eighteenth- and early nineteenth-century European thought. Battle is so often seen in terms of technologies—the influence of the horse on medieval warfare, or of the bow; of gunpowder; of ironclad ships; the machine gun; the atom bomb—that it is often assumed that the people who take part in it are a neutral or at least constant element, a given. Men, it is thought, are simply men;

> “Men, it is thought, are simply men; the only thing that changes in battle is the machinery with which they implement and impose their manhood. This book began with a desire to question that assumption.”

the only thing that changes in battle is the machinery with which they implement and impose their manhood.

This book began with a desire to question that assumption and to ask some more difficult, hazier, less answerable, and wider-ranging questions about one of the most famous battles in English history. Who were the people at Trafalgar? In what sense were they of their time? Was Trafalgar, in short, a Romantic Battle? Did the way it was fought reflect the changing conceptions of virtue and violence so widely apparent in the poetry, art, music, politics, philosophy, even the social life and dress of the period? Was Nelson an aberration, an extraordinary, unlikely, and unrepeatable figure? Or did his remarkable combination of qualities, his ability to move between intense self-control and near-archaic abandon in battle, in fact, reflect the particular cultural circumstances of the English frame of mind in the years leading up to Trafalgar?

These are not the questions usually asked of warriors, or about war, but the excitement of writing this book lay essentially in the repeated sensation I had, when reading the papers of many naval officers, that their own assumptions were deep and articulate reflections of precisely these cultural currents. And when I came to look at naval war in the eighteenth century, I was struck by how much the way it had evolved mirrored all sorts of other, nonmilitary changes in taste and behavior at the same time. Could that parallelism be pure chance? Or is war, somehow, fought according to deep and scarcely conscious rules which are themselves subject to cultural control? Is it the men, in fact, who shape the battles they fight?

Some people question why we continue to celebrate a ferocious battle between two nations that would be unthinkable in today's world. How would you answer them?

In part, I would agree with them. How can you celebrate the killing of people? And certainly one of my intentions in this book was to draw no veil over the bloodiness and nastiness of battle. The people who took part at Trafalgar left descriptions that are graphic enough for anyone's tastes. Nelson himself of course had no illusions about battle, or the sort of battle which would bring the conclusive victory he required. Nelsonian battle is without elegance or finesse: it is utterly destructive, and prepared to accept terrifyingly high level of casualties, because only in the murderously destructive environment of extremely close engagement could a British fleet be sure of bringing about the deeply ▶

damaging victory which would result in British dominance of the world's oceans.

Nor in fact is this book a celebration. It looks at the battle of Trafalgar as a moment of terrifying imposition of force; as a supremely efficient piece of military organization; as a place in which heroism—a cool and phlegmatic doing of violence—was required for victory; and as a set of scenes in which the constraints of normal everyday life and civilization were suspended. Battle cuts a hole in the social fabric; this book is in part an exploration of the ragged edges of that hole. The qualities that are on display in these circumstances are admirable, more than likable. I am not sure that Nelson or many of his captains were very likable people.

But however one might feel about the nastiness of battle, there is no reason, I think, to turn away from it, to regard it as too nasty to consider. In the scale of courage and violence on display here, there is something shockingly and grippingly watchable. There is a kind of beauty in violence, in the destruction of beauty, and it is not possible to understand human nature without understanding how men behave in these extremes; what leads them to this condition; how they react once they are in it; how, in the gut of battle, people find themselves excited or disgusted, terrified or capable of imposing terror on people who, even minutes before or minutes after, they were just as likely to care for and protect. Battle is a mysterious place; it is not to be celebrated in any naive or jingoistic way, but to be examined as deeply as one might look at, say, love or God.

Does the notion of the hero as somebody who strengthens the fabric of our society hold true today? Or do we judge our heroes according to different criteria?

Our society is radically different from the world of 1805; if the theory this book explores has any validity at all, it must be true that our idea of a hero and Nelson's idea of a hero are different. And by far the biggest difference between now and then is our attitude toward class. "Working-class hero" is not a term that would have made sense in 1805. The hero in 1805, drawing on profoundly elitist ideas inherited from Greece, Rome, and medieval Europe, was necessarily a gentleman. In the navy he was an officer and a man of honor, someone who felt at ease with the formal equipoise of his stance on the quarterdeck and who had learned not to flinch, let alone lie down, as the enemy shot came in; he wore his silk stockings and pumps because that kind of drawing-room grace was the mark of the gentleman-hero in battle.

By 1805, this elitist idea of the hero was already coming under strain. Nelson's whole battle style, in fact, was the opposite of this poised elegance. He scrambled into battle, and once there he wanted his captains to fight with a street fighter's hunger and energy, with no concern for the grace or elegance of the conflict. Naval warfare was in many ways dirty, ruthless, and unheroic; as a result, naval officers sometimes struggled for the status of gentleman in late eighteenth-century England.

But perhaps Trafalgar itself, and Nelson's perfectly scripted death at the moment of victory, marked a crucial shift in the idea of the hero. After Trafalgar, the hero was no longer a man who behaved honorably in battle but someone who did his duty, who risked and perhaps even sacrificed his life in the service of his country. And as that definition of the heroic changed, the status of hero opened up to people who weren't gentlemen. Heroism became a quality to which non-gents could aspire. With the increasing democratization of nineteenth-century Britain and the rise in standing and self-confidence of the middle classes, anyone, of either sex, could become a hero. Florence Nightingale, for example, is a figure whose life and standing would have been inconceivable in 1805.

What has survived the deep structural changes in society over the last two hundred years is the idea of duty. Duty, in fact, remains central to any modern concept of the hero. It doesn't have to be duty to one's country, but may be to one's family, one's village, or perhaps the needy and the poor of the world. In 1805, the idea of heroism was not at all foreign to the ideas of self-promotion, of glory, of making oneself into a great figure. That is what a hero had always been, from the age of Homer onward. Nowadays, though, self-promotion and heroism are thought of as almost polar opposites. Any hint that a modern hero is looking for glory, in fact, disqualifies him. Heroic self-promotion is now thought to be disgusting; in 1805 it was thought to be marvelous. And the idea of giving a hero a great deal of money for his heroism, as happened with the heroes of 1805, would today be laughable. Modern heroism must be modest and self-demoting. It must be a form of social service, a concept that would have puzzled anyone in 1805. ▸

A Conversation with Adam Nicolson *(continued)*

Do you have any modern-day heroes?

A modern hero needs to squeeze into a difficult place: his life must be led in the active service of high ideals, in circumstances of extreme difficulty, sustained over a length of time and with no obvious benefit to himself—beyond, of course, the martyr's benefit, which is the honor that attaches to self-denial.

This has narrowed the ground on which modern heroes can stand. They must be courageous, honorable, modest, persistent, and self-denying, while nevertheless of a scale, as people, which allows them to stand up to the wrongs of the world, and even to move beyond them. They must be immense, but we cannot allow them to recognize their own immensity.

Who in the real world can match such a catalogue? Perhaps only Nelson Mandela, named after Nelson by his teacher, has the nobility of spirit to qualify. His life has been in service of high ideals, in circumstances which could scarcely have been worse. He has sustained that service over many years and he has behaved with monumental integrity. Like Horatio Nelson, he has a coolheaded view of violence. It is interesting to read what he had to say about violence and sabotage at his trial for those crimes in South Africa in October 1963. This was the trial at which he was convicted and sent to Robben Island for life. One of the most deeply admirable qualities of this great man is that he admitted quite freely that he was guilty of what he was accused of. "I do not deny that I planned sabotage," he told the court. "I did not plan it in a spirit of recklessness, nor because I have any love of violence. I planned it as a result of a calm and sober assessment of the political situation." He felt that violence was inevitable on the part of the black population: "Without violence there would be no way open to the African people to succeed in their struggle." The leaders of the African National Congress (ANC) felt they had no other option. Mandela quoted Chief Lutuli, who had led the ANC in the 1950s: "Who will deny that thirty years of my life have been spent knocking in vain, patiently, moderately, and modestly at a closed and barred door? What have been the fruits of moderation? The past thirty years have seen the greatest number of laws restricting our rights and progress, until today we have reached a stage where we have almost no rights at all."

It is largely forgotten now, but Mandela was a warrior. He received guerilla training in Algeria. The notes he made from the lectures he was given there were produced in court. He studied Clausewitz, Mao Tse-tung, and Che Guevara. He prepared himself, quite coolheadedly, as he told the court, for guerilla warfare. "I wanted to be able to stand and fight with my people to share the hazards of war with them." It never came to that point because he was caught and imprisoned before battle could be joined. The sabotage of government buildings and electricity pylons, and setting up the training regimes for recruits was all he was responsible for.

Mandela's heroism consisted in the ability, first, to have engaged quite consciously with that dreadful need and, after twenty-seven years in prison, to come out into the light, understanding that the need was over. Nelson Mandela's slow, smiling walk from prison was, I think, the most heroic act in the modern world, a move to a higher plane where the grounds for conflict were dissolved. It was a decision fueled by the same resolved sanity which more than thirty years before had moved him toward violence in the first place. That consistent integrity which seems to bridge all categories—no compromise in the fight, humanity after victory—is, maybe, the mark of the hero.

What should we take away with us from the battle of Trafalgar? What lessons does it teach us that could be applicable in today's world?

Trafalgar, above all, was an exercise in the imposition of power. As such it was supremely successful and there is no doubt that its most potent lessons are for modern power brokers. Power worked in Nelson's hands for all the reasons this book describes: the ground was laid with immense care; the moment of battle, and the ways of prevailing within it, were deeply and fully preconceived; and the captains in Nelson's fleet were given their autonomy in a way that only great leaders can effect, an act of trust which summoned from those captains their deepest reserves of courage and enterprise. Those three factors—preparation, imagination, and trust—were the three ingredients of the British victory. None of them would have meant anything without a fourth: money. Nelson's fleet sailed on a sea of government money—taxed and borrowed—which his French and Spanish opponents could only dream of. That money had entirely reequipped the Royal Navy with the modern guns which destroyed the enemy ships at Trafalgar. And that money would not have been forthcoming from the British middle classes who provided it unless they had believed in and trusted the government which was spending it on ▶

their behalf. This is the deepest of all the political lessons of Trafalgar: imperial power depends on political unity in the imperial state.

Allied to that is another, more humane lesson: the imposition of power involves immense suffering. Empire sheds blood. The situation of Britain in the early nineteenth century in some ways mimics that of America in the early twenty-first century: Anglophone, entrepreneurial cultures, drawn toward total, unipolar, global domination, driven by a thrusting commercial energy, utterly convinced of the God-given rightness of their cause as the agents of freedom, fairly uninterested in the nuances of the cultures they aimed to dominate, widely loathed for their hypocrisy, their philistinism and their smugness, and on the whole enormously successful. The story of Trafalgar, if it has a role as a morality tale, is the story of an empire being made. No empire is winnable without the shedding of blood, whether to create the American imperium in the twenty-first century or the British in the nineteenth century.

The third lesson of Trafalgar is simpler still: the exercise of power is at the same time the most horrible and beautiful of spectacles.

And After Trafalgar . . . ?

by Adam Nicolson

EVEN AS THE FIRING DIED AWAY on the afternoon of Trafalgar, a mood of exhaustion and lassitude settled on the British fleet. Edward Codrington, the elegant and gentlemanly captain of the *Orion*, wielding his speaking trumpet, had exchanged jokey remarks with his friends on other ships as he passed them during the course of the battle. Now, all he could see before him was "fatigue, anxiety and distress of mind." Many wept; more sat staring vacantly into space.

In the course of an afternoon they had destroyed French maritime power. The French possessions in the Caribbean were now exposed to British interests. From this moment, the Spanish Empire began to fall apart. The course of the nineteenth-century British Empire was set. The effect of Trafalgar, in other words, was to take the tension and crisis out of naval life. In London, the new predicament of the naval officer was seen in a way that was at once clearheaded and, to our ears, strangely Romantic: letter after letter arrived at the Admiralty expressing envy at Nelson's lot. He had died when he should have. That part of the drama had been well written. What more perfectly sealed end to a life could one imagine than death at the point of victory?

Edward Codrington by Sir Thomas Lawrence, reproduced courtesy of the Mary Evans Picture Library

He was not the only one. Two of his captains had been killed in the battle: John Cooke of the *Bellerophon*, who had received two musket balls in the chest and died on ▸

And After Trafalgar . . . ? ***(continued)***

his quarterdeck with the words "Tell Lieutenant Cumby never to strike" on his lips; and George Duff of the *Mars*, whose head had been removed by a cannonball early in the afternoon, whose body had lain where he fell, covered by a Union flag, for the rest of the afternoon, and whose thirteen-year-old son, Norwich, a midshipman serving on the *Mars*, afterward wrote his mother, Sophia, the most poignant of all Trafalgar letters: "My dear Mama, You cannot possibly imagine how unwilling I am to begin this melancholy letter: however as you must unavoidably hear the fate of dear papa I write you these few lines to request you to bear it as patiently as you can . . . he died like a hero having gallantly led his Ship into Action. . . ."

Marble plaques on church walls in Donhead in Wiltshire (for Cooke) and Edinburgh (for Duff) as well as memorials in St. Paul's enshrined the moment of service. For the rest of the cast, there was a slightly bereft sense of being left on stage after the drama was over. For none was that truer than Cuthbert Collingwood, Nelson's second-in-command and successor as commander in chief of the Mediterranean Station. Collingwood, a Northumberland man, whose career had intersected with Nelson's at every turn, received all the prizes. He was made Baron Collingwood of Caldburne and Hethpool, awarded £2,000 a year for life, his widow £1,000 a year after his death, £500 to each of his two daughters. (You can multiply these figures by up to 150 for a modern equivalent.) But he never returned home to enjoy the fruits of battle. He remained at sea, blockading the Spanish in Cádiz and Cartagena, then the French in Toulon. For years after Trafalgar, Collingwood slogged away at the dreariness of blockade duty in the Mediterranean. He dreamed of home, of his garden and trees. He had no son and begged the authorities to allow his title to descend through the female line. They refused him. He wrote anxiously to his wife about their sudden elevation to the nobility: "How we are to make it out I know not, with high rank and no fortune." He did not have Nelson's luck, failing to catch French fleets as from time to time they scooted around the edges of the Mediterranean, just out of reach. He ground away at his paperwork: "I hardly ever see the face of an officer, except when they dine with me, and am seldom on deck above an hour in the day, when I go in the twilight to breathe fresh air." In 1810, he was summoned home to England, but he died before he got there. He was fifty-nine.

For most Trafalgar captains, the routine of naval life led seamlessly into a relatively uneventful and largely prizeless future. Knighthoods of the Bath were distributed, a baronetcy for Captain Hardy of the *Victory*,

Cuthbert Collingwood by H. Howard, reproduced courtesy of the Mary Evans Picture Library

progress up the ladder of rank was guaranteed, if slow, as captains dropped off the other end; the various stations on which the Royal Navy was engaged required ships and men to captain them. The eastern seaboard of the United States, the Caribbean, South America, West Africa, the Cape of Good Hope, the East Indies, the Adriatic, the dreariness of the blockade outside Toulon (known in the navy as "Too-Long") the Channel, the North Sea, the Baltic—all of these mopped up year after year of naval officers' lives. Hardy, Charles Bullen of the *Britannia*, Richard King of the *Achille*, and Edward Hargood of the *Belleisle* (who had the consolation of knowing that his wife, Maria, the daughter of an immensely rich banker, was at least untroubled by any money worries at home)—all of them lived a post-Trafalgar life of very nearly unbroken service at sea, many of them only returning to jobs ashore, or to the plum command of a royal yacht, in the 1820s. By then, sliding by automatic promotion into the ranks of the admirals, their knighthoods transmuting into KCBs and eventually GCBs, they commanded dockyards or, in Hardy's case, as First Sea Lord in the 1830s, Greenwich Hospital, where he [Hardy] abolished the yellow coat with red sleeves which until then had been forced on any sailor pensioner who was found drunk on Sunday. Hardy, who in his time had been one of the most brutal floggers in the fleet, found in old age a kind of humanity.

If, for most, it was life lived in a long, post-Trafalgar glow, there were others who, still in the spirit of Nelson, sought what glory there was. ▸

And After Trafalgar . . . ? ***(continued)***

Henry Blackwood, the great frigate captain at Trafalgar, very nearly died in February 1806, when his Ship the *Ajax*, then in the Dardanelles, caught fire when a drunken steward knocked over a candle. The *Ajax* was totally destroyed, and almost half the ship's company died in the catastrophe. Blackwood himself was picked up hanging onto an oar, almost dead with cold, after nearly an hour in the water. He was offered a cozy sinecure at the Navy Board as pay commissioner, but he refused it for a life at sea in the Mediterranean, and eventually as commander in chief in the East Indies, which remained one of the most lucrative of stations. Thomas Fremantle, a fighting dog of a captain, beloved by Nelson and a ragingly fierce disciplinarian, made the Adriatic his own between 1812 and 1814 in the style of freebooting naval dominance that reeked of an earlier age; back in the lovely house in Buckinghamshire decorated with souvenirs from the ships defeated at Trafalgar which his prize money had bought, he presided over the beginnings of a dynasty which would continue to find fame in the navy until the twentieth century. There he could reminisce over his triumphs: "Every place on the coasts of Dalmatia, Croatia, Istria, and Friuli had surrendered to some part of the squadron under my orders." Fremantle had captured more than a thousand guns and taken or destroyed between seven and eight hundred enemy vessels. But even Fremantle, the most hardheaded of all these men and one who had complained to his wife of Nelson's death on the grounds that it would affect his own career prospects, could not escape the hazards of a naval life. He died of a fever in Naples in 1819 while serving as commander in chief of the Mediterranean, the job Nelson had made the most famous and glamorous in the navy.

For some, the post-Trafalgar world was far from easy. The firebrand Eliab Harvey of the *Temeraire*, who as a young man had lost £100,000 in one evening—winning £90,000 of it back that same night—was promoted to rear admiral in 1805, but lost none of his fire. When in 1809, he heard that Lord Cochrane, his great rival, had been appointed to lead a special mission in an attack on the French fleet with fireships, which Harvey thought he should have had himself, he first marched into his admiral's cabin and "used vehement and insulting language," then "expressed his anger so publicly and violently on the quarterdeck of the flagship" that he was court-martialed and dismissed from the navy. He was only forty-nine at the time and until 1830 lived a life of undiminished and largely purposeless rage.

In a navy with far too many officers and clogged at the top after the wave of promotions made after Trafalgar, there is only one man whose life could be envied. Henry Bayntun had been captain of the *Leviathan* at the battle and had performed prodigies of humanitarian courage in the storm which followed, saving many thousands of French and Spanish lives from the battered prizes that were being driven onto the Spanish coast. He scarcely had a navy career afterward. Bayntun had himself painted wearing his Trafalgar sword and medal, and he retired to Bedfordshire, where his papers are still to be found in the county record office: the 1805 log for the *Leviathan*; her musterbook, every man listed; his atlas of charts of the Spanish coast, still marked in pencil with the transits he drew on them. The collection constitutes a strangely touching archive belonging to an old captain who could comfort himself by looking back on his one moment of heroism and glory.

Have You Read?
More by Adam Nicolson

GOD'S SECRETARIES: THE MAKING OF THE KING JAMES BIBLE

A net of complex currents flowed across Jacobean England. This was the England of Shakespeare, Jonson, and Bacon; it was the era of the Gunpowder Plot and the worst outbreak of the plague. Jacobean England was both more godly and less godly than it had ever been, and the entire culture was drawn taut between those polarities. This was the world that created the King James Bible. It is the greatest work of English prose ever written, and it is no coincidence that the translation was made at the moment Englishness, specifically the English language itself, had come into its first passionate maturity. The English of Jacobean England has a more encompassing idea of its own scope than any form of the language before or since. It drips with potency and sensitivity. The age, with all its conflicts, explains the book.

"Adam Nicolson's re-creation of this context is beyond praise. In *God's Secretaries* he brings off a brilliant freehand portrait of an England more rich yet insecure, more literate yet superstitious, more urban yet still rural in rhythm, more unified yet riven with factions."

—Christopher Hitchens,
New York Times Book Review

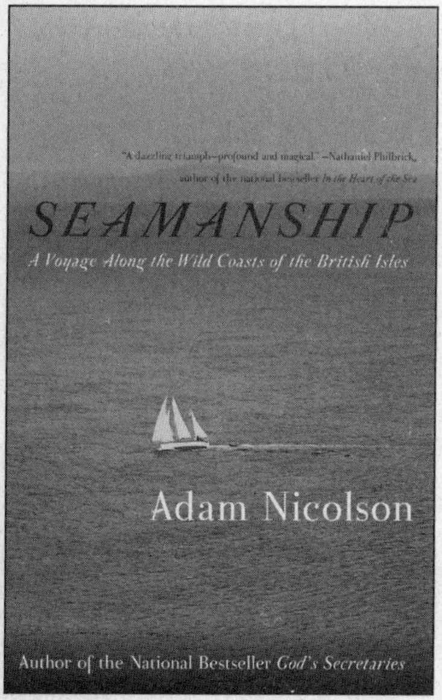

SEAMANSHIP: A VOYAGE ALONG THE WILD COASTS OF THE BRITISH ISLES

Wanting to experience the feeling of being "a single hair on the world's skin" that only the ocean can give you, Adam Nicolson decided to sail along the west coasts of Ireland and

Have You Read? ***(continued)***

Scotland, through the Shetlands, Orkneys, and Faroes. He teamed up with an old friend, George Fairhurst, and shoved off aboard the *Auk*, a forty-two-foot wooden ketch. Their voyage lasted one year and spanned 1,500 miles; they encountered fierce conditions and struggled to manage not only their small boat but their friendship.

Seamanship is more than a travel journal. What Nicolson has written describes an inner journey as much as an outer one. Disasters and revelations greet him at every turn: sacred landscapes and modern visionaries; encounters with the animals living on the wild edge of the Atlantic; and at least one moment when the prospect of death strolls aboard the *Auk*. *Seamanship* is about the gaps that open up between those who go and those who stay at home.

"A superb book, as wise as it is beautiful."

—Bernard Cornwell

"A dazzling triumph—a profound and magical account of a voyage along the wild edges of the British coast."

—Nathaniel Philbrick, author of
In the Heart of the Sea,
winner of the National Book Award